T0349851

Contributions to Economics

The series *Contributions to Economics* provides an outlet for innovative research in all areas of economics. Books published in the series are primarily monographs and multiple author works that present new research results on a clearly defined topic, but contributed volumes and conference proceedings are also considered. All books are published in print and ebook and disseminated and promoted globally. The series and the volumes published in it are indexed by Scopus and ISI (selected volumes).

Takuya Nakaizumi

Impact Assessment for Developing Countries

A Guide for Government Officials and Public Servants

Takuya Nakaizumi
Kanto Gakuin University
Yokohama, Japan

ISSN 1431-1933 ISSN 2197-7178 (electronic)
Contributions to Economics
ISBN 978-981-19-5493-1 ISBN 978-981-19-5494-8 (eBook)
https://doi.org/10.1007/978-981-19-5494-8

This Springer imprint is published by the registered company Springer Nature Singapore Pte Ltd.
The registered company address is: 152 Beach Road, #21-01/04 Gateway East, Singapore 189721, Singapore

Preface

The purpose of this book is to introduce impact assessment (IA) for improving regulation, especially in developing economies. IA[1] is a process that prepares evidence for decision-makers on the advantages and disadvantages of possible regulatory options by assessing those options' potential impacts.

The most important purpose of IA is to improve regulation by identifying regulatory issues and assessing costs and benefits at an early stage of regulation making. Even rough estimates can contribute to improving regulation. Furthermore, because developing countries face a higher degree of resource scarcity and must, therefore, endeavor to use resources more efficiently, it is more important for the developing world, as compared to the developed world, to establish a regulatory system that is as efficient as possible.

My specialty is economics, specifically contract theory (organization economics) and the economics of regulation. I wrote this book based on my theoretical background and many years of experience introducing IA in Japan and Pakistan, disseminating IA, and conducting interviews with relevant officials in the United Kingdom, the United States, and other Organization for Economic Co-operation and Development (OECD) countries. Appointed by the Japanese government in 2000, I began my professional duties by interviewing Dr. John Morral III, chief of the Office of Information and Regulatory Affairs (OIRA) in the United States Office of Management and Budget (OMB) at that time. He was kind enough to fulfill my request, and he shared important information regarding IA. He also introduced me to several important US government officials, for example, Dr. Neil Eisner and Dr. Bob Klothe of US Department of Transportation (DOT), Dr. Brett Snyder of the US Environmental Protection Agency (EPA), and Dr. Randall Lutter at the American Enterprise Institute (AEI) in 2000, Food and Drug Administration of US Department of Health and Human Services (FDA) in 2004, Resource For the Future (RFF) in 2011. I have visited them several times in 2000s. Each graciously introduced me to several important persons, including Dr. Dominic Mancini. The information they imparted

[1] Several countries use the terms "regulatory impact assessment" or "regulatory impact analysis" instead of IA; however, these are basically the same.

to me encompasses the key concept of implementing IA to produce better regulation. Of course, any mistake is my own. Thereafter, I tracked IA progress in OECD countries. This entailed conducting several interviews with US and UK officials. My Japanese government contacts graciously introduced me to several important persons, including Dr. Sean Ennis in the US Department of Justice and Dr. Andrei Greenawalt, former vice officer of OIRA.

After the Japanese government mandated IA in 2008, I focused on competition assessment, which entails assessing whether regulation unnecessarily restricts competition. I was appointed to a Japan Fair Trade Commission study group, and I conducted several interviews with the above officials in the United States (in 2009) and the officials of Competition Market Authority(CMA) or other Ministris in the United Kingdom (in 2018) regarding competition assessment.

I was also appointed regulatory reform adviser in Pakistan by the Japan International Cooperation Agency (JICA). My objective was to help the Pakistan government introduce IA and regulatory reform within the period 2013–2015 based on my aforementioned experience. Thanks to the excellent teams in Pakistan, I had a memorable time there. I would like to thank all the staff of JICA Pakistan and the IERU, including Mr. Aamir Qawi, Dr. Natasha Jehangir Khan, Ms. Hiba Haider Zaidi, Komal Kenneth Shakeel, and my counterpart and consultant, Dr. Naveed Iftikhar. These people were members of the best team that I have had the honor of working with and are also good friends. I am particularly grateful for the special support I received from former Chief Justice Tassaduq Hussain Jillani of the Pakistan Supreme Court.

This book is a practical guide for better IA and competition assessment toward improved regulation. I describe the essence of such assessment and simplify the important aspects including the underlying philosophy and best practices for government officials, especially those in developing countries who wish to introduce or I or are already implementing IA.

We take the rather conservative view that we can realize any achievement by learning incrementally from poor choices. Additionally, we focus on the concept of the baseline and system design for conducting IA appropriately, rather than on detailed analysis methods.

The progress and spread of evidence-based methods, on the other hand, have been remarkable in recent years, and strategies for incorporating them into IA constitute an important issue. The novel coronavirus (COVID-19) epidemic has also made strategies for incorporating crisis management into policy assessment a pressing issue. This book mentions them, but there is vast literature explaining methods and institutional design. While I refer to that literature as much as possible, the main purpose here is to clarify the whole picture.

In Part I of this book, we introduce IA. Chapter 1 explains the relevance of IA and provides an outline that includes several remarks on introducing IA in developing countries.

In Chap. 2, we describe the philosophy. The appendix to Part 1 lists the basic principles of IA.

In Part II, we introduce IA procedure and institutional design, mainly referring to European Union, UK, and US governments. To improve regulation, it is essential for IA to coincide with early-stage regulation making and that adequate reviews are provided.

Part III describes the IA method, while the assessment viewpoint is addressed in Chap. 8. Firstly, IA entails analyzing the necessity of a measure and then demonstrating its sufficiency via cost–benefit analysis. An assessment report is produced, showing correction points identified through public commentary, as well as compliance issues. Here, necessity means ascertaining whether there has been any market failure, imperfect competition, or other distortion that the private sector has failed to address. After justifying the necessity, one needs to establish sufficiency to introduce the proposed regulation by quantifying and monetizing costs and benefits as much as possible, after accurately formulating the baseline and the counterfactual. Evidence-based policy making (EBPM) plays an important role in cost–benefit analysis. Thus, we describe how to use the recent development of causal inference in EBPM to assess the benefits and costs of regulation.

In Part IV, we explain competition assessment. It is difficult, however, to quantify the economic impact, and mainstream competition assessment is based on economic theory. In developing countries, the market economy is weaker than in developed economies because there are few operational firms, resulting in imperfect competition. In some markets in Pakistan, only state-owned firms and foreign-owned enterprises operate. If foreign direct investments were heavily regulated, foreign-owned enterprises' position would be weakened, causing market monopolization. Thus, weak market conditions require greater competition considerations. Hence, competition assessment is more important in developing countries than in developed economies.

Part V addresses current issues such as nudge (Chap. 11), the COVID-19 pandemic and crisis management (Chap. 12), and regulatory reform and the digital transformation (Chap. 13). Concluding remarks are given in Chap. 14. Using the example of the COVID-19 pandemic, we explain strategies for dealing with problems that are so urgent that decisions must be made immediately before evidence can be obtained.

Among my contacts are several Japanese researchers and government officials who provide me with access to important information, discussions, and opportunities. I would like to thank Tokyo University emeritus Prof. Yoshitsugu Kanemoto, emeritus Prof. Akira Morita, Prof. Tanabe Kuniaki of Tokyo University, Prof. Atsuo Kishimoto of Osaka University, Prof. Tatsuya Ono of Tottori University, and Mr. Masamichi Takasaki of MUFG (in 2007), Dr. Yohei Kobayashi of MUFG, along with many government officials at the Ministry of Internal Affairs and Communication (MIC), Ministry of Economy, Trade and Industry (METI), Japan Fair Trade Commission (JFTC), and Japan International Cooperation Agency (JICA) in Ministry of Foreign Affairs of Japan (MOFA). This research is heavily based on interviews with government officials from several countries, as well as on cooperation with my fellow researchers. And Wendy Huang, Chieko Kehoe, Marc-Anthony Isaacs who helped me to sum up the interviews as assistants. I express deep thanks to all those officials and researchers. This work was supported by JSPS KAKENHI Grant Numbers JP15K00473, JP19K01562, JP17H02501, and JP20K01643.

Yokohama, Japan Takuya Nakaizumi

Contents

About the Author

Professor Takuya Nakaizumi, Kanto Gakuin University, College of Economics, earned a Ph.D. in economics, from the Graduate School of Economics, the University of Tokyo. His specialty is contract theory (organizational economics) and the economics of regulation. He was a former member of the Commission of Administrative Evaluation Bureau, Ministry of Internal Affairs and Communications, Japan, helping to introduce impact assessment (IA) into Japanese government. He disseminated IA to the Government of Pakistan as a regulatory reform advisor in Pakistan appointed by the Japan International Cooperation Agency (JICA).

Part I
Outline and Significance of Impact Assessment (IA)

Chapter 1
Outline and the Necessity of Impact Assessment (IA)

Abstract We explain IA and its importance, especially in developing countries. IA should be conducted at the early stage of regulation making. Even rough estimates can drastically improve the effectiveness and efficiency of regulation. We demonstrate this using several examples from my experiences introducing IA in Japan and Pakistan. We also discuss developing economies' limited ability to conduct IA and formulate regulations.

1.1 Why Impact Assessment (IA) Matters in Developing Countries?

This book is written with the intention of providing a reference for the introduction of Impact Assessment (IA), and highlights its principle, process, scope, content, and management, including Competition Assessment. IA is a set of logical steps to be followed when you prepare policy proposals, mainly proposing regulation. It is a process that prepares evidence for political decision-makers on the advantages and disadvantages of possible regulatory options by assessing their potential impacts. The results of this process are summarized and presented in the IA report. Competition Assessment, on the other hand, is aimed to assess whether the regulation unnecessarily restricts competition or not, if so, it is recommended to develop alternative policies that achieve the same objectives, with lesser harm to competition.

Although there are some regulatory departments, especially in the US, that conduct detailed and sophisticated analysis, the most important aspect of IA is to improve the regulations themselves by sorting out the regulatory issues and assessing the costs and benefits, even if it is only a rough estimate.

The most important thing is to sort out the problem of regulation and predict its costs and benefits, even if it is a rough estimate, so that the regulation itself can be improved. This is to show whether there is a need for government intervention at first, then to consider what options are available for involvement, what methods are desirable, and to assess whether the methods introduced are more effective than those not introduced. The goal is to confirm the appropriateness of introducing the regulation by estimate the costs and benefits based on a precise setting.

T. Nakaizumi, *Impact Assessment for Developing Countries*, Contributions to Economics,
https://doi.org/10.1007/978-981-19-5494-8_1

It is difficult to conduct a rigorous analysis even in developed countries. So is more difficult in developing countries, where there are various constraints. However, there is often improvement in conducting such a study much more than not conducting it. In addition, developing countries may have stronger incentives to use resources more efficiently with smaller budgets and resources. An official from Food and Agriculture Organization of the United Nations (FAO) states that international food aid is literally always facing a trolley problem,[1] always facing the decision of who not to starve. In this situation, it is even more important than in the developed world to achieve a regulatory system as efficient as possible.

IA—or all ex-ante policy analyses—provides an objective basis for decisions, thereby helping make effective policy decisions. Emotionally driven decisions can cause long-term damage; it is important to make evidence-based, objective decisions. Truncating emotional decisions and ensuring evidence-based policymaking are essential to support policy decisions of political judgments.

The COVID-19 pandemic has highlighted the importance of evidence-based approaches. For example, even in Japan—a developed country—the novel coronavirus (COVID-19) pandemic has exposed various policy contradictions. For instance, the uptake of vaccines is slower than that in other developed countries by the mid of 2021. Furthermore, Japan is fortunately surrounded by the seas; therefore, if the entry into the country is reasonably controlled, controlling new COVID-19 cases is much easier than in land-locked countries.

However, due to various problems, not only the conventional alpha variant but also the delta variant entered Japan in early 2021. The polymerase chain reaction (PCR) test had limitations. The false negative rate, especially in asymptomatic individuals, is as high as 70%. Therefore, no matter how many PCR tests are conducted, they do not lead to complete quarantine. Strict isolation for more than two weeks is essential for complete quarantine. However, due to human rights protection priorities and budgetary issues, a strict two-week quarantine was not implemented, and people were allowed to stay at home and asked to use a smartphone app to ensure contact.

In March 2021, when the threat of the delta variant became more serious, it was necessary to tighten immigration control. However, effective protection would have been achieved by implementing a strict two-week quarantine, rather than relying on PCR tests or contact confirmation apps. In practice, no quarantine measures were taken, except for the requirement of certificates by PCR or other tests before boarding a flight to Japan. Furthermore, the quarantine measures for returnees were far from strict because of the malfunction of the contact confirmation app and insufficient reporting of location information. After the delta variant was found in community-acquired infection, quarantine measures were finally implemented for up to 10 days. However, it was too late to prevent the delta variant from entering the country through quarantine. Unfortunately, the Olympics had to be held without an audience.

---

[1] The trolley problem is a series of thought experiments in ethics and psychology, involving stylized ethical dilemmas of whether to sacrifice one person to save a larger number. https://en.wikipedia.org/wiki/Trolley_problem.

Strict quarantine measures are considered to be the biggest problem from the perspective of human rights and the difficulty in securing a budget for quarantine. However, in the case of an improper certificate, passengers were denied boarding or deported, even if they were not infected with SARS-COV-2. If quarantine is a violation of human rights, then deportation—which is more serious—should be executed. Due to the sense of human rights, isolation is a problem, but deportation is more incomprehensible.

Especially in the case of the COVID-19 pandemic, many illogical measures have been taken. One example is conducting the Fuji Rock Festival, while the Suzuka Grand Prix of Formula-One in Japan is canceled. During the quarantine period, restaurants will be asked to refrain from alcoholic beverages with a certain degree of compulsion; vaccine intake will be at the individual's discretion, and the government is skeptical about even holding an event wherein only vaccine recipients are allowed to participate, much less consider a vaccine passport.

The main reason for such asymmetric synthesis is that policy decisions are primarily based on coordination with a narrow group of stakeholders. Although evidence-based policies are being implemented in Japan to a certain extent, they are inevitably influenced by the claims of specific interest groups and emotional decisions (see Greenawalt (2015)).

IA can overcome such incompatibilities by introducing transparency and quantitative evaluation into policymaking, although it does not come out overnight, pointing to the need to involve the research community in the regulatory process on a usual basis.

As ITU (2014) pointed out, "It can be a time-consuming exercise in itself, which often requires a shift in the behavior of government officials: from procedure oriented to a more performance-oriented." The IA system is based on this idea of an evidence base, and it provides objective and quantitative information that provides bases for not only regulation but all the policies and makes them improving.

While IA is an evidence-based and performance-oriented approach, the IA process is a systematic approach. Implementing IA into institutional procedures makes the performance-oriented approach more systematic and procedure-oriented. It is best used as a tool to improve the quality of political and administrative decision-making.

IA is conducted to discern the factors that maximize net benefits (benefits minus costs) for society. To realize efficient regulations, policy systems, and budgets that are cost-effective for society without being bound by specific interests, you should be based on such an evidence-based approach, and realizing efficient policies and regulatory systems.

However, it is not always possible to identify what is optimal. It is a prerequisite that the method of identifying the optimum is based on an evidence-based approach. However, the consensus should be taken into account.

IA should be conducted in close cooperation with planning and making of regulations, and it is imperative that both be improved together. Furthermore, it is ideal to make policy decisions involving citizens. Therefore, the efficacy of IA is not only to improve regulation but also the regulation-making process.

To make IA more systematic and provide better assessment, there are four components of essential institutional design: (1) establishing the ground rules of IA, (2) providing guidelines on how to conduct IA, (3) building separate institutions that review and improve the IA process, and (4) involve economists or other scientific researchers. We describe this in detail in Part 2.

Ideally, IA—as a means of ensuring transparency and accountability—is expected not only as a means of information disclosure, but also of providing materials for public involvement. Additionally, it can pave the way for the improvement of policies and regulations through feedback from the general public, and may encourage more accurate decision-making by providing costs and benefits information in advance when the public is asked for its opinion.

When conducting the assessment, proportionality is essential, which means that more important regulations should be assessed with more substantial analysis. Thus, the impact of the regulation should be understood at the beginning of regulation making.

Although accountability and transparency are necessary and public involvement is ideal, IA or policy analysis is also useful for managing policy decisions for efficient decision-making and regulation. Therefore, especially in developing countries, the focus should be on improving policymaking within the organization so that it does not have priority to disclose all the information to the interests of specific stakeholders.

Causal inference, meanwhile, has substantially developed over the past 20 years. These methods provide an inference comparing with and without regulation and derive robust scientific results that are available in broader and time-invariant situations, as they are available for IA, wherein both with and without situation must be estimated. We explain how to incorporate Causal Inference into IA in Chap. 8 of Part 3.

1.2 What is Impact Assessment (IA)?

IA or regulatory impact assessment (RIA) is an ex-ante analysis of regulation, which is mainly called IA in the EU or the UK. Regulatory impact analysis (or economic analysis) is used in the U.S. Regulatory Impact Assessment; on the other hand, Regulatory Impact Assessment is used in Canada and Australia, all of which are designed to incorporate to improve regulation making.

We refer to the ex-ante assessment of regulation as IA in this book. From EU guidance of IA, it is defined as a procedure itself or created document before a new government regulation is introduced, by detailed and systematic appraisal of the potential impacts of it in order to assess whether the regulation is likely to achieve the desired objectives and justify the cost by benefit. The need for IA arises from the fact that regulation commonly have numerous impacts and it is often difficult to foresee them without detailed study and consultation with affected parties. The central purpose of IA is to ensure that benefits will exceed costs from the viewpoint of the evidence base and improve regulation.

It identifies and assesses the problem at stake and the objectives pursued by the regulations. It helps to identify the main options for achieving the objectives and analyzes their likely impacts in the economic, environmental, and social fields. It outlines the advantages and disadvantages of each option and examines possible synergies and trade-offs.

It consists of a set of logical steps to rationalize the proposed regulation. Testing the need for intervention by any government level and examining the potential impacts of a range of policy options should lead to improvements and simplification of the regulation. It assesses the potential impacts of new legislation or policy proposals in the economic (including competitiveness), social, and environmental fields.

In Japan, we call IA Regulatory Impact Assessment (RIA). It was mandated in October 2007. RIA in Japan was introduced in reference to other OECD countries, especially the US and the UK. We introduce a rough sketch of the IA procedure referring to RIA by Japanese government, based on Nakaizumi (2007) & (2013) and Institute of Administrative management (2008).

The Cabinet Order of the Japanese government specifies the Regulation as any effect of restricting the rights of the public or imposing obligations on the public (excluding any effects pertaining to taxation, judicial proceedings, and procedures for application for subsidies). This means not only order but also law except legislation by Diet members is mandatory to conduct RIA. The Japanese government set the Implementation Guidelines for ex-ante Evaluation of Regulations, in which it is important to improve the quality and deepen the understanding of regulations among not only interested parties but also the general public by releasing the results of the ex-ante Evaluation of Regulations. For evidence-based assessment, it is desirable to quantify or express costs and benefits in monetary value to the maximum extent possible. If this proves impossible, the costs and benefits should be explained qualitatively.

The guidelines require that an evaluation report shall contain the following:

- Purpose, contents, and necessity of regulations
- Analysis of costs and benefits.

Setting the "Baseline," analyzing each element of costs and benefits, and including secondary or indirect impacts.

- Analysis of the cost-benefit relationship using cost-benefit analysis, cost-effectiveness analysis, and cost analysis.

Comparison with alternatives is desirable and the views of experts and other related matters and the time or conditions for review must be described.

For a better understanding, one of the brief Practices of IA in Japan is shown as an example, which was conducted as a trial in 2007. The IA (RIA) of the regulation is used to check the safety of lithium-ion batteries before shipment.

The regulation aims to prevent accidents caused by lithium-ion batteries in cellular phones. The regulation provides technical standards regarding the safety of lithium-ion batteries and obliges the firms who have registered to check the conformity of the batteries before shipment.

To prevent such accidents, it is important to mandate rules with unified standards that must be made compulsory for checks undertaken before the shipment.

To estimate the costs and benefits, the baseline is specified at first. Then cost and benefit are estimated as follows:

- It is estimated that without the regulation, there will be 100 accidents per year.
- About 10% of them will be serious accidents which will entail compulsory recall.
- Each recall cost is estimated at about 9 million dollars (1 billion yen).

The total cost of accidents each year would amount to more than about 90 million dollars (10 billion yen) in a baseline case, which means the benefits with regulation would amount to about 90 million dollars if regulation eradicates the accidents completely (100%). Moreover, costs are made up mostly of compliance costs which are anticipated to be about 12.6 million dollars (1.4 billion yen) each year, which includes about 3.6 million dollars (0.4 billion yen) of depreciation and about 9 million dollars (1 billion yen) of labor costs of the 100 testing facilities around the country.

Net benefits (benefits minus costs) with the regulation amount to about 78 million dollars (8.6 billion yen). The IA also analyzes the comparison between regulation and self-regulation.

First, with self-regulation, the compliance rate is estimated at 30%, which would bring about 27 million US dollars (3 billion yen) on benefits. The total cost of recalls is estimated to be more than about 63 million dollars (7 billion yen), which is less than the baseline case of about 27 million dollars. Total compliance costs amount to 3.7 million dollars (about 12-million-dollar times 30%). The net benefits of self-regulation are about 9 million dollars (2.5 billion yen).

Consequently, the RIA supports the introduction of regulations because it brings about the maximum net benefit.

These typical IAs are conducted within social regulation, while cost–benefit analysis has more uncertainty of economic regulation. Some countries, such as the United States, focus on competition analysis/assessment, which mainly examines the effects on competition by regulation.

1.3 Importance of IA and Ways to Introduce it to Developing Countries

1.3.1 Importance of IA in Developing Countries

Regulation is fundamental to governing societies and economies in all countries. Better regulations have become a crucial goal of policymakers. In regulatory processes, policymakers need to balance competing interests and have been critical to the development of democracy and the modern state. In contrast, regulatory systems are becoming more complex and expanding in response to increasingly complex economic and social activities not only in developed countries but also in developing countries. More sophisticated and performance-based regulatory management is required to improve regulatory quality in complex regulatory systems.

IA is a powerful tool for regulatory management to improve regulation because it is a performance-oriented approach. IA plays an important role in evidence-based policy, which drastically improves regulation and heightens social welfare. It could help dramatically reduce poverty and improve economic performance in developing economies. As Sutcliffe and Court (2006) state, "the government of Tanzania implemented a process of health service reforms informed by the results of household disease surveys; this contributed to an over 40% reduction in infant mortality between 2000 and 2003 in the two pilot districts. On the other hand, the lack of IA or evidence-based policy has caused widespread devastation. The HIV/AIDS crisis has deepened in some countries because governments have ignored the evidence regarding what causes the disease and how to prevent it from spreading."

IA requires a shift in the behavior of government officials, from being procedure-oriented to becoming more performance-oriented. However, IA is a systematic approach, and it makes the performance-oriented approach more systematic and procedure-oriented by inserting IA into institutional procedures. Thus, the IA process converts a performance-oriented approach into a systematic routine process. This is one of the reasons why developing countries should introduce IA to improve regulations.

With the growing number of opportunity accessible to international markets and increasing budgetary constraints, it is essential to minimize not only the government budgetary cost but also market immaturity and realize maximum effects in the economy. Regulatory quality contributes to good governance in not oly private sector but also the public sector, which is increasingly recognized in assessments of a country's competitiveness and attractiveness for investment. Additionally, IA is helpful in attracting not only domestic politicians and interest groups but also international organizations and international funds that help the emerging economy to grow.

1.3.2 Ways to Introduce IA Into the Government in Developing Countries

IA does not in itself determine decisions but provides empirical data that can clarify the options available to a decision-making process. It is a tool that can be used to transform stakeholders' understanding of what action is appropriate and can help define the role of the modern state. IA attempts to clarify the factors relevant to policy decision-making. It pushes regulators to make balanced decisions that solve complicated economic and distributional goals.

IA should be supported by a dynamic and well-conceived regulatory policy, strong regulatory institutions, and other complementary and supportive regulatory tools that ensure transparency and accountability at all stages of the process.

IA can be improved by using a variety of tools to assess existing or proposed legislation and regulations, which promote transparency and accountability. Regulatory tools should be mutually supportive and should work together to help producing more effective regulations.

IA systems should apply the benefit-cost principle to all regulatory decisions to support decision-making. The step-by-step approach helps to install the benefit-cost principle as routine, even if this analytical method poses practical and conceptual difficulties in the short term. IA guidelines should consider including and weighting all the principal effects.

Data collection is the most critical part of IA. A poor data collection strategy hinders effective analysis. It is essential to collaborate with academics to gather data and develop precise and straightforward strategies to achieve a successful, quantitative IA. Gathering data is more difficult in developing than in developed countries. Research projects of international organizations, such as the World Bank or IMF, are helpful in gathering data. The practices of OECD countries should be referred to, although there is still gap of supply and demand of RCT, the gap between researchers conducting RCT or other causal inference analysis and government officers who make regulation in developing countries, see Cameron et al. (2016). As Martin Ravallion, Former Director, Development Research Group World Bank made a statement that "It must be acknowledged that the set of research questions that are most relevant to development policy overlap only partially with the set of questions that are seen to be in vogue by the editors of the professional journals at any given time…academic concerns that overlap imperfectly with the issues that matter to development practitioners" from Aoyagi (2017).

The information required by IA can be collected in numerous ways. Public consultation is an important collection method, but it must be carefully structured; the information it provides should be carefully reviewed and tested for quantitative analysis. Regulators can ensure better data quality by involving expert groups, such as academic and other research bodies. This is not only because they are experts in gathering data, but because they do not have strong sectional interests in the issue.

IA should be integrated into the policymaking process at the earliest stage. Where IA is not integrated with the policy-making process, IAs merely justify decisions, or becomes meaningless paperwork. Integration is a long-term process that often leads to significant cultural change within regulatory bodies especially, decision makers.

The assumptions and data used in IA can be improved if they are tested through public disclosure and consultation. Releasing IAs along with draft regulation as part of the consultation procedure is a powerful way to improve the quality of the information available about new regulations, and thus improve the quality of the regulations themselves.

In Part 3, we introduce the typical organization procedure of IA in some countries, including review systems and guidelines from the viewpoint of institutional design, and we refer to the guidelines in Part 4 regarding analytical issues. Organizations vary among countries, based on government organization and political system. From several countries' procedures, we extract the general form and show how to bring an IA system into developing governments.

1.3.3 Obstacle of Introducing IA Into Developing Countries

In conducting IA, however, there are large gaps between developing and developed countries. In particular, there were two illustrious problems. The first is the limited capacity of the government. The second is a less developed economy and a low educational standard for the people. Some developing countries still have low literacy rates.

In developing countries, administrative organizations have various resource constraints as well, making it even more difficult to achieve policy assessment goals. Laffont (2005) examined the limitations of regulation. Estache and Wren-Lewis (2009) summarize the limits of regulators that affect regulation as follows.

We argue that the key aspects of institutional failure affecting regulation in developing countries can be grouped into four broad limitations: regulatory capacity, commitment, accountability, and fiscal efficiency. In developing countries, the size and nature of these four limitations often dominate the regulatory outcomes. Furthermore, since the relative importance of each of these areas varies across developing countries, there should not be a uniform approach to regulatory policy.

i. Limited regulatory capacity: This means the developing nations' limited ability to implement policies. Regulators are generally short of resources, usually because of a shortage of government revenue. This prevents regulators from employing suitably skilled staff or hiring good consultants. Beyond the regulator itself, an underdeveloped auditing system and an inexperienced judiciary place further limits on implementation.
ii. Limited accountability: Institutions in developing countries are often less accountable than those in developed countries. Less accountable institutions, including regulatory agencies, may not be answerable to their principals and, hence, are free to carry out their own objectives. Thus, collusion between the government and various interest groups, including regulated firms, is more likely to occur. In reality, there is abundant evidence of corruption in both the privatization process and regulation in developing countries.
iii. Limited commitment: Laffont's work further reveals that he was convinced that the institutional framework in many developing countries makes it impossible to rely on contracts. The difficulty is demonstrated best by the prevalence of contract renegotiation. Fear of future renegotiation is a serious impediment to attracting private sector participation. Moreover, the inability to rely on contracts

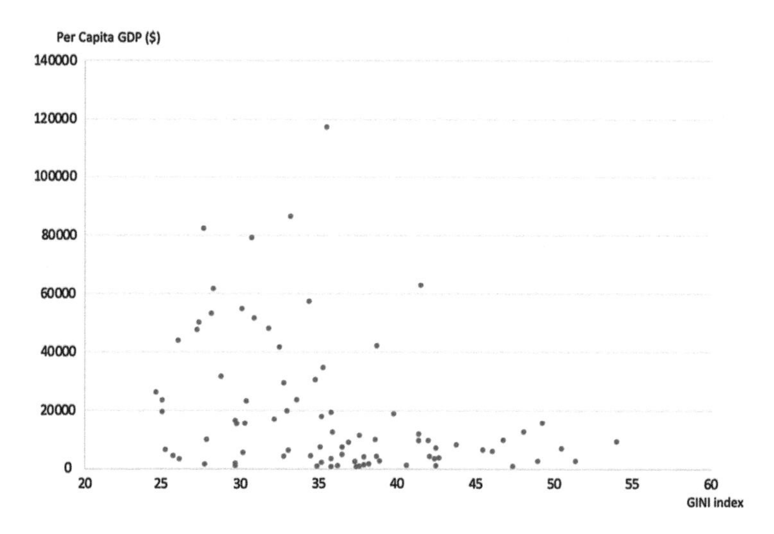

Fig. 1.1 Correlation between income (per capita GDP ($)) and income disparity (GINI Index) among nations in 2018 (source from World Bank).

is particularly damaging, given the greater uncertainties about cost, demand, and macroeconomic stability that exist in developing countries.[2]

iv. Limited fiscal efficiency: The final source of institutional failure explicitly addressed by Laffont is the weakness of fiscal institutions. In infrastructure, this limitation is apparent in the slow progress that state-owned enterprises have made in increasing access to networks. When both fiscal surpluses and the ability to pay for the majority of users are limited (as is often the case in sub-Saharan Africa, for instance), the speed at which investment can be financed is much slower than when governments can finance any resource gap.

In regulation making, these limitations should be considered, and the regulation should aim to maximize social welfare subject to those restrictions (Fig. 1.1).

As for the second concern of the obstacle for better regulation making, among a less developed economy with a low educational standard for the people, some developing countries still have low literacy rates. More than 60 countries have a literacy rate of less than 90%.[3] Generally speaking, in developing countries, not only low income but also higher income disparity emerges. In fact, there is a correlation between low-income and income disparity.

There are two important benefits of IA, the rational management of regulation and promoting transparency and accountability. However, it is more difficult to realize transparency and accountability in developing countries, because it is difficult for

[2] J.J. Laffont analyzed empirically in the last couple of years of his life. With Guasch and Straub, he investigated why, in Latin America between 1985 and 2000, more than 40% of concessions (excluding the telecoms sector) were renegotiated, a majority at the request of governments.

[3] From World Population Review website, https://worldpopulationreview.com/country-rankings/literacy-rate-by-country.

people to access and understand IA and for the government to make the IA well known and coordinate with the people adequately because of limited ability. However, it is beneficial to introduce IA to realize more efficient regulation and regulation making. The principle of transparency and accountability of IA must bring enough benefit to progressing democracies in the future. By exercising leadership and showing ideal regulation based on the theory or world standard, they should conduct IA when it is more difficult to gather information through public consultation.

Thus, first, we focus on rational and efficient regulatory management by introducing IA and providing more efficient regulation and regulation making. However, it is important to ensure transparency and accountability. IA is not a decision material but support for decision-making. Transparency and accountability for the public are directly applicable to decisionmakers. Thus, transparency and accountability of IA are still important, even if it is a long way to achieve more commitment by the people, such as public involvement.

Since independent regulators have jurisdiction over specific regulations, they have become more significant over the last decade. They contribute to improving regulatory quality, transparency, stability, and expertise. It is easier to introduce IA because they operate in the same disciplines as the IA process.

1.4 Lesson Introducing IA: Pakistan and Japan

Many transition-and-emerging economies have introduced IA to improve their regulatory structures. We refer to Japan and Pakistan according to my experience and summarize them into a generalized statement.

Many case studies have been introduced; for example, Korea in Rodrigo (2005) and many other cases in The World Bank Group (2019). I have been engaged in several projects introducing IA in Japan and Pakistan. Thus, more concrete points are partially shown by my informal experience in both Pakistan and Japan.

The Pakistani government has good institutions, including regulatory authorities. Regulatory reform and the introduction of IA are much more successful than I expected. Developing countries with stronger leadership may introduce IA more easily and we sumed up the reform proposal in Implementation and Economic Reform Unit, Ministry of Finance, Government Pakistan (2014).

However, lower incentives and fewer trained people within regulatory authorities and the government could prevent IA from a sustainable and systematic process. Even if regulatory reform is implemented, the lack of conflict management and the territorial battle might cause the reform to lose its substance. Despite excellent analysis and good IA, less ability of implementation makes regulation powerless.

In Pakistan, there are many areas of philistine change, such as changes in the powers of the regulator. In such cases, several important institutions are changed so much that consistent and continuous policymaking is difficult to maintain.

The Japanese regulation-making system has some consistency and rationality among specific stakeholders. However, it is short of transparency and an evidence-based approach. Thus, the Japanese government introduced the IA system. Although the IA system in Japan is based on formal legal authority, the initial IA is not submitted to be reviewed and integrated with the policy-making process. IA is written only in the final stage. Thus, IA merely justifies decisions after the fact, leading to meaningless paperwork.

Japan succeeded in catching up to a certain extent after 1950; this has led to the persistence of those systems to date. However, they are obsolete and prevent current economic development.

The biggest problem in Japan is that the original system has been preserved to the maximum extent possible, and new reforms have been added as much as possible without changing the old system.

Japan's legal system is complicated and difficult to revise. The concept of modularization should be introduced into the legal system. Furthermore, the establishment law, ordinances, and regulations in Japan are very rigid, making it difficult to do anything illegal. Concurrently, it also makes fine-tuning the system difficult once established. Consequently, in Japan, where the status quo bias is strong and the legal system is rigid and complex, people will choose to simply add to it rather than modify it.

In the case of IA, especially early modification by the assessment is essential for meaningful regulations; it is meaningless unless it is done at the same time and in collaboration with regulations as Shah et al. (2015) pointed out. At present, however, it is done almost as an excuse when the regulations have been virtually fixed.

Therefore, in order to make IA work, it is necessary to change the conventional way of regulation making to some extent, that is, to involve the public more widely and enact regulations based on evidence rather than coordinating interests with specific stakeholders, as Langer et al. (2015) pointed. However, it is difficult to make such a change in a rigid system, when there is uncertainty about the benefits of such a change.

Now that the COVID-19 pandemic has revealed the fatigue of the system in many ways, I think it is time to reform the procedure of IA in Japan. This also applies to the introduction of digital networks as a basis for government infrastructure. It is meaningless to introduce tablets without going paperless in the first place. It would be even more difficult in a country where the legal system is so complex that it is difficult to change.

Thus, the problem in Japan is the rigidity of the existing system. IA itself was introduced as an adjunct to the existing body type. As Rodrigo (2005) pointed out, if IA is not linked to policymaking, and commitment to policy is insufficient, the IA process is very tedious.

We can find a direction in which we can maintain consistency as much as possible and reform in accordance with the times. Despite various limitations, Impact Assessment is being conducted in various countries. Since the circumstances vary across countries, most factors with regard to each country must be considered. Additionally, since published IA describe the results and do not usually show the process of analysis, it is necessary to consult the original sources for a more detailed analysis if you need to use it as a reference.

If you understand that there is a disparity, limited ability, and immaturity of the economy as well as citizenship, it might be easier to change the government institution and introduce IA in developing economies than in developed countries because of demonstrating leadership.

References

Aoyagi (2017) Tojōkoku kaihatsu bun'ya ni okeru ebidensu no katsuyō. In: RIETI EBPM symposium. https://www.rieti.go.jp/jp/events/17121901/pdf/2-2_aoyagi.pdf

Cameron DB, Mishra A, Brown AN (2016) The growth of impact evaluation for international, development: how much have we learned? J Dev Eff 8(1):1–21

Estache A, Wren-Lewiss L (2009) Toward a theory of regulation for developing countries: following Jean-Jacques Laffont's Lead. J Eco Literat 47(3):729–770

European Commission, Impact Assessments. https://ec.europa.eu/info/law/law-making-process/planning-and-proposing-law/impact-assessments_en

Greenawalt A (2015) The regulatory process in Japan in comparison with the United States. https://www.rieti.go.jp/en/columns/a01_0431.html

Institute of Administrative Management (2008) Kisei no jizen hyōka handobukku yoriyoi kisei ni mukete chosha-mei. Institute of Administrative Management, 333 page

International Telecommunication Union (ITU) (2014) Using regulatory impact analysis to improve decision making in the ICT sector. GSR14 Discussion Paper. ITU, Geneva. https://www.itu.int/dms_pub/itu-d/opb/pref/D-PREF-BB.RPT5-2014-PDF-E.pdf

Implementation and Economic Reform Unit, Ministry of Finance, Government Pakistan (2014) Institutional design of regulatory bodies: diagnostic and reform directions

Kishimoto A (2018) Kisei eikyō hyōka (ria) no katsuyō ni mukete: Kokusai-tekina dōkō to Nihon no genjō to kadai. Keizaikei, vol 275. Research Institute of Economics and Management, Kanto-Gakuin University, pp 26–44

Laffont J-J (2005) Regulation and development (Federico Caffe Lectures). Cambridge University Press, p 268

Langer L, Stewart R, Erasmus Y, de Wet T (2015) Walking the last mile on the long road to evidence-informed development: building capacity to use research evidence. J Dev Eff 7(4):462–470

Nakaizumi T (2007) Toward better regulation making by introduction of RIA. In: Regulatory impact analysis: toolkits and methods for cross-cutting policy development, implementing successful regulatory reform: a political economy perspective regulatory impact analysis: toolkits and methods for cross-cutting policy development peer review of regulatory frameworks in Brazil public service delivery in China: OECD experiences and policy options. OECD Headquarters, New Conference Center, Paris, France

Nakaizumi T (2013) Introduction and principle of regulatory impact analysis: for better regulation making. Keizaikei, vol 255. Research Institute of Economics and Management, Kanto-Gakuin, pp 49–67. https://kguopac.kanto-gakuin.ac.jp/webopac/NI30000416

OECD Regulatory Impact Assessment page. https://www.oecd.org/regreform/regulatory-policy/ria.htm

Rodrigo D (2005) Regulatory impact analysis in oecd countries challenges for developing countries. In: South Asian-third high level investment roundtable Dhaka, Bangladesh. https://www.oecd.org/gov/regulatory-policy/35258511.pdf

Shah NB, Wang P, Fraker A, Gastfriend D (2015) Evaluations with impact: decision-focused impact evaluation as a practical policymaking tool. In: 3ie Working Paper 25. New Delhi, p 3ie

Sutcliffe S, Court J (2006) A toolkit for progressive policymakers in developing countries. Overseas Development Institute, London

The World Bank Group (2019) Global indicators of regulatory governance: worldwide practices of regulatory impact assessments. https://documents.worldbank.org/en/publication/documents-reports/documentdetail/905611520284525814/global-indicators-of-regulatory-governance-worldwide-practices-of-regulatory-impact-assessments

Viscusi WK, Harrington JE Jr, Sappington DEM (2018) Economics of regulation and antitrust. Fifth edn. MIT Press, 1000 page

Chapter 2
Role of Evidence-Based Assessment in Democracy

Abstract While policy evaluation needs to be evidence-based, it also faces conflicts involving various stakeholders. Whether to prioritize interest alignment or evidence and objectivity in assessment is a major issue. In this chapter, we show that, in accordance with economic principles, the highest priority should be given to deriving socially optimal outcomes based on evidence, regardless of conflicts of interest. This is because it is desirable to conduct objective analysis in accordance with the relevant principles, even when information asymmetry exists between policymakers and stakeholders. We should recognize the existence of information rents based on the revelation principle and guarantee a certain amount of gain for providing correct information. Furthermore, encouraging evidence-based and voluntary citizen involvement will promote the resolution of the implementation problem.

2.1 Introduction

While policy assessments need to be evidence-based, analysts also face conflicts with various stakeholders in the process of IA. It is a big question whether to prioritize, adjust interests or follow evidence-based policy and objectivity. This section shows that, according to economic principles, the highest priority should be to derive socially optimal outcomes based on evidence and scientific methods, regardless of the conflict of interests. In addition, even if there is a problem of asymmetric information between policymakers and stakeholders, evidence-based assessment and accountability are more important when recognizing that important information needs to guarantee a certain gain as compensation. Furthermore, by encouraging voluntary participation of citizens in policy making, even implementation issues will be diminished. Thus, transparency and promotion of public involvement are the ultimate goals of IA. In the next section, we explain why the highest priority should be to derive socially optimal outcomes, regardless of the conflict of interests. Section 2.3 refers to information asymmetry. Sect. 2.4 concludes the chapter.

T. Nakaizumi, *Impact Assessment for Developing Countries*, Contributions to Economics,
https://doi.org/10.1007/978-981-19-5494-8_2

2.2 Optimality of Evidence-Based Policy in Democracy

Developed modern countries are governed by representative democracy. Democracy is based on a majority vote. It is no exaggeration to say that the majority is constantly exposed to the possibility of oppressing the minority. In fact, even in Myanmar, where democratization has progressed, the crackdown on the Rohingya continued rather than disappeared. Therefore, many systems have been introduced to prevent such domineering of the majority. The most important institutions are the constitution and rule of law. Evidence-based policy-making (EBPM) aims to deter such a majority's domineering. In other words, there is a tendency to prioritize evidence over the opinions and interests of individual people, just as the Constitution prioritizes respect for the basic human rights of all people, including the minority, over the opinions of the majority.

However, even though it is evidence-based, policymaking should ideally be based on the consensus of the people. Thus, it is important to disclose information and ensure accountability so as to reach a consensus that the IA should depend on. It is impossible to make policy decisions that ignore the consensus of the people. What kind of IA should be carried out if there is a conflict between public opinion and evidence? Does the pursuit of evidence-based policy produce more desirable results than the consensus of the majority?

Even if an analysis that accurately reflects the majority's interests is conducted, it does not necessarily represent the interests of the whole society. Apparently, the maximization of social welfare and of the majority may differ. First, the interests of the majority and minority may differ significantly in the first place, and the damage of the minority may be far greater than the interests of the majority. Second, the majority has no incentive to consider the minority's minimum rights as guaranteed by constitutionalism. Therefore, reflecting only the claims of the majority may result in enormous infringement of the minority's human rights and cause enormous harm, such as the Rohingya problem. Third, while current democracy limits voters to adults, there are other human stakeholders, such as non-eligible people, future generations, and foreign people. It is possible to improve social welfare by considering non-human beings, such as the environment. Without altruism, the majority of voter has no incentive to consider other stakeholders.

These stakeholders cannot be ignored when considering sustainability and ensuring diversity for future growth. An easy-to-understand example is the problem of global warming. Considering these factors may be beneficial for social welfare. Fourth, from a behavioral economic point of view, when people's discount rate is different from the social discount rate, it is better to analyze using an appropriate discount rate to improve social welfare.

Majority voting does not always bring socially optimal outcome. Based on the concept of economic theory, the purpose of the IA is to maximize social welfare as a complement of majority voting and deter such a majority's domineering. If it theoretically maximizes social welfare, then even analysis results that differ from the interests of the majority should be analyzed and concluded based on EBPM. This is because whatever conflict of interest exists, it is socially optimal to distribute the total surplus based on efficient outcomes calculated with evidence-based regulation making. The bottom line is that the IA should always be based on the best outcomes. This is summarized in the following proposition:

Proposition 2.1 If there is a means by which gains can be transferred, achieving efficient outcomes and distributing them will be more optimal for society than distributing from any other outcome. Therefore, efficiency and distribution can be separated, and it is best to achieve optimal outcomes and then decide who to distribute to.

Proof Let A be the outcome of an inefficient policy, and A* be the outcome of an efficient policy. Changing A to A* causes an increase in gain, assuming that the increase in gain is distributed in society and can be Pareto-improved by allocating it by any method.

Therefore, it is a major premise of IA to always consider what is best in any situation. In general, IA and decision-making should be distinguished, and while IA is based on maximizing social welfare, it is the policy decision that ultimately implements and decides the policy or regulation. Therefore, it can be said that evidence-based impact assessment is ensured by leaving the final decision to the political judgment of the policymaker and placing a cushion between policy decisions and objective policy evaluations.

However, there is tension between policymakers and analysts in the analysis of IA to modify the analysis for the convenience of policymakers. It is also true that such pressure cannot be ignored in the IA analysis. In addition, even if there is little evidence that differs from the majority's interests, it is almost the case that conflicts of interest are faced when conducting IA, and that the results are contrary to specific stakeholders.

Of course, efficient outcomes cannot always be properly allocated, so another outcome may be the best in the sense of a second best when considering allocations. However, even in that case, comparison with the best policy is always important, and objectivity can be ensured by clarifying the problem.

Moreover, developing countries often face cases in which policies cannot be realized due to imperfect implementation and various government limitations. Furthermore, the accumulation of human and social capital has a significant influence on the optimal solution. If so, these constraints should also be considered. Even in this case, it is possible to understand the constraint by comparing it with the optimum solution. This is a very general economic idea in the second theorem of welfare economics and Nash bargaining solution, (see Muthoo (2008), Feldman and Serrano R (2005) for Nash bargaining solution, and see Samuelson (1947) for the second theorem of welfare economics and Coase (1960) for the course theorem). In addition, to make these perspectives more general, the importance of relying on evidence-based regulation making is that it is more independent of specific stakeholders and emotional judgments that deviate from objective judgments. It is based on the idea that the interests of all the people in the country should not be impaired. In policymaking, even if policymaker agrees with the majority, decisions must almost be made that are immune to the interests of a particular stakeholder. It is based on the idea that even if the specific interests are undermined, it is OK when it will be positive as a whole, and the disadvantage can be fully compensated. Another advantage of policy evaluation is that it can be arbitrarily independent of influence peddling.

2.3 Facing Information Asymmetry and Difficulty of Analysis

In the analysis, however, various constraints and obstacles exist. We expect to derive optimal outcomes by considering various real-world problems. In particular, the problem of information asymmetry, that is, the asymmetry of information between the public and various stakeholders, policymakers, and evaluators, is serious problem. This is not only an issue that occurs during information gathering when formulating policies, but also causes an incentive problem based on the agency problem between policymakers and stakeholders when implementing the regulation.

The fundamental solution to this problem is to enhance accountability and transparency. Promoting transparency in the first place as much as possible is a solution to the fundamental problem of information asymmetry. Promoting transparency and involving many stakeholders at the earlier stage, it is difficult to speak only on behalf of one stakeholder, because it can be repulsive to another, and even difficult to falsify the decision documents. It would be easier to increase transparency if we aim to obtain the optimal solution in society.

However, when important information is unevenly distributed, there are incentives to use that information to favor regulation. In economic terms, information gathering under asymmetric information is based on the revelation principle develoed by Myerson (1979). In other words, it is necessary to design incentives to reveal correct information. In the rest of this section, we discuss the implications of the revelation principle for regulatory assessment. And it is rare that policymakers' interests do not coincide with each other. In such a case, the implications of the results of the cheap talk game are effective. This is discussed in the following section.

Revelation Principle (Myerson (1979)) states that if an outcome of social choice can be realized by any mechanism, then the same outcome can be implemented by an incentive-compatible direct mechanism (a mechanism that reports the truth). This shows that even when considering various mechanisms, the principle is that they should have the properties of incentive-compatible direct mechanisms. Therefore, to obtain correct information, we need to design a mechanism to provide the incentive for stakeholders who know information to reveal it. This implies that it is necessary to guarantee a gain as compensation that is optimal for showing the right information (this is called information rent).

The implication is that effective relationships with stakeholders who have important imformation are essential. If compensation for right information is not provided, it must be recognized that the regulations may be distorted due to a lack of sufficient information. Therefore, it must be recognized that the cooperation of stakeholders who know key information is essential, and that it is necessary to give them something in return for their cooperation. If relationships with stakeholders are long-term, it is difficult to maintain asymmetric information indefinitely. Therefore, it is also effective to eliminate asymmetric information by continuing friendly relationships with those who knows information.

Furthermore, it tends to be more informative when there is little conflict of interest. This is an important conclusion for the Cheap Talk game started by Crawford and Sobel (1982). It can also be shown that in such a situation it is possible to elicit more accurate information from multiple stakeholders.

There are cases wherein information asymmetries make emission tradable permits preferable to Pigouvian tax and subsidies (Miyaoka 2019).

In this section, we discuss the importance of pursuing optimal outcomes and disclosing this information in the context of asymmetric information issues. It should also be noted that in order to have asymmetric information disclosed, a certain amount of compensation to the interested parties who has essential information is inevitable, as economic theory requires that information rents be guaranteed. When asymmetric information exists, there will always be an agency problem between the government and the private sector. Furthermore, owing to the limitations of the government, command and control measurement is not possible. Therefore, it is necessary to design incentive-compatible regulations so that they can be implemented through voluntary activities as much as possible. Therefore, the most promising approach is to promote citizen participation in regulation making while coordinating the conflicts of interest. For this purpose, it is essential to ensure information disclosure and accountability at the early stage of regulation making. Thus, it is expected that Impact Assessment and promoting transparency itself, in addition to information gathering, will be a milestone for voluntary citizen involvement which improve democracy.

Finally, an important issue is the design of incentives that provide policy analysits with appropriate incentives for such analysis. Even then, they should be based on EBPM and accountability. Increasing accountability not only facilitates external checks, but also provides neutral support from many stakeholders, which is the greatest incentive to conduct such an analysis.

2.4 Concluding Remark

While impact assessment needs to be based on an evidence base, it also faces conflicts with various stakeholders. Therefore, a major question is whether to prioritize interest coordination, an evidence base, and objectivity in the analysis. In this section, we show that the socially optimal outcome should be derived on the basis of the evidence base, regardless of the kind of conflict of interest we face, because the allocation resulting from the optimal outcome will always improve in the Pareto criteria over the outcome from any allocation that is less efficient, according to economic principles. In addition, it is important to understand the relationships between policymakers and stakeholders. Even when the problem of asymmetric information exists between policymakers and stakeholders, it is desirable to conduct an objective analysis providing information rents for them to reveal the information based on the revelation principle and guarantees a certain level of gain for compensation. Moreover, it should be pointed out that collecting opinions from multiple stakeholders is a powerful way to clarify facts. Furthermore, in policymaking, both analysis and implementation are important. In policy analysis, it is also necessary to properly design the organization that enhance both analysis and implementation. In particular, I pointed out that encouraging objective thinking and voluntary citizen participation is a solution to the problem of implementation. Finally, this kind of analysis is desirable in terms of providing incentives for policy analysts. Neutral and objective analysis is desirable both in terms of gaining public involvement in the long run, and facilitating analysis with that support.

Appendix of Part 1: Principle of IA

We summarize the principles of IA by abstracting various important guidelines and other documents from OECD countries.

(1) Role of IA (as a political decision-making aid)

IA aims to improve regulation quality and the efficiency of the regulation-making process. IA is, therefore, a political decision-making aid, not a substitute for it. IA informs political decision makers of proposed measures' likely impacts, to allow them to tackle any identified problems, and it allows them to decide adequately.

IA does not make decisions; rather, it provides empirical data that can clarify the available options to smooth the decision-making process. It is a tool that can be used to transform stakeholders' understanding of what action is appropriate and can help define the role of the modern state.

Many countries have legislated the procedure of regulation making including IA. This is one way to encourage a high level of compliance, and it provides tangible evidence of the importance that the government makes constant effort for regulatory reform. Legislating elements of regulatory procedure can also help establish consistent standards and outcomes and ensure that the resulting regulation is highly transparent.

(2) Integration of IA into the regulation-making process

In the early stages of policy development, affected groups should be identified, alongside the provision of IA descrbing the proposed measures' impacts on these groups and the calculation of estimates ordered by magnitude. As one progresses through the policymaking process, refinement of data quality and analytical depth is expected.

In cases involving engagement with stakeholders (e.g., formal consultation), quantification and monetization should be included as far as possible, even if the numbers are indicative.

(3) Transparency and consultation

Wide-ranging consultation with stakeholders is an integral part of the IA approach. Informal consultation with stakeholders may occur at different points in the policy cycle. Draft IA is published at afirst formal public consultation stage. Additionally, this stage should focus on firming up the options being considered and ensuring quantification of the costs and benefits of each option as far as possible, even if the numbers are indicative. Consultation should be used to seek stakeholders' views on the proposals under review, as well as on the cost and benefit estimates and the key assumptions and data that contribute to the analysis.

The concept of a transparent regulation-making process may be satisfied as simply as by notifying the public that regulatory decisions have been taken; this is done to control administrative discretion and corruption. Greater transparency often calls for a better organized legal system, which can be achieved by improving the accessibility and coherence of legislation and by utilizing public consultation.

In developed countries, policymakers are increasingly relying on consultation to collect empirical information for analytical purposes, a development that represents the widespread adoption of IA in recent years and a more general move toward analytical decision-making models. In sum, consultation is vital for decision making.

IA aims to contribute to enhancing the regulation quality and the efficiency of the regulation-making process. Furthermore, it aims to provide the public with sufficient information and a forum for exchanging opinions at the conceptual and planning stages of regulation making to facilitate reflection of the public's opinions and needs in policies and business plans.

(4) Quality control

The IA system aims to help the government improve the quality and transparency of its proposals and identify balanced solutions consistent with community policy objectives, as follows:

1. Coherent analysis of potential impacts
2. Consideration of various policy choices (e.g., to use alternative instruments to "control and command" regulation vs. non-intervention)
3. Assessment of costs and benefits by setting an adequate baseline (counterfactual) to compare scenarios with and without the proposed regulation
4. Consultation with stakeholders and enhanced transparency.

To strengthen IA's quality control, most countries that have introduced it have also established an institution to supervise or review other departments' IA.

In the US, OIRA (Office of Information and Regulatory Affair) within the OMB (Office of Management and Budget) reviews other government departments' regulatory impact analysis (RIA)/IA. In Japan, the Administrative Evaluation Bureau of the Ministry of Internal Affairs and Communications has the authority to review

IA. In November 2006, the European Commission created a new internal quality control function, where the Regulatory Scrutiny Board (RSB) reviews IA.[1] The United Kingdom separates IA review from regulation itself. Specifically, the Regulatory Policy Committee (RPC) reviews IA,[2] while the Better Regulation Executive (BRE)[3] in the Department for Business, Energy and Industrial Strategy (BEIS) reviews regulations.

(5) Which IA rules should be mandated?

The government determines which proposals require IA. For example, in the United States, the executive branch conducts RIA for every rule they make, and the OMB reviews all significant regulatory actions. Executive Order 12,866, which is the basis of EO 13,563,[4] requires an OIRA review before actions take effect. Executive Order 12,866 defines significant regulatory actions as those that: (1) have an annual effect on the economy of USD 100 million or more or adversely affect the economy in a material way, a sector of the economy, productivity, competition, jobs, the environment, public health or safety, or state, local, or tribal governments or communities; (2) create a serious inconsistency or otherwise interfere with an action taken or planned by another agency; (3) materially alter the budgetary impact of entitlements, grants, user fees, or loan programs, or the rights and obligations of recipients thereof; or (4) raise novel legal or policy issues arising out of legal mandates, the President's priorities, or the principles set forth in this executive order.

On the part of agencies, Executive Order 12,866 requires an analysis of the costs and benefits of rules, and, to the extent permitted by law, action based on a reasoned determination that the benefits justify the costs.

However, Congress and the Independent Regulatory Commission have no obligation to conduct IA. Thus, laws and some important economic regulations emerging from the Federal Energy Regulatory Commission (FERC) or the Federal Communication Commission (FCC) etc. are not accompanied by IA, whereas, in the United Kingdom and Japan, it is mandatory to conduct RIA of laws.[5]

(6) Viewpoints in IA

IA begins the description of regulation and explanation of background and the issue to be solved. Then it explains the necessity of addressing current or possible social or economic problems. For this purpose, the rationality of the proposed measures must be verified by clarifying the impact (costs and benefits) of the proposed regulatory revision as quantitatively as possible. In cases where quantification is difficult, efforts should be made to provide as specific and objective an explanation as possible.

However, IA is only used to identify and quantitatively and qualitatively understand impacts, not automatically link the results to policy decisions. In particular, it

[1] https://ec.europa.eu/info/law/law-making-process/regulatory-scrutiny-board_en.

[2] https://www.gov.uk/government/organisations/regulatory-policy-committee.

[3] https://www.gov.uk/government/groups/better-regulation-executive.

[4] https://www.whitehouse.gov/omb/information-regulatory-affairs/regulatory-matters.

[5] In Japan, IA is not required for a bill that a legislator proposes.

should be noted that when quantifying and monetizing costs and benefits (also known as monetary conversion or monetary valorization), some factors are not reflected, such as events that involve uncertainty and even uncertainty in the analysis itself. In the assessment process, efforts should be made to ensure transparency and reproducibility, and clarifying various issues as quantitatively and qualitatively as possible should be emphasized to provide materials for the formulation of a more desirable regulatory system.

(7) Proportionate analysis

IA entails a balanced appraisal of all impacts, whereby the depth and scope of IA—and hence the resources allocated to it—are proportionate to the expected nature of the proposal and its likely impacts.

In UK guidance, the effort invested at each step of IA, particularly the estimation of cost and benefits, should be proportionate to the scale of the costs and benefits, the outcomes at stake, the sensitivity of the proposal, and the time available. Less detailed IA may be adequate when a regulatory proposal is likely to affect only a few firms or organizations or many firms or organizations but only to a negligible degree. The same applies in cases where the costs and benefits are likely to be negligible and can be captured by less evidence. By the same token, more data and analysis are required when the impact is expected to be substantial.

(8) Uncertainty

Ex-ante assessments, including IA, are inherently uncertain because they are estimates predicting future events. Therefore, it is natural that regulations' impacts may not be precisely known. However, even in cases where a regulation's impact is unknown, it is insufficient to simply say, "I don't know." Instead, it is necessary to devise, for example, a forecast that (1) uses mimimum and maximum values for major factors, (2) assumes the worst-case scenario for all major factors, and (3) assumes that there is room for improvement for some major factors. However, when concrete figures are given for matters in which a high degree of uncertainty is involved, it is necessary to indicate the confidence interval in the figures.

(9) Reproducibility

It should also be confirmed that the data and methods used in IA are evaluated at a certain level. The results should be presented, and the impact assessment process should be clarified so that a third party can verify it.

Reference

EU Better regulation: guidelines and toolbox page: https://ec.europa.eu/info/law/law-making-process/planning-and-proposing-law/better-regulation-why-and-how/better-regulation-guidelines-and-toolbox/better-regulation-toolbox_en

References

Coase R (1960) The problem of social cost. J Law Econ 3(1):1–44. https://doi.org/10.1086/466560
Crawford V, Sobel J (1982) Strategic information transmission. Econometrica 50:1431–1451
Feldman AM, Serrano R (2005) Welfare economics and social choice theory. Springer, p 416
Myerson RB (1979) Incentive compatibility and the bargaining problem. Econometrica 47:61–74
Miyaoka A (2019) Prices versus quantities with strategic communication between government and polluting industry. mimeo
Muthoo A (2008) Bargaining theory with applications. Cambridge University Press, p 376
Samuelson PA (1947) Foundations of economic analysis (Harvard Economic Studies). Harvard University Press, p 460

Part II
Procedure and Organization of Conducting Impact Assessment (IA)

Chapter 3
Procedure of Impact Assessment (IA) and Concept of Institution Design for Conducting Impact Assessment (IA)

Abstract We explain IA procedure and the organizational structure of IA and regulation making. The key components of institutional design are (1) establishing IA ground rules, (2) providing guidelines, (3) establishing separate institutions responsible for reviewing and improving the IA process, and (4) involving economists or other scientific researchers. Thereafter, we provide a rough outline of IA procedures in the United Kingdom and the EU.

3.1 Introduction

In this part, we explain the procedure and organization for efficiently conducting impact assessment (IA), illustrating the organization of the US, the UK, Japan, and Pakistan regarding regulation making, including IA. We also consider economists' organizational placements. In this chapter, we explain the IA procedure. Next, we explain the concept of the institutional design for conducting IA. In the next chapter, we illustrate the organization of the US. In Chap. 5, we show the role of economists in the US, UK, and Pakistan regarding regulation making, including the IA. In Chap. 6, we present the issues and experiences of economists' organizational placement based on organizational economics.

In recent years, technological progress has accelerated, and the world has faced drastic changes. For example, electrical vehicles (EV), automated driving, promotion of renewable energy, advances in regenerative medicine, development of virtual reality (VR) and drones, nuclear fusion, and even Mars exploration are realizing.

To fully exploit the results of these technological innovations, flexible regulations are needed. The market can respond to technological progress through scrap and building, with the entry of new firms and exit of old ones. Conversely, the public sector has no mechanism other than elections in democracy. Without strong top-down leadership, changing the traditional way of doing things would be difficult.

Thus, in the UK and the US, attempts for deregulation are currently being made to reduce the number of regulations themselves, in the form of "one in one out or two or more out" in 2010s. Such deregulation began in the US in the 1980s, and the

T. Nakaizumi, *Impact Assessment for Developing Countries*, Contributions to Economics,
https://doi.org/10.1007/978-981-19-5494-8_3

recent restoration of deregulation trends seems to be a response to social changes and rapid technological progress.

Therefore, it is desirable to have an organization in charge of IA that can respond flexibly to the principles of proportionality, an evidence base, and earlier commitment to IA preparation. This would involve collaboration from early stage of regulation preparation and focus on analysis proportional to the importance of the regulation, appropriately assessing the flexibility of the regulations, and being flexible enough to withstand regulatory changes. In this chapter, we explain organization structure to adapt regulation making. Section 3.2 shows the key component of institutional design to conduct IA properly, and Sect. 3.3 provides a rough outline of the procedures of IA in the UK and EU.

3.2 Key Component of Institutional Design for Conducting Impact Assessment (IA)

Improving regulations is the main purpose of the IA. Therefore, IA needs to be prepared in coordination with regulations from the beginning of regulation making. Thus, both regulation and IA should be conducted together within the organization with the jurisdiction of the regulation, with an advice from review authority. Importance of commitment to conduct IA from early stages of regulation making is recognized from various examples. For example, competition assessment estimates the impact of regulations on competition. Moreover, if regulations restrict entry of the market and some firms would have significant market power owing to regulation, measures are used to temporarily postpone introduction of regulations until the number of firms increases. However, attempting to implement such measures while establishing a regulatory proposal will only result in minor adjustments. Conversely, constructing a regulatory proposal when regulations are introduced from a variety of options that do not change the effect other than competition will lead to a more drastic reform. The other example is that moving from design-standards regulations that permit only certain products to performance-standards regulation, which is not only the subject of competition assessment but also recommended in the overall US Regulatory Impact Analysis (RIA) guidelines Circular A-4. That can significantly increase the number of companies that can respond and significantly reduce the competition burden, including potential for entry, compared to regulations based on certain specifications.

Such drastic measures can be achieved by proposing them from the outset of a regulatory proposal, and the primary significance of IA is to promote such choices. The first step for better IA is to design organization to encourage preparation of IAs from the early stage of regulation making and their strong and earlier linkage of IA with draft regulations. Thus, the person in charge of IA should become key in the preparation of regulations.

However, earlier analysis might be a rough outline. Checking whether the analysis has been properly performed will be difficult at an early stage. Therefore, providing incentives to analysts and regulators in the initial stage is important. Such early-stage considerations are the basis for subsequent IA, and quality of later analysis will partially ensure that early considerations are secured.

Quality of regulations themselves should also be appreciated as an adequate consideration of their impacts at the earlier stage. But there might be some cases wherein extensive analysis in the later stages is caused by inadequate initial preparation. This is the reason the US Office of Management and Budget frequently holds informal meetings with each department at an earlier stage, discussing the regulation and ensuring the quality of the regulation itself, although disclosing informal consultations is difficult. The Regulatory Policy Committee (RPC) which is in charge of reviewing IA within the UK government, does not check IA in the draft because of an external body. But BEIS, an internal body, consult on draft regulations.

There are four components of successful institutional design described in Chap. 1: (1) establishing IA ground rules, (2) providing guidelines, (3) building separate institutions that review and improve the IA process, and (4) involving economists or other scientific researchers. Ground rules leagalize 1) process to conduct IA, 2) who conduct IA and 3) how IA is used in the regulatory decision, and 4)who reviews the IA and Draft regulation. And guideline provides how to analize and conduct IA. We explain it in Part 3 and introduce US Guideline Circular A-4.

In the US, Executive Order (EO) 12,866 "Regulatory Planning and Review," issued by President Clinton on September 30, 1993, governs the process of conducting impact assessment (called regulatory impact analysis in the US), wherein OIRA reviews each agency's drafts and guides them to final regulatory actions. The EO aims to enhance planning of regulation making and coordination between each regulatory agencies and OIRA relative to both new and existing regulations and make the process more accessible and open to the public. For all significant regulatory actions, the EO requires an OIRA review before actions take effect. EO 12,866 requires the agencies a cost-benefit analysis of the rules and, to the extent permitted by law, action only based on reasoned determination that the benefits justify the costs.[1]

Building separate institution that reviews and helps to improve the IA process is also necessary, and It should check formally and informally are recommended from the early stage of the preparation of the draft regulations and draft IA. Particularly, it is essential to improve the quality of draft IA and regulation, having a review body that comprehensively checks them.

As assessment of regulations mainly involves analysis from an economic perspective (e.g., causal inference and cost-benefit analysis), early commitment of economists is also recommended. There are many economists in the US government, especially in OIRA, EPA and some Independent Regulatory Commissions. Ellig

[1] Executive Order 12,866 assigns OIRA the responsibility of coordinating interagency Executive Branch review of significant regulations before publication. This is to ensure agency compliance with the principles in Executive Order 12,866, which include incorporating public comment, considering alternatives to the rulemaking, and analyzing both costs and benefits.

(2019) investigated the impact of economists' involvement on regulatory quality and showed positive effects. Even in the US, this is a long way to depend on an economic perspective. However, rational decisions based on an economic perspective improve welfare. Additionally, rational decision-makers tend to favor the long term relationship with specialists in order to prommote evidence-based policy making and improve welfare.

To promote evidence-based policy making (EBPM), the UK government established the What Works Network in 2013, which uses evidence to improve the design and delivery of public services. What Works Centres are located in the What Works Network.[2] The What Work Centres have many economists who are sent to various regulatory authorities to help conduct IA. Such effort to involve economists or other scientific researchers is informative for establishing an organization for better IA. Experts, mainly economists, find what is lacking and what is need to be analized. Hence, increasing participation by these experts is desirable. In developing countries, the help of economists at the World Bank would also be beneficial.

After establishing IA ground rules, providing guidelines for better analysis is necessary. Guidelines describe how to conduct IA, especially for better analysis. Thus, we introduce the US and UK guidelines in Part 3. In the US, some departments, such as the National Oceanic and Atmospheric Administration (NOAA) in the Department of Commerce (DOC), have specific guidelines for the department, while others, such as the Food and Drug Administration (FDA) of the Department of Health and Human Services, make use of only OMB guidelines. Because many parts of the guidelines are obvious to experts, the importance of the guidelines varies depending on how much help economists have. Each country complies with its own guidelines, including the analysis methods in the process to conduct IA, as shown in Sect. 3.3. In the next section, we provide a rough outline of the procedures for preparing an IA in OECD countries, and we describe the US procedure in Chap. 4.

3.3 Rough Outline of the Procedures of IA in the OECD Countries

In this section, we briefly explain the process of conducting IA in three stages. In the US executive office of the president, or the UK and EU regulatory authority, impact assessment is prepared concurrently with regulation making. This process is mainly from the EUROPEAN COMMISSION Better regulation "Toolbox" in the EU (2021a).

(1) **Development and proposal of regulation and IA**
First, an organization with jurisdiction over the regulation writes draft regulations and IA based on the definition of the policy problem, rationale for government intervention, identification of policy objectives, and evidence gathering. Then, they develop options and test these options by engaging with interested

[2] https://www.gov.uk/guidance/what-works-network.

parties ahead of formal consultation. Regulatory authority in charge of regulation making and conducting IA should have close contact with the review authority as early as possible.

(2) **Consultation stage**
Informal consultations with stakeholders may occur at different stages in the policy cycle. The stage should focus on strengthening the options considered, ensuring that there is greater quantification of the costs and benefits of each option as far as possible, even if the numbers are indicative. You should use the consultation to seek stakeholders' views on your proposals for review, your cost and benefit estimates, and the key assumptions and data that contribute to the analysis. Draft regulations and IA are then published.

(3) **Final proposal stage**
After responding to the consultation, both the regulation and IA should be modified. The review authority checks and approves if they are adequate. Then, the final impact assessment and final regulation are published when the government announces its approval.

In the remaining of the section, we refer to the procedure of the UK and EU impact assessment. We will explain the US procedure in the next chapter, where the regulation map in the US from the "regulation.gov" website is helpful for viewing the whole picture of regulation.[3] A more detailed explanation of US rule making is shown in Viscusi et al. (2018).

We briefly introduce the UK government's impact assessment and procedure UK in (a). They illustrated the process for the following five steps, illustrating the ROAMEF cycle in Green Book of UK (The UK HM Treasury (2022)), which is a more complicated version of the PDCA cycle. And EU process is shown in (b)

(a) UK impact assessment process

(1) **Development stage:** Rationale and Objective stages in ROAMEF.
(2) **Options stage:** Broadly equivalent to the Appraisal stage in ROAMEF.
(3) **Consultation stage:** Consultation is also part of the Appraisal stage in ROAMEF.
(4) **Final Proposal stage:** This stage is broadly equivalent to what the ROAMEF describes as "developing a solution" at the end of the Appraisal stage.
(5) **Enactment stage:** This stage is similar to the Monitoring and Implementation stage in ROAMEF.

The process is conducted by the Better Regulation Unit of each Ministry along with discussions with review organizations, such as RPC. There have been several changes in review organizations in the UK. The RPC, an external committee, reviews Impact Assessment since 2012 and Better Regulation Executive (BRE) that belongs to the Department for Business, Energy, and Industrial Strategy (BEIS) review the regulation. As the review

[3] See Reg map: http://www.reginfo.gov/public/reginfo/Regmap/index.jsp.

of the analysis should be done independently, this is separated from policy issues. RPC reviews IA, and regulations are separately reviewed by BEIS. In 2018, the UK Parliament removed the requirement for departments to submit RPC draft IA and Regulation at the consultation stage, despite the importance of earlier commitment for RPC to review the regulation and impact assessment. Only BEIS consults each ministry for draft regulation. This may be attributable to draft IA being difficult to estimate because of uncertainty. However, these decisions should be evaluated in future studies.

(b) EU key procedure steps
Referring to the EU guideline, we show a summary of key procedural steps:

(1) Creation of an interservice group (ISG), which will steer the IA process and collectively prepare an IA report. For these initiatives in the commission's work (or other important/sensitive initiatives), the ISG will be established and chaired by the Secretariat General. A member of the lead director-general's impact assessment support service should participate in the ISG.
(2) Following publication of the inception IA on the Commission's website, stakeholders can provide feedback and evidence relative to the problem, possible policy options, and their likely impacts and subsidiarity considerations. This feedback must be considered and integrated into the work of the ISG as appropriate.
(3) Preparation of a consultation strategy by the ISG included mandatory 12-week internet-based public consultation. The consultation strategy should ensure that stakeholders' views are sought for all key impact assessment questions.
(4) Collection and analysis of all relevant evidence, including data, scientific advice, other expert views, and stakeholder input.
(5) Drafting of the IA report.
(6) Submission of the draft IA report to the regulatory scrutiny board (RSB) for quality review, followed by a revision to consider its recommendations for improvement.
(7) Subject to a positive opinion by the board, submission of the IA report to interservice consultation, and the accompanying policy initiative.

Subsequently, an IA report presents the results of the impact assessment process and accompanies the draft initiative through the commission's decision-making process. The Commission's Regulatory Scrutiny Board, which is in charge of reviewing the IA, scrutinizes the quality of all draft IAs and issues one or more opinions on the draft IA report. Before an initiative can proceed, a positive opinion of RSB is required. The final IA report was published and transmitted to a legislator.

References

Ellig J (2019) Agency economists. Final Report. https://www.acus.gov/sites/default/files/documents/Ellig%20Agency%20Economists%20Final%20Report%20September%202019.pdf

EUROPEAN COMMISSION (2021) Commission staff working document better regulation guidelines. https://ec.europa.eu/info/sites/default/files/swd2021_305_en.pdf

European Commission (2021a) Better regulation: guidelines and toolbox, general principles. https://ec.europa.eu/info/law/law-making-process/planning-and-proposing-law/better-regulation-why-and-how/better-regulation-guidelines-and-toolbox_en

European Commission (2021b) Chapter III guidelines on impact assessment. https://ec.europa.eu/info/sites/default/files/better-regulation-guidelines-impact-assessment.pdf

European Commission, Impact Assessment page. https://ec.europa.eu/info/law/law-making-process/planning-and-proposing-law/impact-assessments_en

Institute of Administrative Management (2008) Kisei no jizen hyōka handobukku yoriyoi kisei ni mukete chosha-mei. Institute of Administrative Management, 333 page

Nakaizumi T (2012) Kisei sakusei ni okeru kisei eikyō bunseki (ria) no jūyō-sei: Beikoku no jirei o sankō to shite' hyōka ni tsuite no kōen gaiyō hyōka kuōtarī dai, vol 23. Gyoseikanri kenkyu, ippan zaidanhōjin gyōsei kanri kenkyū

OECD Regulatory Impact Analysis page. http://www.oecd.org/gov/regulatorypolicy/ria.htm

OECD (1997) Regulatory impact analysis: best practices in OECD countries, 280 pages. https://doi.org/10.1787/9789264162150-en

The UK impact Assessment guidance page. https://www.gov.uk/government/collections/impact-assessments-guidance-for-government-departments

The UK government What Works Network. https://www.gov.uk/guidance/what-works-network

The UK HM Treasury (2022) The green book and accompanying guidance and documents. https://www.gov.uk/government/collections/the-green-book-and-accompanying-guidance-and-documents

USA OIRA, OMB, RegInfo.gov-Reg Map. http://www.reginfo.gov/public/jsp/Utilities/faq.jsp

USA OIRA of OMB, Circular A-4. http://www.whitehouse.gov/omb/circulars_a004_a-4

USA (1993) Executive order 12866. http://www.plainlanguage.gov/.../eo12866.pdf

Viscusi WK, Harrington JE Jr, Sappington DEM (2018) Economics of regulation and antitrust, Fifth edn. MIT Press, 1000 page

Chapter 4
IA Procedure and Organization in the U.S.

Abstract We explain IA procedure in the U.S. First, we explain EO 12,866, ground rules of IA(RIA) in the U.S. Then we introduce OIRA (Office of Information and Regulatory Affair of the US Office of Management and Budget (OMB) as a review authority and explain the role of that in the process of RIA. Then we explain the procedure within Presidential Department and other issue in conducting IA.

4.1 Introduction

In this chapter, we explain the procedure of Impact Assessment (IA) and regulation making in the US based on my interviews and reserach that began in 2000 and wrote in Morita et al. (2001) and updated in Institute of Administrative Management Japan (2008). Although I have been continuously reviewing the US procedure after that, the basic principle have not been drastically changed since US guideline Circular A-4 was published. Thus, I still refere these studies. Corresponding to how IA is called in the US, we use RIA instead of IA in this chapter.

The US Congress creates laws that often do not include all the details needed to explain how an affected individual, organization, state, or local government might follow it. Thus, Congress authorizes government agencies to create and enforce regulations. Regulations can be applied to individuals, businesses, state or local governments, non-profit institutions, and others. Regulations set specific requirements regarding what is legal and what is not. If the jurisdiction of the regulation belongs to any presidential department, all regulations are accompanied by RIA based on several EOs.

The US has a history of approximately 50 years in RIA, that is, the longest history of IA in the world. The current US RIA system is based on the Presidential EO 12,866 (1993) settled under the Clinton administration, although it was frozen under the Trump administration and revived by the current Biden administration.[1] The latest version is EO 13,563 (2011), promulgated by the Obama administration.

[1] https://www.whitehouse.gov/omb/information-regulatory-affairs/regulatory-matters/.

T. Nakaizumi, *Impact Assessment for Developing Countries*, Contributions to Economics,
https://doi.org/10.1007/978-981-19-5494-8_4

Each presidential department is mainly responsible for so-called social regulations (e.g., environment, safety, and public health regulations). Thus, cost benefit analysis for quantification and monetary evaluation of external effects is a priority when conducting RIA. Based on this premise, EO 12,866 requires that when a regulation is introduced or changed, the benefits of the regulation must be demonstrated to outweigh the costs of its introduction. However, EO 12,866 applies only to residential departments.

Following EO 12,866 and a series of EOs such as 13,563, each department of the Presidential Office in the US government is required to conduct RIA when enacting regulations. In the next section, we present the framework of EO 12,866. In Sect. 4.3, we show how RIA was conducted according to EO 12,866. Section 4.4 describes the process of preparing RIAs and regulations. In Sect. 4.5, we discribe the procedures in several departments. Section 4.6 presents the review process by Office of Management and Budget (OMB). Finally, Sect. 4.7 concludes the study.

4.2 Overview of EO 12866

EO 12,866 is characterized by its strict adherence to the principle of proportionality, limiting the volume of RIA submitted to OMB under review to only "significant regulations." Additionally, while EO 12,866 introduced risk assessment, it leaves room for qualitative analysis when it is not quantifiable and does not require costs to exceed benefits. Furthermore, it has various adjustment provisions to avoid the abuse of the strong authority of the OMB, which has budgetary authority.

In EO 12,866, the improvement of regulation and justifying benefit is shown to exceed cost and is written as the first priority. In Sect. 4.1 (Statement of Regulatory Philosophy and Principles), federal agencies should assess all costs and benefits of available regulatory alternatives, including the alternative of not regulating. However, costs and benefits shall be understood to fully include both quantifiable (that can be usefully estimated) and qualitative measures of costs and benefits that are difficult to quantify.

Section 4.2 shows the organization in which review of Office of Information and Regulatory Affair (OIRA) in OMB is emphasized as important. In the US presidential office, OMB has strong authority with the right of budgetary allocation within presidential departments. Thus, other departments can be more easily controlled by OMB than other review authorities in other countries in the parliamentary cabinet system like Japan. The rule and deadline to review by OIRA in the OMB is the main part of EO 12,866 to implement RIA. Section 4.7 introduces an even resolution of conflicts because the OMB is so powerful that other agencies can make objections. After the definitions are provided in Sects. 4.3, 4.4 shows the timing and deadline for consultation. Conversely, in Sect. 4.6, the deadline of the review process is described.

The history of RIA in the US began with the introduction of the "Quality of Life Review" in 1971 under the Nixon administration, which requires a comparison of costs between proposed regulations and alternatives. Subsequently, in 1974 and

1976, under the Ford administration, a request was made to analyze in advance the impact of major regulatory proposals (where the concept of economic impact of $100 million or more was presented for the first time). In 1978, under the Carter administration, a cost-benefit analysis of regulations was introduced. In 1981, under the Reagan administration, EO 12,291 was promulgated as a means of deregulation and reform policy to achieve economic recovery.

EO 12,866, issued under the Clinton administration and the current US system of regulatory impact analysis is based on EO12,866 and requires that each department of the President's Office conduct a regulatory impact analysis. The basic structure of EO 12,866 is generally inherited from EO 12,291. Subsequently, the content of EO 12,866 has been modified by successive EOs and has been followed by the present EO 13,563. Implementation of RIA in the US is based on this series of presidential orders. EO 12,866 stipulates the content and procedures required for each agency. Conversely, guidelines (Circular A-4) prepared by the US Office of Management and Budget stipulate specific evaluation viewpoints and methods. As the practice of cost-benefit analysis by each department has now become more acceptable, there has been little resistance to such analysis.

Although only "major regulations" are required to be submitted to the OMB for RIA, the Department of Transportation, for example, conducts RIAs for all regulations, and conducting RIAs is now widespread among departments. From the OMB's perspective, it seems that they are unable to review all RIA regulations.

It should be noted that Conducting IA is promulgated as EOs and cover regulations under the jurisdiction of the various departments of the Presidential Office. Therefore, in the US, Congress and Independent Regulatory Commissions in Congress Jurisdiction are not obligated to conduct RIA. Thus, many economic regulations under the jurisdiction of law and independent regulatory commissions are not subject to RIA. However, according to Dr. Mancini (interviewed in November 2009), the OMB has the authority to decide whether regulation is a "major regulatory activity." Therefore, even independent regulatory commissions outside the OMB's jurisdiction must provide sufficient information to the OMB and show whether it exceeds $100 million or not or other criteia of major regulatory activity. Additional analysis may also be required to demonstrate by OMB.

4.3 Process of Preparing RIAs and Regulations

RIA was conducted according to the regulatory development process. First, the regulatory body prepares a draft regulation after receiving a request from the industry or Congress, or finding a problem in the department. Prior to preparing draft regulations, each regulatory agency prepares a list of regulations that it plans to implement during the year in the form of a regulatory plan and submits it to the OMB, which in turn coordinates with other relevant departments in advance.

The regulatory agency submits its proposed rule and RIA (alternative proposals and their economic analysis) to OIRA of OMB that reviews it. If the OMB decides that reconsideration is necessary, the proposal may be referred to as a regulator for reconsideration of the regulator's analysis. After the review, the proposed regulation is published in the Official Gazette for public comment. After the comment period, the regulatory agency prepares a response to the comments and proposing a final rule and RIA with considering the comments. The final rule and RIA were then submitted again to the OMB for review. After OMB review, the final rule is submitted to Congress for deliberation and is published in the Official Gazette, after that regulation becomes effective.

Public comments are subject to procedures outlined in Section 553(c) of the Administrative Procedure Act. While public comments are not required at the final rule stage under the Administrative Procedure Act, and publication in the Official Gazette occurs at each stage of the proposal rule and final rule, public comments are conducted only once at the proposal rule stage. However, the regulatory body may be published in the Official Gazette and provide public notice at several stages.

Public comments were received not only from interested parties but also from government agencies. Competition authorities such as the Federal Trade Commission (FTC) and Department of Justice (DOJ) do not have the authority to oversee competition analysis which is equivalent to competition assessment on regulation. Hence, other than informal consultations, commenting through public comment is the only formal opportunity to get involved. The impact of the comments is significant as they are known to public.

At the minimum, OMB will review the proposal twice: once for the proposal and once for the final rule. In principle, an OMB review should be conducted within 90 days. However, OMB usually discusses regulations and RIA in the preliminary stages of rule making (e.g., notice of inquiry or an advance notice of the proposed rulemaking). OMB will not conduct its own analysis of the regulation but will review the proposed regulation and RIA and, if there are any questions or advice regarding the analysis, consult informal or formal discussion with the regulatory agency.

In addition to EO 12,866, the Regulatory Flexibility Act requires the agency to assess the economic impact of regulations on small businesses. Regulators also followed these individual laws in their assessments. In 1996, as part of the Small Business Regulatory Enforcement Fairness Act, the Congressional Review Act was enacted, which requires a copy of the regulation or "significant regulatory activity" before the final rule takes effect. Before the final rule goes into effect, Congress requires OMB to send a copy of the regulation and materials, including whether it is a "significant regulatory activity" to the General Accounting Office and both houses of Congress. Congress can vote to disapprove major regulations after the final rule is published, delaying their effective date for at least 60 days.

In the US, it is customary to consider "significant regulations" over a sufficient period of time, and it is common for final rules to take 2–4 years to be developed. The National Emission Standards for Hazardous Air Pollutants in the Cement Industry (Portland Cement Manufacturing Industry) was initially proposed in 1998, but amendments were considered and final decisions were fixed in 2018.[2] The webpage on government regulations was well developed in the 2010s, such as "Regulation.gov",[3] which provides a detailed analysis of RIAs and all the documents, including public comments and responses regarding regulation making. Best practices and guidelines were also updated as appropriate.

4.4 Procedures of Each Department

In this section, we provide an overview of the procedure in each agency of the Presidential Office by illustrating several agencies, such as the Department of Transportation, including the roles of OIRA. In Sect. 4.4.1, we explain the procedure of the US Environmental Protection Agency (EPA), Sect. 4.4.2 National Highway Traffic Safety Administration (NHTSA) in the Department of Transportation, Sect. 4.4.3 National Marine Fisheries Service (NMFS) of the National Oceanic and Atmospheric Administration (NOAA), and Department of Commerce (DOC). This subsection is mainly based on Morita, et al. (2001) and Institute of Administrative Management Japan (2008). Therefore, some facts might not be updated. But it I emphasize that it is not the purpose to show latest procedures but introduce the typical procedure of RIA.

4.4.1 US Environmental Protection Agency (EPA)

We briefly describe the procedure of IA in the EPA based on the CBO (1997). A regulatory impact analysis (RIA) at the Environmental Protection Agency (EPA) originates in one of the program offices, the Office of Solid Waste. Each office has a division responsible for conducting regulatory analyses. To illustrate the process, the Office of Solid Waste's Economic Methods and Risk Analysis Division (EMRAD) is picked up to represent these divisions and the tasks they perform.

First, the division considers whether the resources required to conduct the RIA (i.e., the number of experts required) can be provided within the division and selects either (1) in-house, (2) with the participation of staff from other divisions within the EPA, or (3) outsourced. In case (3), EMRAD and the ordered party usually communicate frequently from the initial stage of the RIA and proceed with the RIA work in a collaborative manner through discussions on both sides, and no clear division of roles exists between the two parties.

Next, in the process of review within the EPA, a work group (with members of the relevant department and legal advisor) was involved. A work group (with members of

[2] https://www.epa.gov/stationary-sources-air-pollution/portland-cement-manufacturing-industry-national-emission-standards#rule-history.

[3] https://www.regulations.gov/.

the responsible department and legal counsel and even staff from other departments) will be established to review the proposed analysis. Members of general counsel will be involved in all regulatory decisions made by the EPA. Depending on the complexity of the issue being addressed, the number of people can range from 2 to 25. The responsible office might request a review from outside experts, such as the EPAs Science Advisory Board.

The work group's report and other relevant studies (materials) supporting the proposed regulation were sent to the EPA administrator. After the Secretary's approval, they are submitted to the OMB for review under EO 12,866.

As mentioned, the proposed rule will be published in the federal register for public comments. After the public comment period, comments are then examined, and the department in charge will prepare the final draft of the regulation, following the same procedure as in the proposal rule.

4.4.2 National Highway Traffic Safety Administration (NHTSA) in Department of Transportation

The Department of Transportation (DOT) has approximately 55,000 employees.[4] In 2009, according to our interview with the DOT secretary, in the jurisdiction of DOT, approximately 75 were important regulations, 100–200 less important regulations, and 4,000–6,000 were routine regulations in a year.[5]

The DOT constantly collects and accumulates data and information through its own statistical departments and testing organizations, facilitating identification of problems and establishment of issues.

In the NHTSA, the process of developing regulations and conducting RIAs is conducted through the following groups' joint efforts. The first is research and development, which is divided into two groups: (1) those that conduct tests, such as crash tests on passenger cars, and (2) those collecting data and information on personal injury and other crashes throughout the US. The second is the collection of data, which is an important basis for benefit analysis. The cost of collecting this data is high, ranging from $15,000,000 to $20,000,000 yearly. Second, in the rule-making process, a group of engineers will propose new standards and possible solutions using the information gathered by the first group as a reference. A support paper was then prepared for the rule-making process. Third, a group of legal experts drafted the appropriate regulatory language. The fourth group was the department in charge of RIA.

Before 2000, the work of each group was divided, but since 2000, there has been an increase in interaction between the groups in charge of rule making and the RIA department, and both departments have held discussions and worked together to create the proposed regulations. In other words, the RIA department not only reviews

[4] https://www.transportation.gov/administrations.

[5] Based on the Interviews at Department of Transportation in 2000.

the draft regulations prepared by the department in charge of rule making but is also involved in the entire regulatory development process, requesting further necessary tests at the information gathering stage and discussing them during the regulatory development process.

Once the proposal rule is finalized within the NHTSA, it is reviewed by the department's legal advisor. The legal advisor is composed mainly of legal experts who comment on the analysis but do not review the analysis itself, rather, it reviews the entire proposed regulation from a policy and political perspective. When RIA is finalized as a DOT, it is submitted to the OMB. After submitting the OMB, the general procedures written in EO are followed.

4.4.3 National Marine Fisheries Service (NMFS) in NOAA of DOC

Subsequently, we present the procedure of the National Marine Fisheries Service (NMFS) in the National Oceanic and Atmospheric Administration (NOAA), Department of Commerce (DOC), based on the guidelines[6] (NOAA 2007) and NOAA web page, as an example of the regulation-making process, including RIAs, in each region of the US.

The waters under the jurisdiction of the federal government are divided into eight regions. Each region is the jurisdiction of the Regional Fishery Management Councils[7] in the US. These councils develop fishery management plans (FMPs), which will be developed for the proper conservation and management of fishery resources in the waters under their jurisdiction.

Thus, fishery management and other marine-resource management in the US are implemented through fishery management plans (FMPs) developed by the Regional Fishery Management Councils.

In most cases, the first step in developing federal fishing regulations occurs at the Council; the final steps are implemented by NOAA Fisheries. The general process for developing federal fishing regulations is mainly as follows:

1. The Council gathers suggestions and ideas regarding fishery problems, needs, or identified issues. Reasonable alternatives were identified through this process.
2. A committee convened by Council develops actions and alternatives, and the Council drafts supporting documents.
3. After alternatives are developed for plans and amendments, public hearings are held to gather feedback on the potential impact of the proposed options or suggestions for alternatives.

[6] APPENDIX B: Typical Regulatory Process, Guidelines for Economic Review of National Marine Fisheries Service Regulatory Actions, March 2007 https://media.fisheries.noaa.gov/dam-migration/01-111-05.pdf.

[7] http://www.fisherycouncils.org/.

4. A committee makes recommendations on the Council's final action. Before a council votes, the public is invited to speak on the action. The council votes for adopting or amending the action. Once the Council votes to adopt a management action, the action is presented to the NOAA Fisheries for review, approval, and implementation.
5. NOAA Fisheries reviews the Council's action for compliance with the Magnuson-Stevens Act and other federal laws and then proposes a regulation by issuing a Notice of Proposed Rulemaking. The public can then consider this and submit their comments accordingly.
6. After considering public comments, the regulation was revised as needed, and a final rule was issued. This final rule was also published by the federal register.
7. The regulation is then codified in the Code of Federal Regulations (CFR), which is the official record of all federal regulations.

If some regulations are considered significant, they are sent to OMB, which is described later. The OMB reviews all the rules it considers significant under EO 12,866. NMFS prepares a listing document for the OMB, which indicates whether NMFS considers the rule to be significant. This was sent to the OMB during the initial evaluation of the proposed rule.

If OMB concurs with NMFS on whether the rule is not significant, the OMB review process ends. However, if the OMB overrules the NMFS determination of "not significant" and determines that the rule is significant under EO 12,866, the OMB advises the Office of General Counsel/Department of Commerce (OGC/DOC) and the OGC/DOC informs the NMFS. The OMB must provide clearance before any proposed rule determined to be significant is published.

When the rule is determined to be significant, the analysis goes through more scrutiny by the OMB to ensure that the requirements of EO 12,866 are satisfied. If any part of the required analysis is missing, the OMB requests an additional analysis to correct this deficiency. If OMB determines that rule making is significant under EO 12,866, it also reviews and clears the final rule before publication in the Federal Register. The OMB usually reviews the rule only, but, occasionally, it also reviews the FMP or amendment.

4.5 OMB/OIRA Review for RIAs

The Office of Information and Regulatory Affairs (OIRA) within the Office of Management and Budget (OMB) oversees the RIA of all the presidential departments and agencies. Because OMB is the apex of the hierarchy in the Office of the President and is responsible for preparing budget proposals and managing federal administrative agencies, the OMB has strong control over regulatory agencies and has strong authority in reviewing RIAs. The OIRA is comprised of four departments.[8] In total, OIRA reviews approximately 500–700 regulatory proposals per year, with a focus on approximately 70–100 important proposals per year (from Morita et al. (2001)).[9]

4.5.1 Subject of Review

Presidential EO 12,866 states that "significant regulatory" activities cause a significant economic impact of $100 million or more per year and are subject to OMB review. Currently, the criteria have been used to determine whether to review regulations where either the costs or benefits are more than $100 million. Without such criteria, too many regulations would exceed the OMB's capacity. There is also a discussion on amending the EO to introduce an organization that would select regulations for review (by interview with Dr. Mancini in November 2009).

OIRA generally designates between 500 and 700 regulatory actions as significant regulations each year. The entire set of regulations is listed.[10] Generally, requesting amendments to regulations where RIA results in a negative net benefit is usual, as cost/benefit analysis is not the only criterion for determining regulations, and even a negative net benefit may pass the review process.

4.5.2 Relationship Between OIRA/OMB and Regulatory Agencies in the Presidential Office

The OIRA desk officer and budget office staff could communicate within the OMB and undesirable regulations might be treated unfavorably in budget allocation. The strength of the OMB's control also depends on the president's stance on the RIA. The OMB requests and collects missing data from the regulatory agencies during the review process. Since the OMB does not collect information itself, but refers to research papers, the amount of non-biased information collected from regulatory agencies is an important issue in the OMB review process.

It must also be highlighted that the OMB coordinates through formal and informal consultations with regulatory agencies. The government encourages improvement and adjustments through consultations, rather than formally dismissing the case based on the review results.

---

[8] https://www.whitehouse.gov/omb/information-regulatory-affairs/.

[9] https://www.reginfo.gov/public/jsp/Utilities/faq.myjsp.

[10] OIRA Reports to Congress, 2018, 2019, and 2020 Report to Congress on the Benefits and Costs of Federal Regulations and Agency Compliance with the Unfunded Mandates Reform Act https://www.whitehouse.gov/omb/information-regulatory-affairs/reports/.

4.6 Other Issues in Conducting RIA in the US Government

4.6.1 Outsourcing in the DOC and DOT

Most departments outsource to universities and consultants requesting the collection of data, information, and specialized research. Even the analysis itself is sometimes outsourced (from the interviews to Office of Sustainable Fisheries/DOC in 2000). To reduce outsourcing costs, university researchers are often contracted.

Because NHTSA/DOT has accumulated collision data and other data mentioned above, the collection of information necessary for benefit analysis is done within the agency. However, the analysis of costs is outsourced to an external research organization. From the interviews in 2000, Annual budget was $200,000, and contracts are made with 2–3 outside organizations in the whole DOT. As the Office of Plans and Policy/NHTSA does not have a budget for outsourcing, it comes from the budget of the department in charge of establishing the rules.

The Federal Motor Carrier Safety Administration (FMCSA) in DOT sometimes contracts with universities when detailed analysis is required. Moreover, it also conducted tenders to collect such studies. The scope of the work is indicated and posted online. A review committee in FMCSA will then evaluate the proposals, and the authorities will select the consultants to be contracted. This process is performed transparently, and the procedures are strict. Additionally, university scholars will receive funding to promote the research involved. They do not work directly with university scholars on draft regulations or RIAs, as individual cases.

The FMCSA will host conferences and be a member of various academic societies. The regulation and cost-benefit analyses will explore various possibilities. For example, government economists, including university researchers, of the Transportation Research Board gather once yearly for conferences. The FMCSA also organizes workshops, and research projects may be launched to assist in the preparation of regulations.

4.6.2 Data Collection Within the US Department

Data collection tools in each regulatory agency include the following: (1) information collection and accumulation by internal departments; (2) direct collection through interviews with companies; (3) outsourcing to external organizations such as consultants and universities; and (4) collection through procedures such as public comments, public hearings, and deliberations by the advisory committee. The DOT, for example, has a research division in each department; however, it also has an internal Bureau of Transportation Statistics that is independent of each division of the department. Most of the safety data can be procured within the department, and the collection and accumulation of information is quite advanced.

4.6.3 Manpower Dealing with Public Comment

Public comments vary depending on the nature of the regulation. From the interviews in 2000 at DOT/DOC, about 500 comments was received per regulation, with as many as 50,000–60,000 comments. Commenters include researchers, consultants, law firms, non-profit organizations, corporations, local governments, individuals, and other regulatory agencies.

Regulatory agencies must respond to all comments, so they group similar comments, organize them, and respond to each group. This grouping alone is a huge amount of work; therefore, the summarization and classification of comments is outsourced in some cases. Replies were written by experts in technology, law, economics, and so on, according to the content of the comments. Grouped comments and responses are published in the Official Gazette along with the results of the RIA and can be searched at the aforementioned "Regulation.gov."

Public comments may be influenced by opinions representing specific interests; however, as public comments originate from a wide range of people in various fields, comment bias can be largely eliminated. Additionally, many of the comments were technical in nature regarding the analysis and were not politically influenced.

On the influence of comments, the OMB and regulatory agencies emphasize the importance of public comments. Changes have been made in the final rule in response to comments. Hence, although comments sometimes result in the change of proposals, the agency considers various data-based factors (e.g., safety standards and manufacturers' manufacturing conditions) to arrive at its decision and does not make decisions based on comments alone.

In addition to formal public comments through publication in the official gazette, each regulatory agency holds public hearings to solicit external stakeholders' opinions, either according to individual laws or informally, at the discretion of the regulatory agency for important regulations. Public hearings can be either oral or written. The first step is gathering the necessary information and seeking solutions through public hearings and discussions at the advisory committee, which is voluntarily established by each regulatory agency at the stage of drafting the proposed rule. In the advisory committee, representatives of various organizations, including industry and consumer groups, gather to negotiate solutions to problems. Engineers, lawyers, economists, and lobbyists are considered representatives. Moreover, because experts in technical issues are gathered, this is an effective method for gathering information and discussing the analysis itself. Additionally, even at the stage of considering the content of comments after the public comment period is over, if a particular opinion requires further consideration, the details of the opinion may be heard.

4.7 Concluding Remark

Within four components of successful institutional design described in Chap. 3, the first component is (1) the ground rules is EO 12,866 and (2) guideline Circular A-4 and (3) separate institutions that review IA the OIRA of the OMB. Almost 50 years of history is enough to penetrate the concept of economics and cost-benefit assessment into regulation making. The US Government has many economists, especially OIRA in OMB. Many economists are involved in regulation making and conducting IA at the early stage within each department. OMB has strong authority with the right of budgetary allocation within presidential departments and agencies. Thus, the US organization involved in the IA process has most advantage in all the countries in the world.

However, even for the US government, several issues remain. First, Congress and the Independent Regulatory Commissions are not compulsory to conduct RIA, although they should make adequate analysis based on the act of establishment and provide sufficient information to the OMB and show whether it does not exceed $100 million.

Even in the US, rational decisions based on economics or other sciences are defeated by populism even before the Trump administration. For example, OMB once attempted to modify the static value of life, trying to decrease the value of older people. However, this was not realized because of the strong opposition of older people. RIA and evidence-based policy making will take time to penetrate the regulatory body.

In the next chapter, we explain economists' involvement and other scientists in the process of regulation making and IA, illustrating several examples: the US, the UK, Japan, and Pakistan.

References

CBO (1997) Regulatory impact analysis: costs at selected agencies and implications for the legislative process appendix b how the environmental protection agency conducts a regulatory impact analysis, 71 page. https://www.cbo.gov/sites/default/files/105th-congress-1997-1998/reports/1997doc04-entire.pdf

Institute of Administrative Management Japan (2008) Kisei no jizen hyōka handobukku yoriyoi kisei ni mukete. Institute of Administrative Management, 333 page

Morita A, Tanabe K, Nakaizumi T, Harada H, Kubo H (2001) Kisei eikyō bunseki ni kansuru chōsa kenkyū hōkoku-sho. sōmu-shō daijin kanbō kikaku-ka

NOAA web page: Guidance for Conducting Economic and Social Analyses of Regulatory Actions. https://www.fisheries.noaa.gov/national/laws-and-policies/guidance-conducting-economic-and-social-analyses-regulatory-actions

National Marine Fisheries Service, NOAA (2007) APPENDIX B: typical regulatory process, guidelines for economic review of national marine fisheries service regulatory actions. https://media.fisheries.noaa.gov/dam-migration/01-111-05.pdf

NOAA, Understanding How Federal Fishing Regulations Are Made. https://www.fisheries.noaa.gov/insight/understanding-how-federal-fishing-regulations-are-made

OIRA Reports to Congress, 2018, 2019, and 2020 Report to Congress on the Benefits and Costs of Federal Regulations and Agency Compliance with the Unfunded Mandates Reform Act. https://www.whitehouse.gov/omb/information-regulatory-affairs/reports/
OIRA, OMB in The US, RegInfo.gov-Reg Map. http://www.reginfo.gov/public/jsp/Utilities/faq.jsp
OIRA, OMB in the US, Circular A-4. http://www.whitehouse.gov/omb/circulars_a004_a-4
OMB in the US (1993) Executive order 12866. http://www.plainlanguage.gov/.../eo12866.pdf
The U.S. Environmental Protection Agency, Portland cement manufacturing industry: national emission standards for hazardous air pollutants (NESHAP). https://www.epa.gov/stationary-sources-air-pollution/portland-cement-manufacturing-industry-national-emission-standards#rule-history

Chapter 5
Economists' Role in IA in The United States and The United Kingdom

Abstract We explore the involvement of economists and other specialists in IA. Even rough IA of regulation at the early stage requires basic economics skills and well understanding of economics. Thus, economists' involvement in IA is very helpful. We show that in the United States and the United Kingdom providing some examples of their role.

5.1 Introduction

We explore how economists and other specialists are involved in Impact Assessment (IA). The IA core concept is well described with and without regulations. Quantifying or monetizing the cost and benefit imperfectly is acceptable if adequately specified with and without regulation. However, even specifications and rough assessments require basic skills and well understanding of economics. Thus, economists should be involved in the analysis. Without involvement, asking other specialists or scientists for assistance might be inevitable. Assessing the cost and benefit of regulation by comparing alternatives as early as possible is essential for good IA and regulation, even if there is a rough outline of specifying the benefit and cost. Proper consideration of alternatives is important, especially for minimizing the impact on competition, as in a previous example of performance-based regulation instead of design-standard regulation. On competition assessment, economists' involvement is more important. Opportunities to hire consultants to conduct IA are many, even if economists belong to the regulatory body. The person in charge of IA and regulation making should have complete understanding of the content of the analysis, despite some part of the analysis being outsourced.

The analysis of costs and benefits should be quantified as much as possible and even converted into monetary terms using monetary units. However, it takes a long-term perspective to accumulate a large amounts of studies which form the base for not only quantitative estimation but also methods of monetary conversion. Such research is likely difficult, especially in developing countries. Hence, it is recommended to divert similar studies from OECD countries and adapt them to one's own country, referring to existing studies, or to request the World Bank for research.

T. Nakaizumi, *Impact Assessment for Developing Countries*, Contributions to Economics,
https://doi.org/10.1007/978-981-19-5494-8_5

In the next section, we introduce the role of economists in the UK, such as the What Works Center. In Sect. 5.3, we explain the scale and positioning of economists in the US, and Sect. 5.4 concludes the chapter.

5.2 Economist in UK Government and Role of What Works Center

5.2.1 Economists in the UK Government

In the UK, as shown in Fujita (2014, 2015), attempts to increase the professionalism of civil servants have been made since the Blair Administration proposed a systemic reform in 2005 called professional skills for government (PSG). Below is an overview of the recent situation (late 2010s), based on Uchiyama et al. (2018), regarding the deployment of economists. According to the National Audit Office (2017) and Fujita (2017), the number of professionals assigned to each ministry in 2016 was 942 for economists, 1,583 statisticians, 540 social survey specialists, 578 operational researchers, and 11,486 scientists. Additionally, the number of so-called generalists, who are positioned as policy professions, is 16,573. These form groups of specialists, and government economists form a group called the Government Economic Service (GES), which is mainly responsible for IA.

Analytical professions, mainly economists, occupy a strong position in the UK government. These professionals form a professional network group that transcends the boundaries of ministries and agencies. Owing to the organizational structure, wherein each professional belongs to a ministry and a horizontal professional group, each professional enjoys the benefits of belonging to a broad professional community while also being well integrated into each ministry. Interagency exchanges of manpowers are frequent, and training is conducted by these professional groups. However, formal authority is difficult to assign because they belong to multiple organizations.

The role of the HM Treasury (Ministry of Finance, UK) has strong influence on the overall organizational structure of the executive branch. HM Treasury disseminates policy analysis guidelines to each ministry through the Green Book. The business case (so-called budget request) requires policy appraisal, wherein economists from each ministry analyze benefits and costs, and the analysis is then reviewed by economists within the HM Treasury.

Moreover, the role of institutions outside the regulatory body is crucial. The Parliament's Select Committees were established for each ministry to monitor other ministries. In these committees, ministries are required to undergo rigorous questioning of the evidence of their policies. In December 2013, the National Audit Office (NAO) released a document called the Evaluation Government, which evaluates policy quality by ministry. This external body should be able to monitor and ensure the quality of evidence in regulation making and IA.

In cost-benefit analysis, quantification and monetary conversion of benefits require collaboration with academia and research institution. Therefore, it is essential to encourage such research on a regular basis and to constantly solicit academia to apply for related projects. In the UK, to promote the supply of evidence by researchers, each ministry prepares and publishes an area of research interest (ARI) that summarizes the issue in annual regulatory plan for research. Additionally, some ministries have visited universities and research institutions to explain their expectations.

Among groups of specialists, What Works Centre (WWC) is an organization that has been key in promoting Evidence-Based Policy Making (EBPM) in recent years and plays an important role in impact assessment and regulation making. The following subsection provides an overview of WWC's focus on providing information for a cost-benefit analysis.

5.2.2 *What Works Centre (WWC)*

The What Works Centre (WWC) is an initiative launched by the UK government in 2013 to assess the existing evidence base in specific policy areas and offer advice on effective practices. Currently, WWC consists of nine member agencies and four affiliates (April 2021),[1] and each has diverse areas of activity and approaches. All WWC organizations are responsible for generating evidence, translating, creating actionable guidance, and supporting decision-making.

1. Activities of the WWC
   From WWC (2018), the activities of WWC are as follows: (1) generating evidence through randomized controlled trials, (2) assessing the quality of existing evidence and organizing the facts from existing evidence, and (3) comparing the effects of different policies and practices and organizing them in a format that can be easily understood by all. (4) delivering the evidence to end users by publishing the results; (5) supporting policymakers and practitioners in using the evidence; (6) supporting policymakers and practitioners in applying the evidence to their evaluation activities and practices. During the six stages of these cycles, if evidence is not sufficient for decision-making by policymakers and practitioners, it will be identified and repeated for new issues.
2. What Works Team (WWT) leading the WWC
   From Uchiyama et al. (2018), WWC established the What Works Team (WWT) in the Cabinet Office, with three full-time staff members and four What Works National Advisers heading the Behavioral Insights Team. WWT is run by three full-time staff members and the head of the behavioral insights team. Despite the small team size, WWT plays the following roles in promoting WWC activities and EBPM. One of the WWT's mission is the operation of the trial advice panel.

[1] https://www.whatworksnetwork.org.uk/about-wwn/.

The trial advice panel consists of approximately 50 researchers and professional government officials who provide advice to ministries and agencies on policy effectiveness measurement. In 2017–2018, the trial advice panel has supported 18 projects, including a large-scale randomized controlled trial with the Department of Revenue and Customs, to determine what mailings are most effective in encouraging prompt payment of taxes. The second is to provide training programs for public officials. They provided training on analytical skills and effective evidence use in a custom-made workshop format.

Additionally, the WWC is not the only organization of economists and other experts. Many economists are also engaged in organizations dealing with economic analysis, such as the Competition Market Authority in the UK (see Part 4). The number of economists in the UK government has been increasing since the Blair administration, and the increasing number of economists has contributed to the promotion of EBPM and improvement of IA. However, conducting a rigorous competition assessment and IA is difficult. The most effective way to improve regulation is for economic thought to be widely shared and for problems to be addressed at an early stage in regulation making. Therefore, hiring more economists is an easy way to promote economic thought, and the quality of IA and regulation are improved in the UK. We then turn to the Economist in US regulation making and (regulatory) impact assessment.

5.3 Economists in the US Government Agencies

In this section, we explain the role and manpower of economists within the US government regarding regulation making and impact assessment (regulatory impact analysis). Currently, the US has the world's highest level of economic analysis. Taking long time, Economic thought took root. Evidence-based policy has been gradually prevailing in the agencies since RIA was introduce almost 50 years ago. We explain OMB/OIRA in Sect. 5.3.1, the Department of Transportation in Sect. 5.3.2, the Federal Communication Commission in Sect. 5.3.3, the Environment Protection Agency in Sect. 5.3.4, and the National Oceanic and Atmospheric Administration in Sect. 5.3.5. We should note that we got these numbers mainly from the interviews in 2000 and summed up to Morita et al. (2001). But they are not drastically changed after that.

5.3.1 OIRA of OMB

OIRA (introduced in Chap. 3) reviews the regulatory impact analysis of all US presidential departments. OIRA consists of four departments,[2] each of which is

[2] https://crsreports.congress.gov/product/pdf/RS/RS21665.

staffed by one or two full-time economists with Ph.Ds and five to ten staff members with Ph.D. or master's degrees, mainly in public policy, who are involved in the RIA review (meta-analysis).

Overall, OIRA reviews approximately 500–700 regulatory proposals per year around 2000, focusing on approximately 70–100 important proposals per year. The ratio of Ph.D. holders to Master Degree holders is about 50–50, including those with a Ph.D. in public policy. Some of them have doctorates in law, and toxicologists and epidemiologists joined the staff. We should note that we got these numbers from the interviews in 2000 and summed up to Morita et al. (2001) or from the interviews in 2009 and summed up to Nakaizumi (2010). But it is still helpful for government officers in developing countries to refer the manpower of economists in the US regulatory system at that time. And due to the follow up interviews in 2010's there is likely no any drastically change after that.

5.3.2 Department of Transportation (DOT)

The DOT[3] has approximately 100,000 employees in total, of which 40,000 are engaged in air traffic control, approximately 15 economists in RIAs, and 89 employees in the general counsel of the DOT. As for the Office of Regulatory Operations, the NHTSA/DOT has 620 employees, of which four are economists. The Office of Plans and Policy/NHTSA/DOT, which is in charge of preparing RIAs, has six staff members in charge of RIAs. Among these, two were economists. Additionally, there are two engineers: a statistician and a social scientist. In 2000, when I interviewed the secretary of the DOT, there were approximately 75 important regulations, 100–200 less important regulations, and 4,000–6,000 routine regulations.

Despite the large number of departments mentioned above, only 15 economists worked on RIA (in 2000). Although the Federal Aviation Administration (FAA) alone had about 10 economists, identifying only the economists involved in the analysis is difficult because they are simultaneously working on RIA and regulatory design. For example, at the Federal Highway Administration, economists are responsible for both fund allocation related to regulatory design (life-saving devices, security, etc.) and cost-benefit analysis. Several consultants are hired to compensate for this. For example, the National Highway Traffic Safety Administration (NHTSA) had many economists; however, other agencies hire consultants on a project basis, thereby reducing the number of internal economists.

The Federal Motor Carrier Safety Administration (FMCSA), which is responsible for regulating the trucking industry, had five economists in the analysis office of its research and technology division focusing on regulatory compliance issues. They also sent their staff to state partnership departments and carriers to conduct field inspections. This is comprises the majority of the budget and resources of the FMCSA.

[3] https://www.transportation.gov/administrations.

In 2000 and 2003, I interviewed the National Highway Traffic Safety Administration (NHTSA). The organizational structure then was discussed below. In 2003, the Office of Plans and Policy/NHTSA/DOT, which was in charge of preparing RIAs for NHTSA, had six staff members in charge of RIAs: two economists, two technicians, a statistician, and a social scientist.

Although many regulations have been enacted by the Department of Transportation, most economists are in charge of other tasks, and few economists are in charge of RIAs. One of the reasons for this is that DOT has a smaller percentage of regulations requiring analysis more complex than that used in EPA and other agencies. Simple analyses that do not require professional judgement are either outsourced or conducted by staff who are not economists.

The expertise of the staff is secured by hiring experts such as Ph.D. holders rather than through training programs. However, follow-up of the latest research is always conducted, and workshops are often held. Workshops not only provide technical guidance or training but also exchange information and standardize the analysis. Additionally, although not conducted for economic analysis, contracts may be made with university scholars when new research is being conducted on the social costs of automobile accidents, such as the value of life. For example, regarding the enactment of regulations on the hours of service for pilots in the aviation industry, latest research on the body clock has led them to seek the opinions of university experts on what kind of rest and work systems and flight hours are desirable. Note that the consulting company they contract for has contracts with many university professors and university officials. Therefore, these experts are rarely hired directly.

5.3.3 Federal Communication Commission (FCC)

The FCC's work was governed by the Communications Act of 1934. It has jurisdiction over all interstate communications, both wireline and wireless, including cable television, international communications, and cellphones. The wireline division is responsible for wireline regulations; the telecommunications division is responsible for interstate communications, international communications, and the introduction of competition into local markets; and the wireless division is responsible for all commercial licensing related to wireless, including mobile and fixed-line telephony. The International Division has jurisdiction over regulations related to satellite and international wireline communications. Regulations were established by the Communications Act and by other requirements.

Based on the interview at FCC in November 2009, FCC was organized into seven organizations: (1) consumer protection, (2) enforcement and compliance, (3) wireline, (4) wireless, (5) international, (6) media, (7) public safety. Furthermore, FCC has 12 other offices, including the Secretariat and the Office of Strategic Planning and Policy Analysis, a think tank within the FCC. The FCC has twelve offices with their own functions, and all offices have economists on staff and visiting professors from universities on a 1- or 2-year term. They advise the FCC on economic analysis.

Unlike the Department of Justice (DOJ) and the Federal Trade Commission (FTC), every department and office has Ph.D. economists. For example, based on the interview in 2009, the wireline division had 18 economists assigned to it, and FCC had 60 in total. The number may decrease due to retirement, but it is rising. Lawyers have also been trained to conduct competition analyses. For example, in trade clauses, a group in the bureau includes lawyers in the analysis. Competition analysis was commonly conducted by a lawyer with expertise in competition analysis or by an economist.

There were fewer economists than lawyers. The FCC had 1,800 staff members, of which 60 are economists, which is a very small percentage. Lawyers had a little more to do. One of the tasks of economists is to conduct competition analysis. As it relates to competition, data for periodic reports on FCC issues were organized. Some of the topics in the reports relate to regional, broadband, and cell phone and cable TV competition. Economists are also tasked to create radio-wave maps. For example, in the cell phone department, economists trace cell phone licenses and the areas they cover and, in some cases, work on issues related to the media. A variety of tasks remain, and only seven or eight of the 60 economists were engaged in economic analysis in 2009. However, if a large project is launched, more economists will be engaged. For example, a huge merger would require many procedures, and economists doing other work would help. After that more economists became engaged to competition analysis. That will be mentioned in next chapter.

5.3.4 Environmental Protection Agency (EPA)

When we interviewed the EPA in 2000, nearly 100 economists throughout the EPA assisted in policy making through the preparation of RIAs and had primary responsibility for the exercise of RIAs. Additionally, several departments in EPAs share experts in the preparation of RIAs.

In the Office of Policy, Planning, and Evaluation in EPA, there were approximately 30 economists. Some have degrees in public policy, but most staff are economists, and many are Ph.D. holders in environmental economics and other environment-related fields. The Office of Policy, Planning and Evaluation has no legal professionals, but the department collaborates with regulatory departments by providing information and advice. However, owing to a lack of resources, the office often outsources data collection and research to universities and private consultants.

5.3.5 National Oceanic and Atmospheric Administration (NOAA), Department of Commerce (DOC)

Based on an interview in 2000, the DOC had a total of 44,766 staff members and 450 economists, but rather than being engaged in preparing RIAs, most of them are involved in economic and statistical work within the DOC, analyzing and reporting on GDP, trade balance, and so on. On regulatory business units, the NOAA/DOC had 31 economists; the DOC's overall general counsel was composed of 145 lawyers, and the NOAA/DOC's general counsel was composed of about 90 lawyers.

5.4 Concluding Remarks

To assess regulations, quantifying and monetizing the impact corresponding to the benefits is necessary for calculating the benefits. For example, if the introduction of a certain regulation leads to a reduction in traffic accidents, estimating the number of lives saved is necessary. To conduct further cost-benefit analyses, converting these figures into monetary terms is ideal. However, making these figures convincing overnight is impossible, and constant research is essential.

For special markets (e.g., the electric power market), applying a simple supply and demand analysis directly is problematic. This is because electricity cannot be stocked, so prices are known to be highly inelastic in the short term, resulting in stronger market power than other markets with many suppiers.

This situation has been analyzed and clarified by many researchers since the California electricity crisis in the US. Thus, to improve impact assessment, including competition analysis, constant research by the academic community and feedback on the results are essential. For regulatory assessment and reform, conducting analysis based on the basic concepts of economics is crucial, and regulators who are actually in charge need training to acquire such analytical skills. This kind of training is something universities should provide.

Some of the economic analysis of the local government in developing countries might be more advanced than that of the federal government, and, in some respects, the university in the region is playing a important role in the research. Despite this, the federal government's policymaking in Pakistan, for example, has been very closed, and there has been very little that can be observed from the outside. Therefore, to ensure the transparency of regulatory bodies, developing interactions with these universities is necessary.

Such accumulation of research outcomes is difficult, especially in developing countries. In such cases, similar studies from OECD countries should be diverted to suit one's own country. Alternatively, requesting existing studies from the World Bank or new projects for this purpose is an option.

References

Federal Communication Commission (2002) EchoStar-DirecTV merger page

Fujita Y (2014) "Igirisu kōmuin seido kaikaku ni okeru "senmonshokuka no igi" kikan gyōsei kanri Kenkyu, vol 146

Fujita Y (2015) I Seisaku-teki jogen seisaku keisei no senmon-sei wa doko made jōshiki-ka dekiru ka? - Igirisu kōmuin seido kaikaku ni okeru porishī purofesshon no sōsetsu. nenpō gyōsei kenkyū, vol 50

Fujita Y (2017) "Ebidensu ni motodzuku seisaku keisei" o sasaeru jinzai ikusei" Jinjiin geppō, vol 816 (Heisei 29-nen 8 tsuki-gō)

Guidelines for Economic Review of National Marine Fisheries Service Regulatory Actions (2007h). https://media.fisheries.noaa.gov/dam-migration/01-111-05.pdf. https://www.fisheries.noaa.gov/insight/understanding-how-federal-fishing-regulations-are-made. http://www.fisherycouncils.org/

Morita A, Tanabe K, Nakaizumi T, Harada H, Kubo H (2001) Kisei eikyō bunseki ni kansuru chōsa kenkyū hōkoku-sho. sōmu-shō daijin kanbō kikaku-ka

Nakaizumi T (2010) Beikoku de no kyōsō bunseki jitchi chōsa hōkoku-sho

National Audit Office (2017) "Capability in the Civil Service" https://www.nao.org.uk/wp-content/uploads/2017/03/Capability-in-the-civil-service.pdf

OIRA of The U.S. Office of Management and Budget (2003) Circular A-4. http://www.whitehouse.gov/omb/circulars_a004_a-4

The U.S. Office of Management and Budget (1993) Executive order 12866. http://www.plainlanguage.gov/.../eo12866.pdf

The US Envornmental Protection Agency, (2021) Guidelines for preparing economic analyses. https://www.epa.gov/environmental-economics/guidelines-preparing-economic-analyses

USA OIRA, OMB, RegInfo.gov-Reg Map. http://www.reginfo.gov/public/jsp/Utilities/faq.jsp

Uchiyama T, Kobayashi Y, Taguchi S, Koike T (2018) Igirisu ni okeru ebidensu ni motodzuku seisaku keisei to Nihon e no shisa: ebidensu no 'juyō' to 'kyōkyū' ni chakumoku shita bunseki. RIETI Policy Discussion Papers Series 18-P-018

What Works Network (2014) What works? Evidence for decision makers

What Works Network (2018) "The What Works Network: Five Years On" https://assets.publishing.service.gov.uk/government/uploads/system/uploads/attachment_data/file/677478/6.4154_What_works_report_Final.pdf

Chapter 6
Economists' Optimal Placement Within Relevant Organizations

Abstract We discuss the role of economists and their placement in the organization to improve IA based on organizational economics. In order to introduce Evidence Based Policy, it is highly recommended to assign economists or other specialists to conduct early analysis from a standpoint that is as neutral as possible. But Incentive and ground rule, and top-down initiative to make all the officers to consider economic analysis is most essential for instilling economic thought and evidence-base, while organizational change has only limited effects.

6.1 Introduction

Relative to institutional design toward desirable regulation making and impact assessment, this chapter discusses the role of economists and their placement in the organization to improve IA based on organizational economics (see Milgrom and Roberts (1992)). In regulation making, identifying who has jurisdiction over the issue and who the stakeholders are and coordinating the interests between stakeholders considering the petitions from politicians are primary concerns. Thus, legal experts naturally occupy a central position in regulation. Moreover, lawmakers should have a good understanding of economics.

Policy is the first and foremost interest adjustment from the lawmakers' perspective, wherein stakeholders are key in regulation making. However, they do not reflect the overall impact on society. Evidently, the position of stakeholders should not prioritize those with the loudest voices. It is effective to eliminate such biased effects, assign economists or other specialists to conduct early analysis from a standpoint that is as neutral as possible. Hence, economists and other experts should be involved in the analysis as early as possible to prevent small, strong stakeholders from distorting the regulations to suit their own needs.

However, when economists are involved in the preparation of an IA, (1) having economists analyze it after making a decision and (2) having economists analyze it as a mere excuse are unnecessary, as Ellig and Morrall (2010), Hahn and Tetlock (2008) pointed out.

T. Nakaizumi, *Impact Assessment for Developing Countries*, Contributions to Economics,
https://doi.org/10.1007/978-981-19-5494-8_6

Economists and other experts should be involved as early as possible in regulation making, and result-oriented analysis must be avoided. A possible countermeasure is either to (1) place economists widely in each department to facilitate information gathering and communication with other staff members or to (2) implement countermeasures to organize economists into one department to strengthen their influence, improve quality, and better reflect their analysis results in decision-making.

However, a trade-off exists between the two measurements. Neither measurement completely solves this problem. Thus, it is more essential to establish guidelines and make cost-and-benefit analysis mandatory. Strong leadership is also important for implementing the procedure based on the guidelines in accordance with the performance review of the staff who is in charge of promiting the quality of IA and regulation. Changing organizational structure has limited effects on improve the quality of IA and regulation.

External pressures may also be effective. Froeb et al. (2009) highlighted that the opinions of decentralized economists become influential when the OIRA's requirement for correct economic analysis become strong. Ellig (2019) introduces two examples to improve economic analysis owing to external pressure. One is the case of the Securities and Exchange Commission (SEC) and the other is the Federal Communication Commission (FCC).

The SEC mandated the Cost-benefit Analysis partially because of the judiciary Judgement of Chamber of Commerce v. SEC (412 F.3d 133 2005) and American Equity Life Ins. Co. v. SEC (572 F.3d 923 2010). Simultaneously, the SEC's economic analysis was subject to critical assessments by the Government Accountability Office (GAO 2011, 2012) and the SEC's Inspector General. Congressional leaders criticized the SEC's economic analysis. Thus SEC introduced legislation to impose new analytical requirements (Kraus and Raso 2013).

In contrast, the FCC historically had the most common role for economists in rulemaking to furnish attorneys in the rulemaking bureaus with research or data to support decisions that had already been made. However, after President Obama issued EO 13,579, which requested that Independent Regulatory Commission conducts benefit-cost analysis when developing regulations, Chairman Genachowski directed the FCC staff to follow the order (Copeland 2013).

Conversely, in developing countries, manpower constraints must first be considered. Room is less for economists. If economists are scarce, they will likely have to be assigned to the organization in charge of the review. However, in such cases, it is difficult to get economists involved at an early stage. Therefore, it is difficult to ensure sufficient quality of IA. The discussion below is based on the condition that a certain number of economists can be hired.

In the next section, we will first list issues related to the organizational placement of economists based on the recent economic theory of organizations. Section 6.3 presents examples from Ellig (2019) and Froeb et al. (2009) for the regulatory management organization within the US Government. Section 6.4 concludes and enumerates the solutions.

6.2 Perspective Arguments Based on the Economics of Organization

Organizational economics[1] classifies the decision-making processes into three major categories. (1) gathering and proposing information necessary for a decision, (2) considering alternatives and approval, and (3) implementing.

The IA and regulation-making process is narrowed down to only "(1) gathering and proposing information necessary for an adequate decision" while taking the 3rd part into account. Hence, in order to improve the results as much as possible, organizational economics focuses on four aspects: (1) delegation of authority, (2) information processing (gathering, analyzing, and transmitting information), (3) incentives, and (4) decision-making. Since an extremely large number of issues affect how an actual organization is designed, we should focus on as few important issues as possible and examine how these issues are reflected in the organizational design. The frameworks of Ellig (2019) and Froeb et al. (2009) consider the issue of either allocating economists in each department to conduct the analysis or gathering economists within a single department to be involved in the analysis. We followed the approach by Ellig (2019) and Froeb et al. (2009), from a theoretical viewpoint on involving economists in regulation making.

If the analysis is conducted by economists in each department, Froeb et al. (2009) define it as (1) "divisional" organization that disperses economists among the divisions, bureaus, or offices that conduct various agency's mission. In divisional organization, collecting information by economists is easy, but supervisors may find it difficult to reflect the opinions of these analysts in decision-making. Conversely, if a department that gathers the economists together can be created, such an organization is defined by Froeb et al. (2009) (2) "functional" organization. Economists are placed in their own divisions, bureaus, or offices. In a regulatory agency, collecting information by economists is more difficult, but the quality of the analysis will be improved and reflected more easily. There is a trade-off between information processing and quality of economic analysis, and we discuss the characteristics of both organizations on information processing, incentives, delegation of authority, and decision-making based on organizational economics.

(1) Information processing (gathering, analyzing, and transmitting information)
If economists are placed in "divisional" organization, collecting and communicating information will be easier than in "functional" organizations. Conversely, if economists are concentrated in "functional" organization, participating in the planning of the initial regulation-making will be difficult for them. Moreover, collecting and communicating with other analysts and attorneys to acquire and analyze information will also be difficult for them.

(2) Delegation of authority and decision-making
Regarding authority, concentrating economists in "functional" organization would be preferable so that their conclusions could be clear and less likely to be

[1] The discussion of the section mainly based on Itoh et al. (2021), and Gibbons and Roberts (2012).

justification of interest coordination and, therefore, more likely to be reflected in decision-making. Additionally, in this case, the discretionary power of the economic analysis increases, so the authority of economists can be substantially enhanced. Furthermore, since the conclusions can be clearly stated and the quality of the analytical method is proportional to personnel effectiveness, it is desirable from an incentive perspective. Conversely, in "divisional" organization, analysis could be only justification of interest coordination and not reflected in decision-making. Informal authority tends to provide "functional" organization more than "divisional" organizations. Thus, to give "divisional" organization the authority as strong as "functional" organization. And guidelines and rules to delegate formal authority should be provided.

(3) Incentives
Incentives are provided through promotions and salaries to each officer based on her/his evaluation. Quality of IA and regulation depends on adherence to the main purpose or goal of the agency. It is important on better incentives to determine clearer goals of the organization. If the incentive becomes stronger, the quality of the IA improves in any organization. The incentive may be greater if economists are concentrated in one department because peer pressure among economists will be stronger and reviewers' viewpoints will depend on the quality and relevance of the analysis.

Therefore, "functional" organizations have economists who collecting information more difficult, while the results of the analysis are more likely to be reflected in decision-making. Additionally, the incentive will be greater if economists are all concentrated in "functional" organizations, as peer pressure can be applied to them. Conversely, "divisional" organization has economists access and gather information easier, while the results of analysis tend to be lower quality and less reflected in the decision-making. In the following, we introduce the characteristics of the actual US government, referring to Ellig (2019).

6.3 Improvement of the Quality of IA and Involvement by Economists Within the US Government

Even in the US organizations, several primitive difficulties in preserving the quality and appropriate usage of IA exist, as reported in Ellig (2019). Several examples from Ellig (2019) are as follows.

(1) As a problem of "functional" organization, economists suggest that "Economists in independent offices also acknowledge a key disadvantage that may reduce the consideration of economic analysis. They are not usually invited to internal program office meetings, where the initial regulatory options are discussed. Hence, many key decisions were made without economists. Independence "allowed economists to speak freely, but on some occasions too late to be heard.

(2) Environmental assessors complained more about the timing of the analysis after decisions were made when dealing with high-profile decisions at the national level.
(3) Ellig (2019) also introduced Williams' (2008) survey that did not focus primarily on organizational structure, but it touched on this issue. Williams (2008) interviewed senior economists at the Federal Agencies, such as the FDA, EPA, DOT, Department of Labor, Department of Homeland Security, Department of Agriculture, and Consumer Product Safety Commission. The following are several notable comments.

   (a) The problem of "divisional" organization is as follows: "One of the economists' major concerns was agencies' tendency to change the economic analysis to support decisions, because the economists are located organizationally alongside the individuals responsible for justifying regulatory decisions. The interviewer also recounted an incident in which he was told on a Friday to reduce costs and increase the benefits of a regulation or not bother to return to work on Monday."
   (b) As for issues of incentive or authority, "being managed by economists would be a luxury as non-economists focus mainly on deadlines and not on quality economics or having economic influence policy' when economists are managed by non-economists. Other economists argue that their agencies would be able to recruit and retain better economists if they were managed by other economists.
   (c) Respondents also highlighted that existence of OIRA reviews gives agencies some incentive to listen to functional economists offices. Finally, they also suggested that economists can produce a better analysis and perhaps have their analysis considered more seriously when they are managed by other economists.

As mentioned, the Independent Regulatory Commission is not mandatory for IA. However, the Securities and Exchange Commission has an internal rule of providing a cost-benefit analysis in regulation making since 2012. This is "not primarily through a change in the organizational structure, but through changes in decision-making authorities, practices, and procedures." Ellig (2019) described that it stemmed from court judgement and assessments by the Government Accountability Office (GAO).

From Kraus (2015), "Prior to 2012, attorneys, rather than economists, took the lead in drafting an economic analysis for rules (Peirce 2013, 582). characterizes the relationship between SEC economists and lawyers at that time as a "stable dysfunctional equilibrium." Economists were not very involved in rule making and focused more on research studies. Rule writers avoided involving economists since the analysis might "limit their policy discretion." This "Siberia effect" is one of the main potential disadvantages of functional organization of economists.

In Kraus and Raso (2013), the D. C. Circuit's Business Roundtable v. SEC decision in 2011 (647 F.3d 1144 2011) provided the primary impetus for emphasizing benefit-cost analysis. Simultaneously, the SEC's economic analysis was subject to critical assessments by the Government Accountability Office (GAO 2011,2012), the SEC's inspector general (SEC OIG 2011, 2012), and independent economists (Fraas and Lutter 2011). Congressional leaders criticized the SEC's economic analysis, too. Thus SEC managed to introduce legislation to impose new analytical requirements.

Subsequently, the SEC's general counsel and chief economist issued new guidance in March 2012 that specifies how economists are involved in the rule-making process. The guidance states that economists should be involved in the earliest stage of the process before a preferred alternative is chosen.

On the FCC case, the most common role for economists in rulemaking has been to furnish attorneys in the rulemaking bureaus with research or data to support decisions that had already been made. Attorneys in a bureau would then be tasked with writing an order justifying a regulation, and they would (sometimes) turn to economists for supporting information. Attorneys did not want to involve economists as they did not realize that economics was relevant to the rule.

After President Obama issued EO 13,579, Chairman Genachowski directed the FCC staff to follow the order, and the agency sought to include benefit-cost analysis in every order. However, these activities were not sufficient to improve IA quality before FCC Chairman Ajit Pai's (2017–2022) set working group. They conclude that economists and economic analyses were not systematically incorporated into regulation making.

In January 2018, based on the recommendation of the working group, the FCC approved an order that largely adopted the working group's plan. The order moved most of the FCC's economists into the new Office of Economics and Analytics (OEA), which settled in December 2018, along with some attorneys, data professionals, and other personnel. The new rules adopted also commit OEA to prepare "a rigorous cost-benefit analysis for every rule making, if it makes an annual effect on the economy of $100 million or more" (FCC 2018, 4–6).

Transitional issues have been highlighted. One is that non-economists are sometimes surprised to find out that the rules they are working on have economic impacts, and they view economists' involvement as simply another layer of review that delays rules. The other is that procedures to coordinate economists' involvement in rule making and other items have not been established before. However, as the OEA and rulemaking bureaus gain more experience operating under the new structure, this issue will be resolved.

The FCC's experience offers lessons. First, placing economists in program offices that write regulations does not guarantee that they are consulted and engaged in regulation making, which is a potential disadvantage of functional organization by isolating the organization and ignoring economics in decision-making. However, this can be overcome with the appropriate leaderships of decision authorities. Second, economists can make a noticeable contribution to the development of regulations simply by being involved in the discussion and design of regulations before any economic analysis of a commission decision is written.

6.4 Conclusion

When economists are involved in the organization of the regulatory body and developing IA, two main alternatives exist. One is a divisional organization that places economists widely in each department who have jurisdiction in making regulations. It facilitates information gathering and communication. The other is a functional organization in which economists are concentrated in one department so that they can improve the quality of economic analysis and reflect the results in decision-making. There is a trade-off in either case, and both do not completely solve the problem.

Thus, the priority is to set guidelines and mandate IA with cost and benefit analysis. Leadership in implementing the IA procedure is also important. A performance review based on the promotion of IA causes administrators to focus on improving IA it should be noted that the effects of changing the organizational structure are limited.

Whatever form of organization is adopted, measures should be considered to mitigate the problems of each organizational structure. The FCC's measures to support functional organizations are helpful in this regard if a functional organization is chosen (Ellig 2019).

To avoid isolating economists from the operating bureaus, functional organizations should be given formal authority in all rulemaking, transactions, enforcement matters, and formal and informal practices.

Owing to budgetary problems or other issues regarding several limited abilities, governments of developing countries cannot hire enough economists. Thus, few economists are likely to gather within a single unit and help regulation making among various regulatory bodies. Following these measurements of FCC are also helpful.

(1) Creation of a joint guidance memo specifying how economic analysis (Impact Assessment) would be incorporated into decision-making and how economists would then be incorporated into project teams.
(2) Development of informal procedures to coordinate economists' work with that of the bureaus and determine how economists will participate in teams that handle rule making, transactions, auctions, and enforcement matters, including the assignment of at least one economist to each team working on major rule making.
(3) Development of guidance documents describing how to apply regulatory impact analysis to communication policy issues.
(4) Production of a separate, non-public memorandum on economic issues to accompany documents circulated to the Commission.
(5) Modification of performance criteria to include effective appreciation of economic concepts and the incorporation of economic analysis.
(6) Inclusion of feedback from non-economist units in economists' performance reviews and expansion of internal training to include regulatory impact analysis and best practices in data management.

(7) Operation of research, workshops, and other activities that address emerging economic issues and policy challenges.
(8) Modification of performance criteria to include effective appreciation of economic concepts and the incorporation of economic analysis.

References

Brennan, Tim. (2017) "Bolstering Economics at the FCC: Will a Separate Office Help?," Technology Policy Institute (September 18), available at https://techpolicyinstitute.org/2017/09/18/bolstering-economics-at-the-fcc-will-a-separate-office-help/

Copeland, Curtis W. (2013) "Economic Analysis and Independent Regulatory Agencies," Report prepared for the Administrative Conference of the United States

Ellig J (2019) Agency economists. Final Report. https://www.acus.gov/sites/default/files/documents/Ellig%20Agency%20Economists%20Final%20Report%20September%202019.pdf

Ellig J, Morrall J (2010) Assessing the quality of regulatory analysis a new evaluation and data set for policy research

Federal Communications Commission. (2018) "In the Matter of Establishment of the Office of Economics and Analytics, Order" (released January 31)

Fraas A, Lutter R (2011) On the economic analysis of regulations at independent regulatory commissions. Adm Law Rev 63:213–241

Froeb L, Pautler PA, Röller L-H (2009) The economics of organizing economists. Antitrust Law J 76(2):569–584

Gibbons and Roberts (2012) The handbook of organizational economics. Princeton Univ Press, 1233 page

Government Accountability Office (2011) "Dodd-Frank Act Regulations: Implementation Could Benefit from Additional Analyses and Coordination," Report No. GAO-12_151.

Government Accountability Office (2012) "Dodd-Frank Act: Agencies' Efforts to Analyze and Coordinate Their Rules," Report No. GAO-13-101.

Hahn RW, Tetlock PC (2008) Has economic analysis improved regulatory decisions? J Econ Perspect 22(1) (Winter)

Itoh, Kobayashi, Miyahara (2021) Soshiki no keizai-gaku. Yuhikaku, 414 page

Kraus, Bruce R., and Connor Raso. 2013. "Rational Boundaries for SEC Cost-Benefit Analysis," Yale Journal on Regulation 30:2, 289–342

Kraus BR (2015) Economists in the room at the SEC. Yale Law J Forum 124(January 22):280–304

Milgrom P, Roberts J (1992) Economics, organization, and management. Prentice-Hall, Englewood Cliffs, NJ

Securities and Exchange Commission Office of Inspector General. (2012) "Follow-Up Review of Cost-Benefit Analyses in Selected SEC Dodd-Frank Act Rulemakings," Report No. 499

Securities and Exchange Commission Office of Inspector General. (2011) "Report of Review of Economic Analyses Performed by the Securities and Exchange Commission in Connection with Dodd-Frank Act Rulemakings"

Uchiyama T, Kobayashi Y, Taguchi S, Koike T (2018) Igirisu ni okeru ebidensu ni motodzuku seisaku keisei to Nihon e no shisa: ebidensu no 'juyō' to 'kyōkyū' ni chakumoku shita bunseki" RIETI Policy Discussion Papers Series 18-P-018

Williams R (2008) The influence of regulatory economists in federal health and safety agencies. Working Paper No. 08-15. Mercatus Center at George Mason University, Arlington, VA

Part III
Analysis and Analytical Viewpoints in Impact Assessment

Chapter 7
Analysis and Analytical Viewpoints in Impact Assessment (IA)

Abstract This chapter describes analysis and analytical viewpoints in IA. IA first identifies current problems, then illustrates the necessity of government intervention. the effectiveness of the proposed regulation is ascertained through objective analysis, which entails quantifying possible costs and benefits. We explain this analytic process using several examples.

7.1 Introduction

This chapter describes analysis and analytical viewpoints in Impact Assessment (IA). IA specifies that the current problems are identified, the necessity of government intervention in solving them is explained, and whether the regulation is actually effective or not is indicated by objectively analyzing the possible costs and benefits of its implementation when introducing or revising a regulation.

Ex-ante assessment of regulation originally started in the US. Once a regulation is created, changing it is very difficult. Therefore, the most important consideration is to conduct an analysis before introducing regulations and provide support to realize appropriate regulations. Currently, IA is the most important among policy evaluation in most OECD countries.

Before making a formal analysis, following the EU guideline, it would be great help to realize that all IAs must answer a set of key questions and respect certain principles. IA should be comprehensive, proportionate, evidence-based, open to stakeholders' views, unbiased, prepared collectively with relevant Commission services, embedded in the policy cycle, transparent, and of a high quality. However, the best way to carry out IA and present its results will vary from case to case, given the widely differing nature of regulation-making initiatives.

The questions an IA should answer are as follows:

1. What is the problem and why is it a problem?
2. Why should the EU act?
3. What should be achieved?
4. What are the various options to achieve the objectives?

T. Nakaizumi, *Impact Assessment for Developing Countries*, Contributions to Economics,
https://doi.org/10.1007/978-981-19-5494-8_7

5. What are their economic, social, and environmental impacts and who will be affected?
6. How do the different options compare (effectiveness, efficiency, and coherence)?
7. How will it be monitored and subsequent retrospective evaluation be organized?

In IA, the necessity of introducing the regulation or other measures is considered first. Necessity implies that government intervention might be needed. Even if the existence of a problem is characterized, the public sector does not have to measure and solve the problem; private sector might be able to measure and solve the problem. Then there is no need and of government intervention, even harmful. If there is no need of government intervention, we do not define it necessity. In other words, it is required to describe why the private sector alone is insufficient. In terms of economics, it is necessary to describe the factors of market failures such as externalities, imperfect competition, and information asymmetry.

If government intervention is inevitable to solve the problem, we go to the next step. This is because it does not necessarily mean that government intervention is desirable. In other words, there are cases in which the introduction of regulations is a necessary condition but not a sufficient condition. Therefore, it is necessary to not only identify the necessity, but also sufficient condition to quantitatively clarify the costs and benefits of introducing the regulation to confirm the introduction of the measure is indeed desirable. Evaluating the costs and benefits, and confirming the effectiveness and efficiency, is also a way of confirming the sufficient conditions for introducing regulations. Effectiveness implies whether the objectives of the measure have been achieved or not. Moreover, efficiency needs to verify there was sufficient cost-effectiveness in achieving the benefit, and the benefits justify the costs.

Thus, after identifying the current problem, we will confirm the necessary conditions by showing necessity and the sufficient conditions by estimating efficiency, and verify whether this measure is really meaningful by the pincer movement.

In the guidelines for IA (Regulatory Impact Assessment, RIA) in Japan, the content including analytical viewpoints of IA includes the following:

(1) Purpose, content, and necessity of the regulation
(2) Identification of costs and benefits
(3) Analysis of the relationship between costs and benefits
(4) Comparison with alternatives
(5) Expert opinions and other relevant issues
(6) The timing or conditions of the review.
(From Japan's Guidelines for Ex-ante Evaluation of Regulations).

At the end of this section, the best and simple practice of assessment is presented. In the case to introduce a brand new important regulation, IA is typically a huge undertaking. However, most new regulations are usually either a small extension or a little modification of the existing ones. Therefore, while there are many examples of proposed regulations and IAs around the world, most of them are only a set of small analysis or modifications. For example, if there was an IA for a regulation that mandates child restraints, the structure would have been relatively straightforward.

However, actual proposals for mandating child safety restraint system have been in the works since the 1970s, and there is no IA consisting of all the analysis; they consist of only a partial revision of the previous regulation, such as FINAL ECONOMIC ASSESSMENT of FMVSS No. 213 FMVSS No. 225 Child Restraint Systems, Child Restraint Anchorage Systems, NHTSA, DOT (1999).

Therefore, in order to illustrate IA of whole project, we take an example that is not an IA, but is very clear and understandable in assessing the costs, benefits, and the concept of IA. It is the "OFFICIAL WHITE HOUSE RESPONSE TO Secure resources and funding, and begin construction of a Death Star by 2016" by Paul Shawcross, Chief of the Science and Space Branch at the White House Office of Management and Budget, which is a response from an OMB science expert that was actually triggered by a petition to the US Presidential office in 2012, and is as follows:

Example 7.1 "OFFICIAL WHITE HOUSE RESPONSE TO Secure resources and funding, and begin construction of a Death Star by 2016."

The Administration shares your desire for job creation and a strong national defense, but a Death Star isn't on the horizon. Here are a few reasons:

The construction of the Death Star has been estimated to cost more than $850,000,000,000,000,000. We're working hard to reduce the deficit, not expand it. The Administration does not support blowing up planets. Why would we spend countless taxpayer dollars on a Death Star with a fundamental flaw that can be exploited by a one-man starship?

However, look carefully (here's how) and you'll notice something already floating in the sky—that's no Moon, it's a Space Station! Yes, we already have a giant, football field-sized International Space Station in orbit around the Earth that's helping us learn how humans can live and thrive in space for long durations.

Omission (of middle part of a text).

If you do pursue a career in a science, technology, engineering or math-related field, the Force will be with us! Remember, the Death Star's power to destroy a planet, or even a whole star system, is insignificant next to the power of the Force.

More formally, we specify the analysis as follows:

(a) Background: In the US, when a certain number of pledges are collected, the government must formally comment on them.
(b) Necessity: Necessity is justified because Death Star has the natural monopoly issue because of economies of scale.
(c) Purpose: Purpose is not justified because Planetary destruction is contrary to the purpose of space exploration.
(d) Efficiency: Efficiency is not justified because The cost is enormous ($85 K), but it has a fundamental weakness in its effectiveness: it can be destroyed by a single manned space fighter. Thus, cost-effectiveness is low.
(e) Alternatives: Peaceful space exploration is currently underway. And the alternative is preferred.
(f) Result: The petition is declined.

Naturally, IAs and regulations must be a part of more important policy decisions to improve national welfare, but there is much to be learned about the methodology from such a simple example. I hope you will understand the core of the analysis from these examples, and undertake the more important and difficult analysis. The remainder of the chapter is organized as follows. Section 7.2 discusses necessity, Sect. 7.3 examines the importance of alternatives, and Sect. 7.4 describes the analysis of effectiveness and efficiency. Finally, Sect. 7.5 presents the concluding remarks.

7.2 Necessity of Regulation

From the Study Group on Policy Evaluation of Regulations Japan—Final Report in the "Standards for Government Involvement" (Administrative Reform Commission, December 16, 1996), "Basic Principle A" states that in principle, what the private sector can do should be left to the private sector. Thus, necessity is not just an explanation that there is a need for a measure, but it must also describe the reasons why the activities of the private sector alone are insufficient, including the private sector cannot do it or leaving it to the private sector will cause problems.

In the terminology of economics, this means explaining the existence of important market failures such as public goods, externalities, market power, imperfect information (information asymmetry), economies of scale (e.g., natural monopoly), or other compelling public need. Guidelines in other countries also often require explanations from an economic perspective. It is true that some regulations cannot be explained from this perspective. However, even in such cases, it is important to explain the necessity of government intervention as objectively as possible through the means of regulation.

We will now explain each factor of necessity. They belong to either imperfect competition or market failure. Imperfect competition implies a situation where the assumption of a perfectly competitive market is not satisfied, for example, monopoly or oligopoly. The other situation is when the market mechanism itself is flawed, even if the assumption of a perfectly competitive market is satisfied. It is called market failure, which contains natural monopoly, externalities (external diseconomies: pollution, etc.), commons(club goods), asymmetric information (adverse selection or moral hazard problem), etc., and we explain it based on US Guideline Circular A-4.

In Circular A-4, the US guideline for regulatory impact analysis, Market Failure or Other Social Purpose is described as follows.

The major types of market failure include externality, market power, and inadequate or asymmetric information. Correcting market failures is a reason for regulation, but it is not the only reason. Other possible justifications include improving the functioning of government, removing distributional unfairness, or promoting privacy and personal freedom.

7.3 Selection of Alternatives

Possible alternatives should be considered while conducting the analysis (comparison of costs and benefits). Comparative consideration of alternatives is expected to play the following two roles depending on the stage of IA. The first is to provide basic information for narrowing down alternatives by listing the alternatives and considering their approximate costs and benefits at the earliest stage of assessment. The second is to be accountable for the superiority of the adopted regulatory proposal over the other alternatives that were not selected for subsequent consideration.

For the former role, it is desirable that a range of alternatives be enumerated as wide as possible at the earliest possible stage of regulation making. As a result of the study, it is desirable that the evaluation includes even the possibility of no government intervention.

For the latter role, in addition to the proposed measures, it is desirable to conduct an estimation that includes two alternatives—one more substantial and one less substantial. Note that in the case of deregulation, at least two alternatives should be considered: one that maintains the status quo or a more modest deregulation proposal, and one that provides further significant deregulation, including the abolition of the regulation.

Alternatives can be set for various attributes of the proposed regulation if the measure envisions regulation. For example, the following types of alternatives could be set. In the subsection of Circular A-4 below, adequate choices of alternatives are illustrated.

"4.1 Alternative Regulatory Approaches" in A-4

Once it is determined that federal regulatory action is appropriate, you will need to consider alternative regulatory approaches. Ordinarily, you will be able to eliminate some alternatives through a preliminary analysis, leaving a manageable number of alternatives to be evaluated according to the formal principles of the Executive Order. The number and choice of alternatives selected for detailed analysis is a matter of judgment. There must be some balance between thoroughness and the practical limits on your analytical capacity. With this qualification in mind, you should nevertheless explore modifications of some or all of a regulation's attributes or provisions to identify appropriate alternatives. The following is a list of alternative regulatory actions that should be considered.

(a) Different choices defined by statute
(b) Different compliance dates
(c) Different enforcement methods
(d) Different degrees of stringency
(e) Different requirements for different sized firms
(f) Different requirements for different geographic regions
(g) Performance standards rather than design standards
(h) Market-oriented approaches rather than direct controls
(i) Informational measures rather than regulations.

7.4 Efficiency Analysis in RIA (Assessment of Costs and Benefits)

7.4.1 *Purpose of the Analysis*

The purpose of IA is to identify and quantitatively understand the problem, and it does not unconditionally lead to results. In particular, it should be noted that there are many factors that are not reflected in the processes of quantification and monetization of costs and benefits. Therefore, rather than making regulatory decisions based on the numerical values obtained from the cost-benefit analysis, the original purpose of the analysis is to provide materials for the quantitative clarification of various issues and to make the regulation-making process more transparent and objective.

In the process of assessing costs and benefits, it is natural to try to quantify and monetize them as much as possible, but it is also inevitable that many factors are not reflected. Therefore, insistence on accurate estimates will not yield sufficient results. Rather, it is more realistic to consider the sufficiency of introducing measures, as seen in the following EPA case study. Even if there are benefits that are difficult to convert into monetary terms, there is no need to force the conversion of other benefits into monetary terms if the specific benefits alone are sufficient to cover the social costs of the entire regulation.

Example 7.2 U.S. Environmental Protection Agency Type 1 Drinking Water Regulations: Regulatory Impact Analysis for Groundwater Use Rule.

"The primary goal of the proposed Ground Water Rule (GWR) is to improve public health by identifying public ground water systems that are now, or are likely to become, fecally contaminated, and to ensure adequate measures are taken to remove or inactivate pathogens in drinking water provided to the public by these systems. This document provides: a description of the need for the rule, a description of the regulatory options, baseline information on ground water systems, estimates of the monetized benefits and costs of the proposed rule, a description of additional unquantified and nonmonetized benefits, analysis of the economic impact of the rule, and a comparison of the overall benefits and costs of the rule alternatives."

The above regulations are beneficial in that it will reduce the treatment cost for health hazards and the number of deaths they cause. Moreover, it may prevent suffering from health hazards and rapid outbreaks of infectious diseases and pests. However, only the first two points are calculated in monetary terms. If the benefits of this exceed the total social costs of the regulation, it is allowed to introduce the regulation.

7.4.2 "Comparison" with Counterfactual, So Called With and Without Analysis

When the regulation is implemented, a major task of IA is to evaluate these costs and effects as objectively as possible. To clarify the costs and benefits, it is necessary to compare the cases with and without regulation, namely, compare the regulation with the counterfactual. We define counterfactual or without regulation as baseline. We illustrate Example 7.3, which is a very understandable example of baseline or counterfactual. Though it is an ex-post analysis, it is also applicable to ex-ante analysis including IA.

Example 7.3 The effect of the introduction of a Connecticut Speeding Crackdown, USA

Based on Glass (1968), we explain the counterfactual or baseline in Connecticut Speeding Crackdown. In 1955, a record 324 persons were killed in automobile accidents on Connecticut highways. On December 23, 1955, Governor Ribicoff announced a crackdown on speeders. New rules of penalty for drivers offending the speed limit are as follows:

First speeding offense: 30-day license suspension,
Third offense: 1-year suspension.

After the introduction of crackdown, fatalities dropped from 324 to 284 in 1956. Governor Ribicoff made a comment that "Connecticut has succeeded in stopping the upward surge in highway deaths, and ... contrary to the national trend, we have saved lives. Fewer people died on the highways this year than in the same period last year, in Connecticut."

Figure 7.1 justifies the governor's claim that the crackdown was effective because the number of fatalities decreased from 324 to 284. Is the governor's claim correct? Unfortunately, this result alone does not tell us anything about whether or not the introduction of the ordinance had any effect.

It would be natural to compare 324 and 284 to conclude that crackdown on speeders worked well. As it is, it is wrong, because 324 and 284 are the number of fatalities in 1955 and 1956, respectively. Correctly, we must compare the number of fatalities if the crackdown on speeders was introduced in 1956 with the number of fatalities if it were not introduced; in IA, both must be estimated ex-ante, but even in the ex-post evaluation, if the regulation is introduced, the counterfactual—the case without the regulation—is not realized. In the case of evaluation of regulations, at least the counterfactuals have to be estimated. This is also an important issue in causal inference, and there has been remarkable progress in recent years in the development of estimation methods and empirical research using them. How to utilize these results in IA will be discussed in Chap. 8.

Therefore, comparing the deaths in 1955 and 1956, as the governor did, does not mean that the effect of the introduction of the rule has been measured. If the circumstances other than the introduction of the speeding ordinance were the same

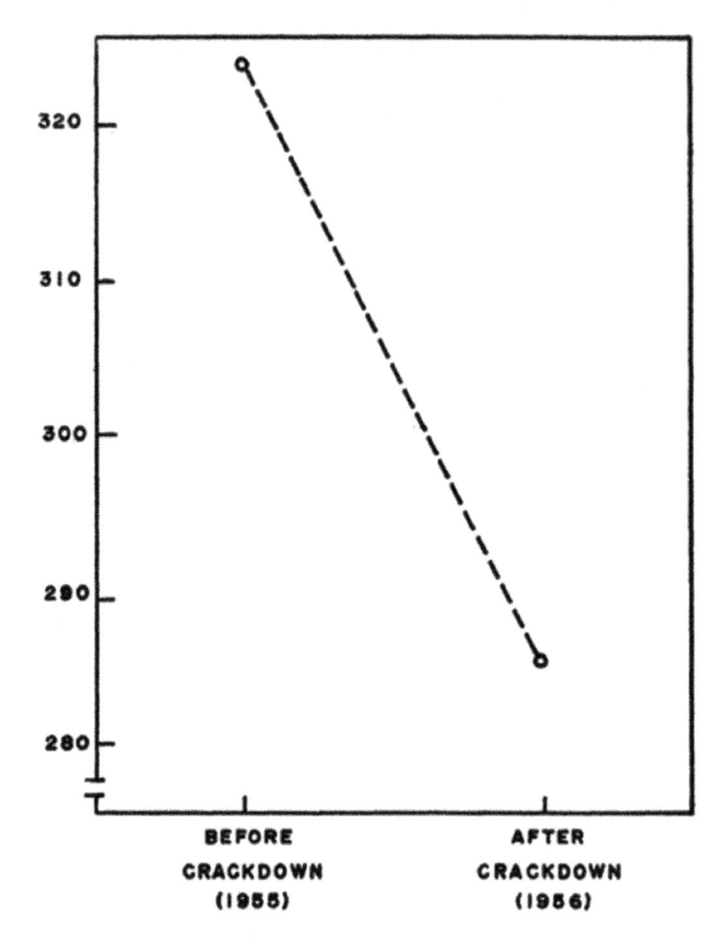

Fig. 7.1 Fatalities before and after crackdown

in 1955 and 1956, it would correspond to the situation where the crackdown on speeders was not introduced in 1956. Such a situation is extremely rare, but if such an assumption is reasonable, we can use 284 as the counterfactual in 1956, that is, the case where the rule is not introduced, and the effect of the regulation is 324 − 284 = 40.

The counterfactuals should be estimated using a strict method of causal inference. However, there is a simple method, which is to extend the period to find the trend without rule. Figure 7.2 shows the number of deaths over time. The number of deaths has been on an upward trend, increasing and decreasing at a constant rate, with a sharp increase in 1955. This raises the question of whether the increase in 1955 was due to weather or some other factors and has only returned, or whether it is just a natural regression of the world system downward.

The other way is to compare cross section data. Figure 7.3 shows how Connecticut, where the ordinance was introduced, compares to other states. It

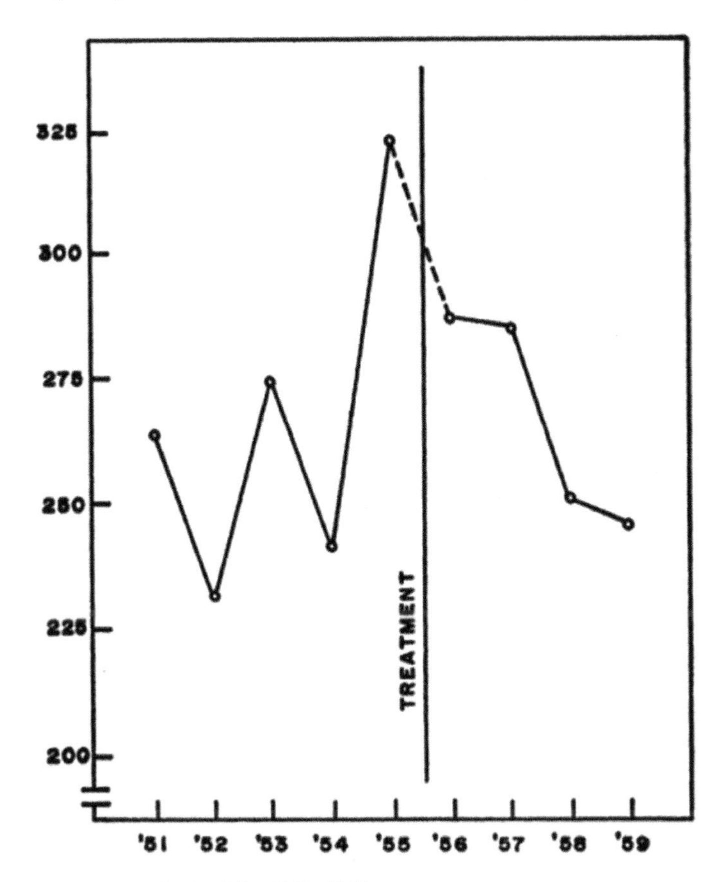

Fig. 7.2 Connecticut traffic fatalities 1951–1959

compares Connecticut with the average of the four states that border it. To compare states of different sizes, the evaluation index is standardized per 100,000 people. The graph shows that the number of deaths in Connecticut has decreased significantly since 1956 compared to the four neighboring states. The lower right graph plots deaths by state, and shows that deaths declined in every state from 1955 to 1956, with Rhode Island showing a greater decline than Connecticut. New Jersey and New York also showed declines after 1956, but the decline in Connecticut was more distinctive.

The real effect here is called the "impact" in IA. In other words, if the change in the outcome indicator, that is, the reduction in the number of deaths, was brought about by the effect of the program to introduce the rule, that is the impact. A more detailed analysis of this case study shows that the reduction in deaths in Connecticut was not entirely explained by the introduction of the ordinance, but it did have a certain impact.

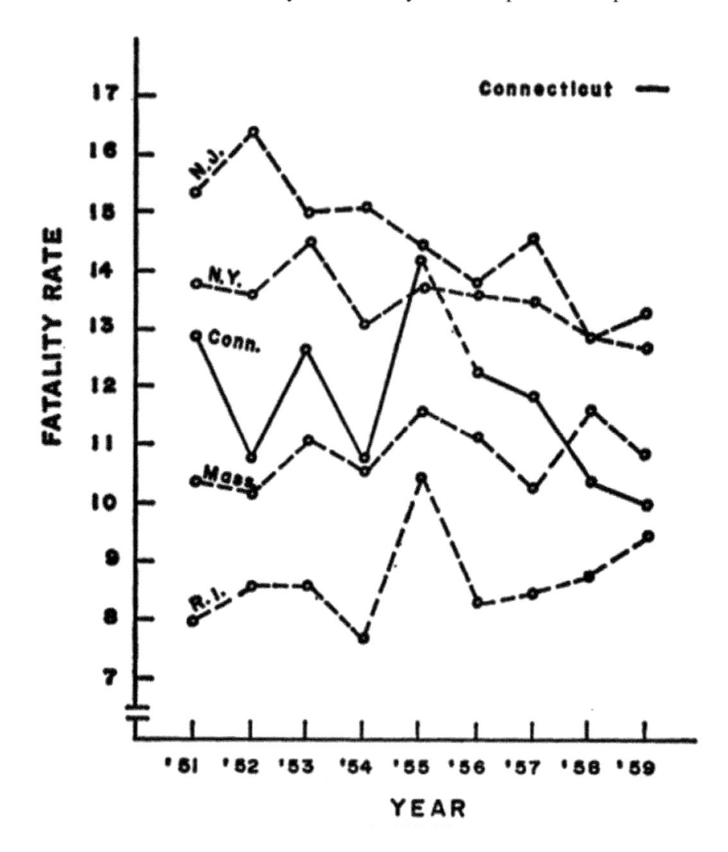

Fig. 7.3 Traffic fatalities for connecticut, New York, New Jersey, Rhode Island, and Massachusetts (per 100,000 persons)

7.4.3 Three Steps to Specify the Impact (Benefits Minus Costs)

In a broad sense of cost-benefit analysis, including cost-effective analysis, the counterfactual of comparison is called the baseline. Usually, the baseline is "if the current system is maintained" (in the UK, this was called "doing nothing" from the interview in 2004). See (3) for key points on the selection of baseline. We illustrate the three steps of assessment of costs and benefits in IA.

Step 1: Identify the counterfactual or baseline and specify the impact of the regulation.
The counterfactual or the case without regulation is identified as the baseline. Subsequently, compare the baseline, that is, the counterfactual, "if the current system had been maintained," with "if measures had been introduced," and identify what changes have occurred.

Step 2: Classify and identify costs and benefits.
Of these changes, classify and organize those that are positive for society as benefits and those that are negative as costs. It is also important to organize the enumerated items so that there is no double counting or overlap.

Step 3: Calculate the monetary value or discounted present value of the impacts.
The costs and benefits classified in Step 2 are quantified and valued in monetary terms as much as possible. Subsequently, the costs and benefits that will be incurred in the future are discounted to present value, and the costs and benefits (or the benefits that have been evaluated monetarily) are compared.

Up to step 2 could be made mandatory (in the U.K. (2004)) The Regulatory Impact Unit of the UK required step 2, that is, whether the various impacts on the economy have been identified, as a minimum requirement.

Example 7.4 Impact Assessment for a regulation on mandatory child seat (child restraint system).

Suppose the government tries to mandate child seat (child restraint system) in cars whenever it carries a child. In this case, the IA could be as follows.

As mentioned, actual proposals for mandating child safety restraint system have been in the works since the 1970s. Moreover, there is no IA consisting of all the analysis of child restraint system in the US; they are only a partial revision of the previous regulation, NHTSA, DOT (1999). Thus, this regulation and IA are simplified virtual examples.

Step 1: Specification of the baseline and identification of the impact of the measure.
Compare "if the status quo is maintained" and "if the measure is implemented."
Status quo is a baseline and counterfactual when a regulation introduced: Child seats will not be installed in each passenger car.
If measures are taken: Child seats will be installed in each passenger car whenever child is carried.

Step 2: Classification and identification of costs and benefits
Benefits of the mandatory installation of child seat include reduction in infant mortality rate, etc.
Cost associated with the purchase of child seat, Cost of compliance (cost of policing), etc.

Step 3: Calculation of the monetary conversion and discounted present value of the effect, and quantification of cost and benefit and conversion to monetary values. Reduction in infant mortality rate will be calculated using experimental data. Child seat production costs and compliance costs will be collected through interviews. Cost-effectiveness of the regulation is calculated by the additional social costs required to reduce infant deaths and injuries.

In the case where costs and benefits occur at different points in time, it is necessary to aggregate all the benefits with different timings into a discounted present value. Child seat can be used for several years once purchased; however, the timing of realizing other costs and benefits differs. Thus, it is necessary to compare them using discounted present value. The following is an example using simple numbers. Suppose the cost per child seat is \$500 and it can be used for 10 years; the benefit per seat in this case is supposed to \$100 per year. Suppose the annual regulatory compliance cost is \$10 per seat. The benefit for each year then is \$100 – \$10 = \$90; further, if the discount rate is 5%, the present value is as follows: $\frac{90}{1+0.05} + \frac{90}{(1+0.05)^2} + \cdots + \frac{90}{(1+0.05)^{10}} \approx 695$

In comparing \$695 with the cost of \$500, since the benefits exceed the costs by about \$195, the introduction of the measure will be justified.

We should note that even if the effect is not translated into monetary terms, the effect that will occur at in the future must be discounted, as OMB guidelines also instruct to discount the effect. Suppose \$100 is equivalent to the reduction of one fatality per 100,000 people per year when baby uses child seat (0.00001 per seat), which means one child fatality is equivalent to \$10 million.

$$\text{The cost is } 500 + \frac{10}{1+0.05} + \frac{10}{(1+0.05)^2} + \cdots + \frac{10}{(1+0.05)^{10}} \approx 577.2$$

$$\text{The benefit is } \frac{0.00001}{1+0.05} + \frac{0.00001}{(1+0.05)^2} + \cdots + \frac{0.00001}{(1+0.05)^{10}} \approx 7.72 \times 10^{-5}$$

By comparing the costs and benefits, cost effectiveness can be calculated:

$577.2/(7.72 \times 10^{-5}) = 7.47 \times 10^6 \fallingdotseq$ \$7.5 million; it implies that a cost of \$7.5 million is incurred to reduce one fatality. It is lower than \$10 million.

Using the concept of depreciation, the cost of purchasing a child seat could be divided into the cost of one year. As it is, depreciation cost could be calculated based on declining balance depreciation, and then divided into periodic costs and compared with the reduction in annual fatality rate.

Regarding the case of child safety seats, based on the concept of straight-line depreciation, the annual cost can be divided proportionally into \$50, and the annual cost is \$60. It can be compared to the annual reduction in fatality rate, that is, 0.00001 per seat. However, the cost to reduce one fatality in this case is \$6 million, which looks more effective than the previous result. This is due to the fact that the interest rate is assumed to be zero in this kind of simplified method. Such a simplified method should not be used for a large initial investment or measures with long term benefits because of the impact of discount rate is substantial.

When deriving the impact, you must extract the direct impact on society as a whole. Analyzing the distribution of impacts is a different perspective of the assessment of costs and benefits in this section. Thus, when you make a distribution analysis, extreme care should be taken because it is more difficult and complicated and double counting may occur.

7.4.4 *Formulation of the Baseline: Assessing the Counterfactual*

When assessing the costs and benefits of introducing regulation, the baseline should be the status quo, that is, "if the current system is maintained." It should also take into account that the baseline must include changes in the market environment, the external environment affecting costs and benefits, and changes in other regulations that would occur if the current system is maintained. After introducing regulation, baseline is counterfactual, which is the same as empirical study included causal inference. Thus, we discuss the concept and methods of the causal inference and how to incorporate causal inference into IA in the next chapter.

After specifying the baseline, we derive the impact, cost, and benefit. It is useful to explain the specification of the impact whether adding the regulation or replacing the previous one.

(1) Impact when introducing a new regulation
The impact caused by the introduction of the regulation only adds to the current situation. In this case, the cost factor is negative and the benefit factor is positive. Assuming that the cost factor is C and the benefit factor is B, if all these factors are converted into monetary terms, the net benefit of introducing the regulation is (B-C).
Example: Establishment of a new regulation for child seat as mentioned above.
(2) Impact of change from an existing regulation to a new regulation
In this case, it is easy to understand to consider the case where no existing regulation is changed to a new regulation, and compare the existing and new regulations.

Current situation: regulatory system of X (that does not change) and Y (that is taken over Z completely).

New regulations: If we introduce a regulatory system called Z instead of Y, the net benefit of the existing regulation is Benefit of Y – Cost of Y. Further, the net benefit of the new regulation using "no regulation exists" as baseline is as follows: benefits of Z – Costs of Z.

Since the baseline is the status quo, the net benefits generated by the introduction of the regulation can be calculated as follows:

$$
\begin{aligned}
&\text{Net benefits from the introduction of regulations obtained by cost} - \text{benefit analysis}\\
&= \text{Net benefits of new regulations} - \text{Net benefits of existing regulations}\\
&= (\text{Benefit of Z} - \text{Cost of Z}) - (\text{Benefit of Y} - \text{Cost of Y})\\
&= (\text{Benefit of Z} - \text{Benefit of Y}) - (\text{Cost of Z} - \text{Cost of Y})
\end{aligned}
$$

When it can be assumed that the benefit of the regulation does not change as a result of the change from the existing to the new regulation (the case where both benefits are the same),

$$\text{Benefit of Y} = \text{Benefit of Z}$$
$$\text{Net benefit of introducing regulation} =$$
$$\text{Cost (benefit factor) of Y} - \text{Cost (benefit factor) of Z.}$$

Moreover, it is sufficient to compare the change in costs. In this case, not only the monetary conversion of benefits but also the quantification of benefits is unnecessary. It is very useful because most regulations are revising existing regulations and the major benefits are the same as the existing regulation. Thus, the assessment in IA regarding such regulations is simpler than in a brand new regulation. We illustrate recycling-related regulation as examples.

Example 7.5 Act on Recycling of Specified Home Appliances in Japan

In the past, people in Japan rarely recovered steel and certain other metals from end-of-life (EoL) home appliances and discarded the rest of the appliances in landfills. In 2001, the Act on Recycling of Specified Home Appliances was introduced. The Act provides for a collection and recycling system for waste of used home appliances in which retailers of home appliances take charge of collecting appliances and their manufacturers take charge of recycling the collected appliances. The following is a summary of the costs and benefits generated in the cases of maintaining the status quo and implementing the Home Appliance Recycling Law. Here, the effects of waste treatment compared to non treatment are almost the same before and after the introduction of the new law. Thus, the analysis can be done by describing only the differences of the costs including benefits of recycling (Fig. 7.4).

Thus, net benefits from the introduction of the regulations obtained by cost-benefit analysis.

$$=(\text{Benefit of Status quo} - \text{Cost of Status quo})$$
$$-(\text{Benefit of the new regulation} - \text{Cost of the new regulation})$$
$$=\text{Net benefits of new regulations} - \text{Net benefits of existing regulations}$$

7.4.5 *Estimating Cost of Regulation*

The cost component can generally be divided into compliance costs and administrative costs. Compliance costs include direct monetary payments such as fees and surcharges paid by the public and businesses to comply with regulations, capital investment costs, running costs, and administrative costs for preparing documents and collecting information. This also includes the costs of impeding competition and market efficiency (market surplus). These are the major cost elements.

Administrative costs are the overhead costs incurred by the central and local governments to formulate and enforce regulations. It includes general administrative

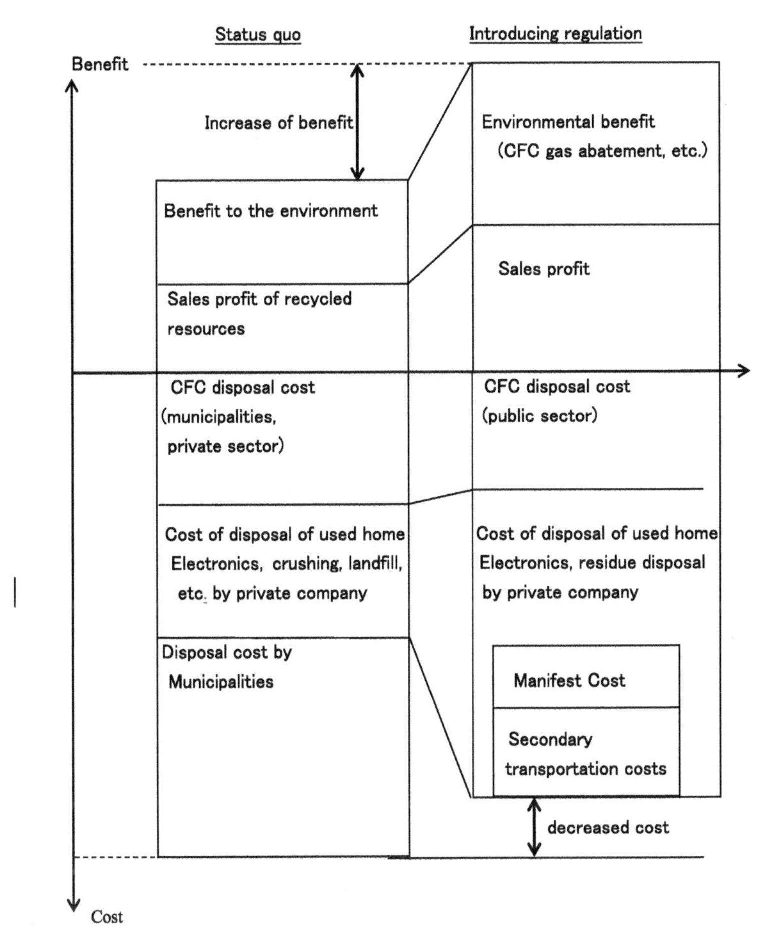

Fig. 7.4 Costs and benefits of the status quo case and the recycling law implementation case

costs in the responsible departments, monitoring and reporting costs, enforcement costs, and in some cases, costs through litigation and other means.

Costs should be accounted for without double counting. Depending on the relationship between the regulator and the stakeholders, information of compliance-costs may be easy or difficult to obtain. In IA, especially in draft IA, you should conduct the assessment even if it is not perfect. We should aim for the most reasonable calculation results possible. Obtaining a rough estimate is more effective than not doing it at all. If you find cost per unit and total number with which the regulation needs to comply, total compliance-costs could be derived to approximate per unit times total number.

7.4.6 Estimating Benefits of the New Regulation

As for the benefits, especially for regulations in the field of environment, safety, and health, it is essential to have a scientific basis for understanding and evaluating the benefits. Such evidence is provided by the research of academic institutions and the knowledge of consulting firms, and obtaining it overnight is almost impossible.

In the case of developing countries, a lack of resources for this kind of research is severer than that in developed countries. In such cases, ideally it is preferable to foster higher research institutions. As mentioned in Chap. 8, the cooperation of economists is also desirable to use the results of such analysis.

However, even in cases where these are difficult, field experiments based on causal inference have been widely conducted in developing countries in recent years, and the number of related World Bank projects is increasing. In addition, the findings of studies conducted in developed countries can also be applied.

Even in developed countries, it is difficult to calculate the benefits of specific regulations, and many analogies are made when they cannot be derived directly. We present two examples from Food and Drug Administration (FDA) of the US Department of Health and Human Services.

Example 7.6 RIA of regulations imposing mandatory ingredient labeling for dietary supplements

Imposing an ingredient labeling requirement is beneficial in that it saves consumers' time in search of medicines. To calculate this benefit, FDA estimates that consumers save 2 min in searching for medicines compared to the time before the introduction of the regulation. Thus, the benefit of the regulation is calculated to multiply this by the average wage as saving the opportunity cost (from interview with Peter J Vardon, Ph.D., FDA, at FDA, February 2004).

Example 7.7 RIA of a regulation on the use of raw and semi-boiled eggs to prevent damage from Salmonella

The benefit of regulating the use of raw and semi-boiled eggs to prevent food poisoning by Salmonella is calculated using the price of sterilized eggs, which has the same effect as the regulation. In other words, they try to explain the benefit of the regulation by the price difference between normal eggs and sterilized eggs based on the purchase of sterilized eggs at a higher price than normal to prevent food poisoning (from interview with Peter J Vardon, Ph.D., FDA, at FDA, February 2004).

7.4.7 Assessment of Costs and Benefits

Methods of aggrigating costs and benefits in IA are mainly "cost-benefit analysis," "cost-effective analysis," and "cost-utility analysis" that is an application of cost-effective analysis. In cost-benefit analysis, not only costs but also all the benefits are converted into monetized values using available values or quantification methods, and all the values are expressed in monetary terms to determine whether the benefits exceed the costs.

The amount obtained by subtracting costs from benefits is called net benefits. If the net benefit is positive, the introduction of the regulation is justified. If there are some available values or quantification methods, cost-benefit analysis would be an ideal method. As it is, it is difficult to evaluate all effects and costs in monetary terms even in the UK and US, where researches have relatively advanced.

Further, "cost-effective analysis" expresses the total social costs to achieve the effects of regulation. It has the advantage that the effects do not have to be completely converted to monetary value. Therefore, cost-benefit analysis seems to be the most applicable in reality. However, since it is difficult to provide decision criteria in cost-effective analysis if the regulation has multiple effects, it is necessary to conduct a cost-benefit analysis by converting them into monetary values or cost-utility analysis using proper quantification methods, quantifying the extent to which various effects provide social benefits as "utility," and comparing them by reducing them to a single scale.

In order to reduce to utility, it is necessary to use objective weights for each effect based on the height of utility. However, as with monetary units, the objective estimation of such weights is difficult and cost-utility analysis has limitations to their use.

Finally, in other countries, the analysis of efficiency perspective is sometimes called cost-benefit analysis. It should be noted, however, that this is more like an assessment of cost and benefit in the sense that it examines costs and benefits, and is not a cost-benefit analysis in which everything is converted into monetary terms as described above.

It is emphasized that the quantification method itself has its limitations, and it is impossible to express all the cost-effectiveness quantitatively. Further, the monetary units for such conversions should be obtained as a result of the long-term accumulation of academic research. The limitations of such quantification and monetization should be fully considered in regulation making and regulatory decision.

In addition, quantification and numerical values alone are insufficient to ensure objectivity and transparency. To ensure objectivity and transparency, the reproducibility of the analysis must be ensured first. In other words, the analysis itself must be made available to the public in a form that can be traced by outsiders. Therefore, efforts should be made to disclose the analysis materials, including the data used, as much as possible.

7.4.8 Cost-Effective Analysis

When it is difficult to convert everything into monetary terms, there is a way to present cost-effectiveness and compare among various options. However, regulations with multiple goals cannot evaluate each option with a different degree of achievement of each goal. Even if a regulation has multiple goals, cost-effective analysis is useful when benefits from existing and new regulations are almost same and all the benefits are offset by changes in regulations in calculating net benefit. (as 7.4.4. (2))

It is another way to determine the relative equivalence between each objective and all the benefits can be shown by a single criterion. It is called cost-utility Analysis. An example is the equivalent fatality used by NHTSA of DOT as shown in next section.

When a large-scale regulation with various objectives is assessed in a single IA, the abovementioned problems in cost-effective analysis are more likely to occur due to multiple objectives. Thus, it is effective to cut down the regulation to measure specific objectives.

In the preliminary stage, it is important to consider alternatives seriously and preferable to propose the various options. If effective options can be proposed, cost-effective analysis is useful in choosing the most effective countermeasure alternatives.

7.4.9 Cost-Utility Analysis

NHTSA, which is responsible for traffic safety, has traditionally conducted cost-effective analyses. However, the goal of the agency's regulations is to prevent accidents and casualties. Therefore, cost-effective analysis must be conducted for the dual goals of reducing the number of fatalities and injuries. To deal with this, the ratio of the social damage caused by fatalities and injuries is calculated in advance using WTP or other estimation. This ratio is called equivalent fatality and is used as a weight to represent death and injury as a single unit. Injury is also divided into several stages, and the same weight is estimated for each stage. This is equivalent to cost-utility analysis and we can compare among the various options. This is an estimation available in NHTSA (1996) (Table 7.1).

Table 7.1 Comprehensive fatality and injury relative values NHTSA (1996)

Injury severity	1994 Relative value* per injury
MAIS 1	0.0038
MAIS 2	0.0468
MAIS 3	0.1655
MAIS 4	0.4182
MAIS 5	0.8791
Fatals	1.000

* Includes the economic cost components and valuation for reduced quality of life

7.4.10 *Cost-Benefit Analysis*

Cost-benefit analysis is the best way to examine and compare costs and benefits. Although it is difficult to convert everything into monetary terms, in the case of completely new regulations with many goals, cost-benefit analysis might be the best way to estimate net benefit. However, IA is a supplement to a decision and is not a decisive one. Thus, if it is not possible to estimate the monetary value objectively, the estimate must be used very carefully.

If you need to estimate monetary value, it is well described in Circular A-4 of the US OMB. We briefly introduce it below. First, if the goods or services directly affected by the regulation are traded in the market, the traded price (or the future price if the future price can be predicted) should be used for monetary conversion (3.a Direct Uses of Market Data in A-4).

However, if the goods or services are not traded in the market, we need several ways to estimate the monetary value. The first method is to indirectly use the data traded in the market (i.e., to use the valuations implicit in the market prices), which is called the indirect market method (3.b in A-4). The second method is to directly ask consumers to assign a value using questionnaires, etc., and is called Stated Preference Methods (3.c in A-4).

The third method is to use the value already estimated by one of these two methods and is called the Benefit Transfer Method (5. In A-4). It is preferable to collect original data on revealed preference or stated preference to support regulatory analysis. Yet, conducting an original study may not be feasible due to the time and expense involved. One alternative to conducting an original study is the use of "benefit transfer" methods. The practice of "benefit transfer" began with transferring the existing estimates obtained from the indirect market and stated preference studies to new contexts.

Other indirect market methods include the comparable market method, the travel cost method, the hedonic wage method, the hedonic price method, the defensive spending method, and conjoint analysis. All of them are described in A-4.

7.5 Important Note for Assessing Costs and Benefits

The purpose of this study is to conduct an IA to examine, on the basis of evidence, whether the benefits of the regulation outweigh the costs and are socially desirable. Therefore, it is not the original purpose to spend a lot of budget and manpower to calculate the benefits. In addition, irrespective of the method used, there is a high possibility that more desirable research exists, and it is questionable whether they will be accepted by the public irrespective of the expense.

Rather, it is more important to consider what options are desirable in the early stages of regulation by conducting multiple trial calculations. This is the reason why, although we have quoted much from A-4 about the possibilities of various options, we have suppressed both quotations and explanations of the monetary valuation method, which provides more explanations than proposals for options.

This book reiterates that setting a precise baseline and identifying the expected costs and benefits are of utmost importance for the analysis of IA, and that it is best to select a more desirable regulatory proposal from among the various alternatives.

Risk analysis, for example, is particularly useful in uncertain situations. It is helpful to be evaluated in a situation where there is not enough evidence. Accountability should be enhanced by conducting a large number of sensitivity analyses to show as many changes as possible in situations different from those for which they were appropriate, such as behavioral changes, while acknowledging their limitations.

7.5.1 Discount Rate

Costs and benefits do not necessarily occur simultaneously. In such a case, simply adding up the costs and benefits chronologically can be misleading. Costs and benefits to be incurred at a future time are less valuable than those to be incurred at the present time, and must be discounted to present value using the discount rate.

Discounting is not done as an adjustment to the rate of increase in prices. The reason for discounting is that benefits accruing in the present are prefer to that accruing in the future, and costs accruing in the future are prefer to costs accruing in the present. There are two rationales for this.

(1) Rate of return on investment
 On average, investments have a positive rate of return. Thus a unit of current consumption is more expensive than a unit of future consumption. This is because if we postpone our current consumption and invest it, we can gain more future consumption.
(2) Time Preference Rate
 People usually prefer one unit of consumption in the present to one unit of consumption in the future. This is called people having a positive time preference, and society as a whole also has a positive time preference.

In a perfect competitive market, the rate of return on investment and subjective time preference will match the market interest rate. However, since real markets are imperfect due to taxation and information asymmetry, it has been proposed to use some form of weighted average of the two, or to use them on a case-by-case basis.

The base year for discounting should be the year in which the regulation comes into effect, unless there is a specific reason not to. The first thing to do is to prepare a list of yearly estimates of the costs and benefits that are expected to result from the regulation. The discounting can then be done by calculating the net benefits (benefits minus costs) in advance for each year and discounting them to present value, or by discounting the costs and benefits to present value, respectively, and subsequently calculating the net benefits.

7.5.2 *The Problem of Double Counting*

Changes in regulations and other policies naturally affect economic activities. In addition, such impacts affect the entire economy through changes in economic activities, especially through change of prices. Dividing this into direct impacts and spillover effects, it makes sense to individually consider the spillover effects. However, in terms of calculating the benefits, adding the costs and benefits of spillover effects to the costs and benefits of direct effects amounts to double counting, which is apparently wrong.

Example: A case in which a price decrease of one good due to deregulation leads to a price decrease of another good (e.g., a decrease in the cost of cell phones due to a decrease in the inspection cost of cell phone equipment, which in turn leads to a decrease in the price of cell phones, which in turn leads to an increase in the price of fixed-line phones: it is incorrect to calculate the increase in the price of fixed-line phones as an expense. A change in the price of fixed-line telephones only generates an increase in income to the supplier and an increase in expenditure to the consumer, each of which offsets the other and is neither a cost nor a benefit to society.

(1) Possible practical problems with double counting

(a) Error of the offsetting costs and benefits.
This includes mistakes in the offsetting costs and benefits, especially by overly considering only the costs and benefits attributed to different entities. In the case of child restraint system in Example 7.4, for the manufacturer who makes the child seat, it appears to be a benefit because it is a job. Calculating this as a benefit is an error that simply forgets to take into account the fact that there will be manufacturing costs. Here, there is no secondary benefit because it is offset by the cost from increased work.

(b) The concept of opportunity cost
As mentioned above, adding the costs and benefits generated by spillover effects to the costs and benefits at the time they are incurred, or accounting for income generated by costs as benefits is a double-counting error. However, the following arguments seem plausible at first glance; therefore, we will explain the problem.

"The cost of regulation provides jobs. For manufacturers and their employers, the situation is even worse, as they would be unemployed if there were no jobs created by the regulation. Therefore, the income from the jobs created by regulation should be considered a benefit."

This comment emphasizes that in the absence of regulation, people will be "unemployed" and, thus, worse off than they are now. This is equivalent to assuming the worst situation as a baseline and arguing that no matter how inefficient the measure in question is, it is desirable because it will be even worse without regulation. Emphasizing this aspect justifies any useless measure. Keynesian economics, which is the basis for economic stimulus, is close to this position and tends to think that it is desirable to implement even useless measures.

However, cost-benefit analysis suggests that even if people lose such jobs, they can find new, more desirable jobs in the long run. In this sense, we believe that working in a job based on useless policies is a sacrifice of time that could be used more effectively. The time sacrificed and the wages earned by more productive works are called opportunity cost. In cost-benefit analysis, we believe that the opportunity cost of wasteful policies is large. Opportunity cost applies to not only wages, but also profit. Therefore, the profit obtained from other jobs, that is, profit opptunity, can also be calculated as a cost with regulation.

7.5.3 Dealing with Uncertainty

(1) Use of risk assessment

The benefits of regulations on safety, environment, health, etc. can also be predicted quantitatively using indicators such as the number of accidents per year, the concentration of chemical substances in rivers, or the number of illnesses per year. For such predictions, risk assessment methods such as those listed below are recommended.

Step 1: Identify the variables that the regulation directly targets and the variables that are indicators of benefits.

(e.g., the emission concentration of chemical A and the number of cases of lung cancer per year.)

Step 2: Qualitatively demonstrate the causal mechanism linking the two.

(e.g., if the emission concentration of chemical A is reduced, its concentration in the air and the amount of exposure is reduced and the risk of developing lung cancer is reduced.)

Step 3: If possible, quantify the causal mechanisms that link the two.

(e.g., reducing the emission concentration of chemical substance A from B to B1 will reduce the risk of developing lung cancer by C1 cases per year.)

Step 4: Simulate the magnitude of the benefits of each alternative measure.

(e.g., reducing the emission concentration of chemical A from B to B1, B2, or B3 will reduce the risk of developing lung cancer by C1, C2, or C3 cases per year.

In particular, multiple indicators of safety and environmental benefits can be employed because regulations go through several stages, from the variables they directly address to the variables they result in. More Indicators of the impact are desirable but, at the same time, are more difficult to predict and increase uncertainty. Therefore, the extent to which they should be predicted should be determined for each individual assessment, applying the proportionality principle discussed in Part I. Examples of the stages of benefit indicators are as follows.

In the case of a regulation to tighten control on drunk driving, the indicators of the effect of the regulation could be (1) an increase in the number of arrests, (2) a decrease in the number of drunk driving accidents, or (3) a decrease in the number of people killed or injured in drunk driving accidents. In terms of the purpose of the regulation, the order of (3), (2), and (1) is desirable, but quantitative prediction becomes more difficult in this order.

In the case of a regulation to set a standard value for the emission of an air pollutant, the indicators of the effect of the regulation can be (1) a reduction in the emission amount, (2) a decrease in air concentration, (3) a reduction in the amount of people's exposure, or (4) a decrease in the number of diseases. For the purpose of regulation, the order of (4), (3), (2), and (1) is desirable, but quantitative prediction becomes more difficult in this order.

(2) Use of sensitivity analysis
When it is difficult to determine future variables, and when the estimates of such variables differ among the interested parties, it is effective to conduct a sensitivity analysis to supplement the estimates. In sensitivity analysis, if a variable (ratio) is uncertain, multiple values such as 0, 1, 5, and 10% are assumed within a certain range, and analysis is conducted for each of these values and compared. The validity of the analysis results can be examined by changing these values.

(3) Monte Carlo simulation
It refers to a simulation in which a variable with uncertainty is given information about its probability distribution, 10,000 iterations are performed, and its 95% confidence interval is estimated. This kind of work can be easily carried out using statistical analysis software. For example, if we consider that there is a large uncertainty in the discount rate and benefits, we can calculate both as a distribution. The discount rate is assumed to be log normally distributed with 1–10% included in the 95th percentile of the distribution, and the benefits are assumed to be uniformly distributed, occurring over 10 years and ranging from 1 to 300 million yen annually. There is no uncertainty about the cost, which is assumed to be 1 billion yen in the first year. Using a Monte Carlo simulation with 10,000 iterations, the discounted present value of the net benefits is estimated to be 700 million yen on average, with a 95% confidence interval of –0.83 to 1.57 billion yen.

7.5.4 Analysis of Spillover Effects

Let us consider the case of deregulation of entry into the telecommunications market (the following is a simplified and fictitious example). In this case, (1) more competition in the telecommunications market, which we call the primary market, is expected to result in lower telecommunications prices. Further, (2) prices of goods and services provided using telecommunications, which we call secondary market, are also expected to fall. (3) In addition, a widespread decline in the prices of goods and services provided using telecommunications will increase consumers' real incomes, which may increase demand in the telecommunications market that we call inducement effect. Here, (2) and (3) would fall under the category of spillover effects or indirect effects.

In the case where each market is perfect, the decrease in the price of goods and services that occurs in (2) will bring benefits to consumers. However, this will be offset when the costs and benefits are aggregated for society as a whole because it will directly result in a decrease in the supplier's income. However, demand shift caused by (3) should be taken into account when estimating the benefits and costs.

It is also possible that the supply of goods and services using telecommunication technology (e.g., music distribution) will increase due to a decrease in telecommunication rates, and the supply using other media (e.g., CDs) will decrease. Such effects that were not initially intended by the new establishment, revision, or abolition of regulations are called secondary effects. In this case, it is equivalent to an indirect impact or indirect effects.

In typical cost-benefit analysis, benefits that occur in the primary market are estimated using the consumer surplus approach that belongs to occurrence-based benefit estimation. In many cases, induced effects are ignored because they are difficult to measure, but estimation methods that take induced effects into account are sometimes used.

Attribution based approach is also possible to measure costs and benefits. This approach takes into account indirect effects for all markets (both primary and secondary), predicts what will eventually happen, and subsequently adds up the increase or decrease in benefits with general equilibrium framework. To predict the impact on the distributional effects, it is necessary to estimate the impact of the measurement on an attribution basis. It is applied general equilibrium analysis. It is important to note that adding the accrual-based and attribution-based measurements results in double counting.

Applied general equilibrium analysis can explicitly consider spillover effects or indirect effects and provide information on the distribution of benefits by region and economic entity. However, the accuracy of the measurement of total benefits is not necessarily higher than that of the consumer surplus approach due to the difficulties involved in estimating the parameters of the model and data limitations. At present, applied general equilibrium analysis is considered to be more effective in supplementing the information obtained using the consumer surplus method and in examining issues such as the relationship of benefits by entity and region, rather than as a replacement for the consumer surplus method.

Since the input-output analysis of Keyinsian flamework does not take supply constraints into account, the direct effect is amplified, and even in cases where there is no benefit at all, calculation results may be obtained as if the gross national product had increased and the benefit on an accrual basis had occurred. Therefore, input-output analysis must not use for the purpose of measuring attributed benefits.

As for the secondary effects, particular attention should be paid to cases where there is a trade-off relationship; for example, banning a chemical substance result in its substitution by a riskier chemical substance (risk trade-off), stricter environmental regulations result in reduced safety (risk trade-off), or stricter safety regulations result in excessive reassurance to people, which in turn compromises safety (risk trade-off) (moral hazard). Further, if the regulation provides not only the benefits directly targeted by the regulation but also other types of benefits, both should be estimated and summed. For example, when emissions of greenhouse gases are reduced as a measure to combat global warming, emissions of ordinary air pollutants may be reduced simultaneously. Both are benefit and should be estimated.

7.6 Evaluation of Economic Regulations

7.6.1 Basic Principle of Economics Regulation

In market-oriented economy, competitive market provide best distribution of resources and allocation in economy. Thus, without any market failure, supporting market for operating efficiently is most efficient for economies and development of the country. It is the primal principle to keep regulation from interfering any market activity preserving perfect competition. Thus, all the regulation to intervene price and quantity should be abolished if there are no market failure.

From Viscusi et al. (2018), "If we existed in a world that functioned in accordance with the perfect competition paradigm, there would be little need for antitrust policies and other regulatory efforts. All markets would consist of a large number of sellers of a product, and consumers would be fully informed of the product's implications. Moreover, there would be no externalities present in this idealized economy, as all effects would be internalized by the buyers and sellers of a particular product. In such circumstance, regulation is rather harmful for operating market."

In US guideline Circular A4, there is a description of The Presumption Against Economic Regulation at the end of B. The Need for Federal Regulatory Action.

"Government actions can be unintentionally harmful, and even useful regulations can impede market efficiency. For this reason, there is a presumption against certain types of regulatory action. In light of both economic theory and actual experience, a particularly demanding burden of proof is required to demonstrate the need for any of the following types of regulations:

price controls in competitive markets;

production or sales quotas in competitive markets;

mandatory uniform quality standards for goods or services if the potential problem can be adequately dealt with through voluntary standards or by disclosing information of the hazard to buyers or users;

controls on entry into employment or production, except (a) where indispensable to protect health and safety (e.g., FAA tests for commercial pilots) or (b) to manage the use of common property resources (e.g., fisheries, airwaves, Federal lands, and offshore areas)."

If market failure happens even in the competitive market, however, market does not provide optimal distribution in economy. Thus, government intervention is justified. Even if there is necessity to intervene the market, government intervention might cause worse outcome. Thus Impact Assessment should be done and check the sufficiency to introduce regulation. We have called such regulation mainly social regulation. We roughly classify social regulations as measures to deal with market failures such as externalities, and economic regulations as measures to deal with imperfect competition such as market power. However, the distinction between social regulations and economic regulations is not a strict one. Economic costs are incurred even in social regulations.

Perfect competition based on mainly four premises. (1) a large number of sellers and buyers of a product, and (2) both sellers and buyers would be fully informed of the product's implications. (3) free entry and exit, (4) there is no product differentiation. If these premises do not apply, some regulations might be justified. Impact assessment or competitive assessment should be recommended to check whether some regulation could violates the premise and dimmish the competitive pressure or not. We introduce two IAs of economic regulation in this section and competition assessment will be described at Part 4.

7.6.2 Evaluation of Economic Regulations

The IA of social regulations mainly focuses on identifying the impact on externalities, whereas economic regulations focus on the consumer surplus of the market using consumer surplus approach because they aim to increase consumer and producer surplus. However, since there is extreme uncertainty to estimate demand and surplus in the market, it is considered practical to use a competition assessment or simplified method using a linear demand curve, as in Example 7.8. In the analysis of economic regulations, especially by independent regulatory commissions, competition analysis is conducted in a appropriate form.

Example 7.8 "Regulatory Impact Analysis: Amendments to the National Emission Standards for Hazardous Air Pollutants and New Source Performance Standards (NSPS) for the Portland Cement Manufacturing Industry Final Report" EPA 2010

Surplus analysis is introduced as part of cost-benefit analysis at the US Environmental Protection Agency. Over the past decade, EPA has increasingly used surplus analysis as part of its cost-benefit analysis. The example is a regulatory impact analysis of the new environmental regulations imposed on the cement industry.

In the first half of 2009, EPA submitted its final proposed regulations (National Emission Standards for Hazardous Air Pollutants from the Portland Cement). In its regulatory impact analysis, EPA assesses the impact of regulation on an oligopoly market, how market share might change, and whether the additional costs of regulation might lead to entry or exit.

In the case of the oligopoly market model, the equilibrium price can be derived using a linear cost function where the marginal cost is constant while the marginal revenue is diminishing. Therefore, the oligopoly model has the advantage that it is easier to perform comparative statics, and a change in price due to a change in cost can also be analyzed using a linear cost function or demand function. A linear cost function is used to analyze price shifting due to rising costs. In addition, the possibility of the exit of small and medium-sized enterprises (SMEs) with high costs and a high proportion of fixed costs and the expected volume of imports are estimated, and based on this, the impact on SMEs is also examined.

Example 7.9 (Draft Version) Regulatory Impact Analysis of the Exemption from License for Use of Radio Frequencies by Public Telecommunications Businesses (May 2002)

The Regulatory Impact Assessment by the UK's Radiocommunications Agency of the Department of Trade and Industry (2002) is IA of deregulation to allow exemption of license for a part of the use of 2.4 Ghz band frequency for access to the Internet by wireless LAN (Wi-Fi), which previously required a license. In the UK, the use of radio frequency bands for wireless communications had been licensed under the Wireless Telegraphy Act, with the exception of low-power short-range radio and cell phone regulations. At that time, there was a growing trend to seek exemption from licensing for short-range broadband wireless access to public telecommunication services, such as for Internet access. In particular, the 2.4 Ghz band is ripe for service provision, both technologically and economically. Therefore, this measure is to revise the current law (in 2002) that prohibits the provision of short-range broadband wireless access as a business, and to promote the spread of wireless LAN.

We explain it by a three-step approach. As a first step, the effects of deregulation can be summarized as follows. The Agency commissioned a study to assess the economic and technical impact of radio spectrum of proposed strategies on present and potential users to allow provision of public access systems using license exempt spectrum. The study estimated the consumer surplus from the introduction of public

RLAN systems to be approximately £500 million. This annex summarizes the calculation of this estimate.Consumer surplus is the sum of all net benefits enjoyed by consumers, namely, the difference between the market price and the maximum price the consumer would be willing to pay for each unit of the product or service used. It is calculated using the following formula:

Step 1: Identifying the effects of the measures.
Maintain the status quo: A license is required for all use of the 2.4 Ghz band frequency. Use of wireless LAN is also not allowed.
Deregulation: Exemption from licensing will be granted for some of the above, and use of wireless LAN will be possible.

Step 2: Classification and identification of costs and benefits

(a) Benefit factors
The first benefit factor is that the release of the 2.4 Ghz band will bring about the expansion of the use of wireless LAN, especially broadband communications. As a result, technological innovation in this technology and the resulting promotion of competition in Internet communications are expected to lead to lower prices for broadband Internet services and an increase in consumer surplus (see below).

(b) Cost (risk) factors
As a cost factor, there is a risk of excessive demand in some areas due to license exemptions that results in congestion problems. Therefore, it is pointed out that existing users may have to purchase new equipment to prevent interference.

Step 3: Quantification of benefits, conversion to monetary values, and calculation of discounted present values. In this measure, the benefits include the generation of consumer surplus resulting from the provision of new services through deregulation. By assuming the demand curve to be linear and calculating the area of the triangle in Fig. 7.5, they estimated the annual consumer surplus generated in the UK as a whole to be approximately 6.4 million pounds. Specifically, the consumer surplus is roughly estimated as below (Fig. 7.5 is added by the author).
Consumer Surplus = (maximum price-minimum price) × No. of subscribers × 1/2

The Agency commissioned a study to assess the economic and technical impact of radio spectrum of proposed strategies on present and potential users to allow provision of public access systems using license exempt spectrum. The study estimated the consumer surplus from the introduction of public RLAN systems to be approximately £500 million. We summarizes the calculation of this estimate.

Consumer surplus is the sum of all net benefits enjoyed by consumers, namely, the difference between the market price and the maximum price the consumer would be willing to pay for each unit of the product or service used. It is calculated using the following formula:

Estimates for the figures of the consumer surplus calculation are based on publicly available data on prices and/or subscriber numbers of existing public RLAN services offered by Jippi and Sonera (Finland), Telia (Sweden), and MobileStar (the US). The Table 7.2 shows the monthly subscription charges to public RLAN systems in Finland, Sweden, and the US. The highest price is considered to be the maximum price consumers would be willing to pay whereas the lowest price is assumed to be the long run equilibrium price, which is equal to the marginal cost.

Table 7.3 shows subscriber forecasts (provided by Gartner) for the number of notebooks with integrated 802.11b equipment shipped in the US in 2005. Assuming the same per capita equipment usage, forecasts for the UK were made. It was assumed that only 50% of future UK users would subscribe to public RLAN services while the other 50% would use the equipment exclusively to access private systems. This leads to an estimate of 1.6 million UK subscribers in 2005. A report by Analysis has forecast at least 20 million public WLAN users in Western Europe by 2006, with more than half of these in the UK, France, Germany, and Sweden. Therefore, the assumption of 1.6 m can be considered reasonable in calculating a lower bound on consumer surplus.

Table 7.4 shows the figures used for the calculation of consumer surplus based on two scenarios. The first and second scenarios consider the cases where the maximum price UK consumers would pay are £98.43 and £82.28 per month, respectively.

The consumer surplus that results from the introduction of public RLAN services was estimated to be around £500 million per annum in 2000. (Note that the use of 2005 forecast data leads to our consumer surplus forecast relating to the year 2005).

Furthermore, the cost factor is due to the aforementioned risk of interference. However, in the process of collecting opinions from stakeholders, the majority of opinions were that such interference problems can be effectively dealt with by service

Fig. 7.5

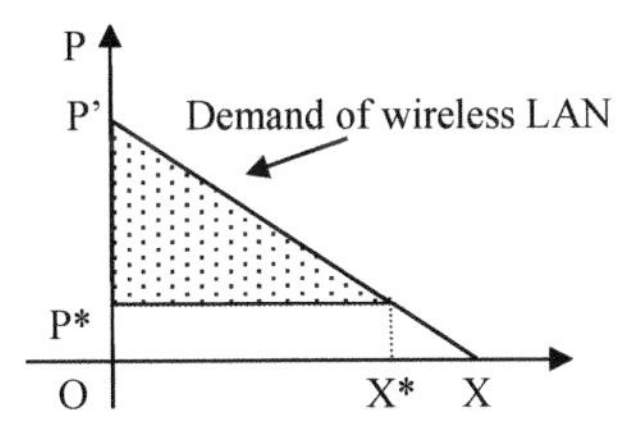

Table 7.2 Subscription charges

Service	Monthly subscription charge
Telia home run	£98.43
MobileStar	£41.12
Jippi freedom	£31.49

Table 7.3 Subscriber numbers

User type	Integrated notebook shipments in 2005, the US	Integrated notebook shipments in 2005, UK equivalent
Small and medium businesses	6,530,000	1,400,000
Large businesses	4,920,000	1,060,000
Education	739,000	159,000
Home	2,970,000	637,000
Total	15,200,000	3,250,000

Table 7.4 Calculation of consumer surplus

	Scenario 1	Scenario 2
Price (£/month)	31.49	31.49
Subscribers (million)	1.6	1.6
Choke price (£/month)	98.43	82.28
Consumer surplus (£ million/month)	53.55	40.63
Consumer surplus (£ million/year)	642.62	487.59

Note Consumer Surplus = (maximum price-minimum price), * No. of subscribers* 1/2

providers individually, and the research results showed that such measures are technically feasible; therefore, it is concluded that such problems will not arise. Therefore, the benefits of introducing new services outweigh the potential costs (risks) of interference, and the deregulation measure should be introduced to allow public providers to use 2.4 Ghz with license exemption.

Thus, the regulatory impact analysis compares the costs (risks) and benefits for society as a whole, and comes to the conclusion that license exemption should be chosen. This is organized as the impact for each entity in Table 7.5. The benefits and costs of equipment suppliers in Table 7.5 are offset from the direct effects and are not recorded as costs or benefits. However, it would be difficult to properly grasp this point when conducting the analysis. For this reason, it is preferable to prepare such attribution tables separately from the work of synthesizing social costs and benefits. They considered three options, Option 1: Full de-regulation, Option 2: A light regulatory regime with limitations on use of licence exempt spectrum for public telecommunication" and Option 3 is baseline. We illustrate only Option 1 to show the distribution chanel.

Option 1: Full de-regulation—use of license exempt spectrum for public telecommunication.

Table 7.5 Expected costs and benefits of option 1

Business sector or user affected	Benefits	Costs	Net benefits
Current end users	Ability to access new services Ability to raise revenue by operating as a public network Ability to choose whether to subscribe to a public network	Charges for new services Potentially lower quality of service for existing private RLAN users due to interference Potentially lower reliability of SRDs due to interference Engineering costs of modifying equipment to mitigate interference or change frequency	Depends on the number of license exempt spectrum users, price and availability of substitutes, and levels of interference in areas of existing use
Public Service Providers	Increased revenues from the ability to provide new services Increased revenues from the ability to enter new geographical markets, e.g., rural Lower barriers to entry will encourage new entrants	Cost of new equipment (albeit relatively low) Operating costs of new network Potential loss of ability to deliver services due to interference	Positive If interference is manageable, benefits are likely to outweigh costs
Public service customers	Ability to access new products and services Ability to choose public or private network Potentially lower prices as a result of increased competition Potential roaming between public and private networks both nationally and internationally Increased social interaction via community networks	Charge for new services (In the US, subscription charges per month are £41.12 whereas they are £98.43 in Sweden. Further, in the US, 802.11b LAN cards for PCs are currently priced at around £100) Potential loss of ability to access services due to interference Cost to business customers of lost revenues if networks are unreliable Cost to customers of replacing unreliable networks	Depends on the willingness to pay for new services in light of quality, interference, and reliability of service Consumer benefits from the introduction of public RLANs were estimated to be £500 m per year (See Annex 1 for the calculation of the consumer benefits of introducing public RLANs) Total welfare gains would be higher if you include the benefits of all new services and the benefits to producers

(continued)

Table 7.5 (continued)

Business sector or user affected	Benefits	Costs	Net benefits
Equipment Manufacturers	Revenues from equipment to support new services Ability to access global market Encourage ongoing technical innovation	Decrease in profits from supplying current license exempt equipment if interference degrades access for all users	Depends on demand and supply of old and/or new equipment

Note Assessing the relative costs and benefits of introducing public RLANs relies on individual demand, location, and existing user density; and can really only be judged on a case-by-case basis

References

Boardman AE, Greenberg DH, Vining AR, Weimer DL (2001) Cost-benefit analysis-concepts and practice, 2nd edn. Prentice Hall

Ellig J, Morrall J (2010) Assessing the quality of regulatory analysis: a new evaluation and data set for policy research

FDA (2004) Final rule declaring dietary supplements containing ephedrine alkaloids adulterated because they present an unreasonable risk. Final Rule US Federal Reg 69(28):6787–6854. https://pubmed.ncbi.nlm.nih.gov/15364637/

Fox J (2007) The uncertain relationship between transparency and accountability. Development in Practice, Taylor & Francis

Fraas A, Lutter R (2011) Can greater use of economic analysis improve regulatory policy at independent regulatory commissions?. http://www.rff.org/events/pages/can-greater-use-of-economic-analysis-improve-regulatory-policy-at-independent-regulatory-agencies.aspx

Glass GV (1968) Analysis of data on the connecticut speeding crackdown as a time-series quasi-experiment. Law Soc Rev 3(1):55–76, (22 pages)

Goldman DP et al (2004) Pharmacy benefits and the use of drugs by the chronically Ill. JAMA: J Am Med Assoc 291:2344–2350

Harrington W, Heinzerling L, Morgenstern RDD (2009) Reforming regulatory impact analysis. Resour Future. www.rff.org/RFF/Documents/RFF.RIA.V4.low_res.pdf

Hahn RW, Burnett JK, Chan Y-HI, Mader EA (1999–2000) Assessing regulatory impact analysis: the failure of agencies to comply with executive order 12,866. Harv J L Pub Pol'y, 859

Hahn RW, Tetlock PC (2008) Has economic analysis improved regulatory decisions? J Econ Perspect 22(1) (Winter)

Institute of Administrative Management (2008) Kisei no jizen hyōka handobukku yoriyoi kisei ni mukete chosha-mei. Institute of Administrative Management, 333 page

Jorgensen T et al (2014) Effect of screening and lifestyle counselling on incidence of ischaemic heart disease in general population: Inter99 randomized trial. BMJ 348:g3617

Kisei no seisaku hyōka ni kansuru kenkyūkai (2007) Kisei no jizen hyōka handobukku yoriyoi kisei ni mukete. Final Report, gyōsei kanri kenkyū sentā

Löfstedt RE (2004) The swing of the regulatory pendulum in Europe: from precautionary principle to (regulatory) impact analysis. J Risk Uncert (Springer)

METI, Japan (2001) Act on recycling of specified home appliances. Effective date: April 2001 (promulgated in June 1998). https://www.meti.go.jp/policy/recycle/main/english/law/home.html

Morrall JF III (2001) Regulatory impact analysis: efficiency, accountability, and transparency, the APEC-OECD Co-operative Initiative

Morita A, Tanabe K, Nakaizumi T, Harada H, Kubo H (2001) Kisei eikyō bunseki ni kansuru chōsa kenkyū hōkoku-sho. sōmu-shō daijin kanbō kikaku-ka

Nakaizumi T (2011) Beikoku ni okeru kisei ga kyōsō ni ataeru eikyō no haaku bunseki shuhō ni tsuite' kōsei torihiki No. 733, 2011–2011. Kosei Torihiki

Nakaizumi T (2012) Kisei sakusei ni okeru kisei eikyō bunseki (ria) no jūyō-sei: Beikoku no jirei o sankō to shite' hyōka ni tsuite no kōen gaiyō. Hyoka Q Inst Adm Manag (23):2012–2010

Nakaizumi T (2013) Progress of competition analysis in the US government, mainly focusing on environmental regulation, (in Japanese). Res Inst Econ Manag (Kanto-Gakuin University) 35:163–173

NHTSA (in the U.S. DOT) (1996) The economic cost of motor vehicle crashes, 1994. https://rosap.ntl.bts.gov › dot › dot_13243_DS1

NHTSA, U.S. Department of Transportation (1999) Final economic assessment of FMVSS No. 213 FMVSS No. 225 child restraint systems, child restraint anchorage systems. https://unece.org/DAM/trans/doc/wp29compendium/9-3.pdf

New York Times (1955) The effect of the introduction of a Connecticut Speeding Crackdown, USA. https://www.nytimes.com/1955/12/23/archives/ribicoff-orders-war-on-speeders-connecticut-first-offenders-to-see.html

OECD Regulatory Impact Analysis. http://www.oecd.org/gov/regulatorypolicy/ria.htm

Radaelli CM (2004) The diffusion of regulatory impact analysis—Best practice or lesson drawing?". Eur J Polit Res 43(5):723–747

Shawcross P, Chief of the Science and Space Branch at the White House Office of Management and Budget (2012) Secure resources and funding, and begin construction of a Death Star by 2016. https://petitions.obamawhitehouse.archives.gov/petition/secure-resources-and-funding-and-begin-construction-death-star-2016/

Shawcross S (2016) Secure resources and funding, and begin construction of a Death Star by 2016. https://petitions.obamawhitehouse.archives.gov/petition/secure-resources-and-funding-and-begin-construction-death-star-2016/

The U.S. Environmental Protection Agency (2010) Regulatory impact analysis: amendments to the national emission standards for hazardous air pollutants and new source performance standards (NSPS) for the Portland cement manufacturing industry final report. https://www3.epa.gov/ttn/ecas/regdata/RIAs/portlandcementfinalria.pdf

The Radiocommunications Agency of the Department of Trade and Industry in the UK (2002) Provision of public telecommunication services in license exempt spectrum. Draft Regulatory Impact Assessment. Mimeo

Umeda J, Ono T, Nakaizumi T (2004) Gyōsei hyōka to tōkei' tsuki zaidanhoujin Nihon tōkei kyōkai

USA (1993) Executive order 12866. http://www.plainlanguage.gov/.../eo12866.pdf

USA OIRA, OMB, RegInfo.gov-Reg Map. http://www.reginfo.gov/public/jsp/Utilities/faq.jsp

USA OIRA of OMB, Circular A-4. http://www.whitehouse.gov/omb/circulars_a004_a-4

U.S. Environmental Protection Agency (2015) Type 1 drinking water regulations: regulatory impact analysis for groundwater use rule. https://www.epa.gov/sites/default/files/2015-10/documents/regulatory_impact_analysis_for_the_proposed_ground_water_rule.pdf

Viscusi WK, Harrington JE Jr, Sappington DEM (2018) Economics of regulation and antitrust, Fifth edn. MIT Press, p 1000

Chapter 8
Role of Causal Inference in IA

Abstract We discuss how evidence-based policy methods can be used in Impact Assessment, identifying causal inference among the EBPM methods. Causal inference shares the idea of comparing counterfactuals with facts, treatmment groups with control groups, and the former with cases where a regulation is introduced while latter with those where it is not. Additionally, causal inference is the preferred validation method, including randomized controlled trials (RCTs). By virtue of its universality, causal inference transcends time and space, and verification of a causal relationship is equivalent to demonstrating the validity of the rationale for introducing the proposed regulation.

8.1 Introduction

Evidence Based Policy Making (EBPM) or Evidence Based Policy is the practice of making policy decisions based on scientific evidence. In this sense, it is emphasized that the promotion of IA will also lead to the promotion of EBPM. However, the recent prominence of EBPM is not only due to its introduction into policy making in the UK as Nakaizumi (2019) pointed out, but also because of the remarkable progress made in recent years in EBPM methods, especially in causal inference methods (see Angrist and Pischke (2008), Ito (2017), Nakamuro and Tsugawa (2017)). It is effective to introduce the methods into conventional policy evaluation. Abhijit Banerjee, Esther Duflo, and Michael Kremer won the Nobel Prize in 2019 for their experimental approach to alleviating global poverty by introducing randomized controlled trial (RCT) into Economic Analysis, especially development economics. Further, David Card, Joshua Angrist, and Guido Imbens won the Nobel Prize in 2021 for pioneering the use of natural experiments—David Card for his empirical contributions to labor economics, and the other half jointly to Joshua D. Angrist and Guido W. Imbens for their methodological contributions to the analysis of causal relationships. They have shown that various methods of causal inference can be applied not only to the economy in general, but also to social fields such as education. They showed it possible to use experiments or other causal inference methods in the fields of education and public health, which were previously difficult to verify. In this chapter,

T. Nakaizumi, *Impact Assessment for Developing Countries*, Contributions to Economics,
https://doi.org/10.1007/978-981-19-5494-8_8

we will discuss how the method of causal inference should be incorporated into Impact Assessment.

First, impact analysis compares the costs and benefits of introducing regulation with the counterfactual case of not introducing it. In the ex-ante assessment, both the cases of introducing the policy and not introducing the policy must be estimated. Comparing the case where the regulation is introduced with the case where it is not introduced is the essense of causal inference. Moreover, the case where it is not introduced corresponds to the counterfactual, which is the key to estimation in causal inference. Therefore, the assessment of costs and benefits has the same basic concept of causal inference. To begin with, it is natural to say that cost–benefit analysis share the same base of causal inference.

However, there are some areas where the current causal inference approach cannot be directly applied to ex-ante evaluation of regulations. In causal inference, the main focus is on ex-post evaluation, in which one of the cases is estimated after a policy is introduced. In the case of ex-ante evaluation, however, it is necessary to estimate not only the case where the policy is not introduced (counterfactual) but also the case where it is introduced. Moreover, in many cases, the data essential for causal inference are not available.

In contrast, there are many cases in which the necessary evidence is already clear from various previous studies, and there is no need to develop new analysis with the methods used in causal inference specifically in the ex-ante evaluation of the relevant regulations.

Furthermore, it is also incorrect to think that one must always use the causal inference method in the ex-ante evaluation of regulations. Rather, the empirical results of causal inferences made based on the general principles are universal. Therefore, it is common to apply these results in the assessment by taking the assumptions on which previous study depends into account. It is most problematic not to conduct IA itself simply because strict causal inference is impossible.

There are also many cases in which the penetration of the concept of causal inference itself is effective for IA and regulation making, even without complex estimation. For example, Japan's Ministry of the Environment claims that illegal ivory trade has not been detected, but this does not make it clear whether illegal trade is not conducted at all or is not simply being detected. In the latter case, we need to fundamentally rethink the whole policy or regulation. These differences are the issue for causal inference to discriminate. The idea that policy decisions should not be based on flawed ideas is highly desirable, as described above.

The remainder of this chapter will focus on the use of causal inference methods in EBPM, especially in IA. Section 8.2 explains how these methods can be used in the analysis of Impact Assessment. Section 8.3 discusses future challenges and prospects. Section 8.4 presents the concluding remarks.

8.2 Several Examples of Methods of Causal Inference

In causal inference, treatment group is usually considered as the case where the regulation is realized, while controlled group is considered as the case where the regulation is not realized and the effect of the policy cannot be measured. In causal inference, the most important point is how to estimate this unrealized situation (counterfactual) in a way that can be scientifically verified. In what follows, I will explain randomized controlled trials (RCTs), which is the most typical method of causal inference.

RCTs test the impact of treatment on subjects. The structure of RCTs is similar to that of comparative experiments in the natural sciences, where the target of the policy is equivalent to the treatment group and the non-implementation target is the control group, and if there is a significant difference between the two, the policy is considered to be effective. However, unlike in the natural sciences, it is impossible to make the control and treatment groups homogeneous. In the social sciences, in particular, individual differences are so large that it has been considered difficult to conduct experiments like those conducted in the natural sciences.

However, even if individual differences are large, by collecting a relatively large number of subjects and randomly raassigning them either control group or treatment group, it is possible to make the control and treatment groups close to the same on average except treatment effects, based on law of large numbers other than the treatment effects. Thus, we derive the treatment effects to compare the two groups even in the field of social sciences.

Thus, the difference is considered as the treatment effect. Meta-analysis, which collects and comprehensively analyzes a variety of studies, has even greater generality. Therefore, conducting such meta-analyses or providing assistance to such meta-analyses in preparation for the analysis within IA will also improve the quality of ex-ante evaluations of regulations.

Empirical analysis in economics has been dominated by the study of how to find causal relationships from correlations. Empirical research based on causal relationships suggested by economic theories has been the main method in the past, and results based on such methods, mainly in structural estimation, are still important. In recent years, research that combines these conventional methods with the base of causal inference has become the mainstream. In such cases, main issue is how to derive causal relationships instead of simple correlations.

Examples include difference-in-difference analysis, which compares the effects of policies before and after assuming that the baseline (counterfactual) is a linear change, and regression discontinuity design and its application to bunching analysis, which compares the effects of policies when they appear at the same point in time and in discrete ways due to institutional discrete change of factors. Instrumental variables are also useful in identifying the causal relationship. The panel data method is a method that realizes a situation similar to that of an RCT from the data, in the sense that it derives the treatment and control groups by averaging and eliminates fixed effect.

These methods derive the impact of regulation from past data and estimated counterfactuals. Naturally, it would be ideal if a large-scale RCT of the same effects as the regulations would be conducted before introduced. In the future, RCTs could become mandatory before the introduction of a regulation, as is currently the case for new drug and vaccine trials. However, at present, even in developed countries, RCTs are rarely conducted in advance of the introduction of nationwide regulations. Furthermore, it is even more difficult in developing countries with budget constraints (Sutcliffe and Julius Court (2006)). Therefore, in the next section, we will focus on two points in conducting IA and regulation making incorporating causal inference: (1) how to link the concept of causal inference to the improvement of IA, and (2) how to use the results of past causal inference, mainly meta-analysis, for IA.

8.3 Use of Causal Inference in IA

In IA, the first step is to outline the regulation and the neccesity for it. It is necessary to explain what problems will occur in the current situation without the regulation and how serious they will be if no measures are taken. The case without regulation amounts to the baseline. It is not an exaggeration to say that it is almost a completion of the preliminary IA to specify the baseline and explain these problems in a quantitative way.

Even in the absence of a formal IA, verbal or descriptive explanations of cost and benefit and necessity has likely been made in any policy-making process in all countries in the world. IA aims to do this in a more systematic way, while simultaneously providing a quantitative and evidence-based assessment of the impact, presenting the issues in a way that is easy to understand for a wide range of people, and enhancing transparency and accountability. In what follows, we sum up the analytical viewpoints in IA refering the methods of causal inference.

(1) Overview of regulations and description of current issues
The current problems form the basis of the baseline. It should identify as specifically as possible what the situation would be if the regulation was not introduced. It is equivalent to identify precisely the case where the regulation is not introduced, that is, the counterfactual.
(2) Necessity
Necessity refers to the fact that the market cannot solve the current problem without government intervention.
(3) Identify the baseline and specify costs and benefits
Next, in the assessment of costs and benefits, the baseline is also used as a basis to compare the situation with the introduction of the regulation, and to identify the costs and benefits. The most important thing in assessing the costs and benefits obtained from the introduction of regulations is that it is difficult to specify

the situation with or without regulations completely. Therefore, in accordance with the principle of proportionality, the focus of the analysis should be on the points that are particularly necessary for measuring the effectiveness of the introduction of regulations.

(4) Effectiveness analysis

Even if the necessity indicates that there is a need for government intervention, it is not necessarily clear whether the measures introduced by the possible regulation will be effective. In other words, sufficiency to introduce regulation is not illustrated.

In the case of metabolic syndrome screening in Japan, Government misjudged that the confounding factor of taking care of one's health had an effect on health, which led to the introduction of a system with little causal relationship and no effect. The main purpose of IA and EBPM is to prevent the introduction of such a system that has no direct causal relationship and does not show effectiveness. In this case, even if it is impossible to conduct an RCT in advance, it is promising to use the results of RCTs conducted in other cases or natural experiments, which is defined that actual cases happen to constitute an RCT flamework.

The lack of causal effects of metabolic screening on health has been shown in two RCTs conducted in Denmark by Jorgensen et al. (2014) and Suzuki et al. (2015). Thus, whether the policy actually achieves its objectives or not must depend on examining whether there is actually a causal relationship and whether effectiveness exists. In doing so, the method of causal inference is crucial.

(5) Comparison with alternatives

In the early stages of regulation making, it is important to propose a variety of alternatives and show how they improve the proposed regulations. Moreover, when asked why the options are not used in the future, the initial discussions leading up to the proposed regulation will be an adequate explanation. In the case of RCTs, it is common to not only compare one option with a symmetrical group, but also analyze various options simultaneously. Therefore, it can also be used as a reference when initially considering various alternatives. See the examples of Jorgensen et al. (2014) for more on this.

(6) Efficiency analysis

When effectiveness is confirmed, the most cost-effective alternative should be selected, taking into account other issues such as fairness and distributional impact. If the impact on the market environment is limited, the costs incurred in the private and public sectors can be assessed and calculated, taking care not to double count.

8.4 Conclusion

This chapter has shown that IA shares a common feature with the method of causal inference in that it estimates both the cases where regulations are introduced and not introduced, and compares them. In this respect, the concept of causal inference is useful in conducting ex-ante estimation of regulations. In addition, it is a powerful method for validating efficacy, including RCTs, when research results on causal inference exist. Causal inference presents the results in a universal manner. Even if there were no causal inference studies conducted as an IA to estimate the effect of that regulation, if the effect is realized in conventional studies and the causal relationship is verified, the effectiveness of the introduction of the regulation has been shown. If the cost is commensurate with the effect, the introduction of the regulation is justified.

The biggest problem is that nothing is done to address them because a perfect analysis is not provided. Even if there are limitations to the analysis, it is much better to be done with explaining what the limitations are. Even a rough estimate is much more useful than doing nothing at all, because it clarifies the problem much more precisely. This is the first point that must be recognized in IA. If there is no any perfect method, it would be beneficial to try various methods. Further, it should be added that taking a weighted average of the results of various analyses does not necessarily lead to the correct conclusion.

References

Angrist JD, Pischke J-S (2008) Mostly harmless econometrics: an empiricist's companion. Princeton Univ Press, 371 page

Ito K (2017) Deta Bunseki no chikara, Ingakankeini Semaru Shikouho. Kobunsha, p 289

Jorgensen T, Jacobsen RK, Toft U, Aadahl M, Glümer C, Pisinger C (2014) Effect of screening and lifestyle counselling on incidence of ischaemic heart disease in general population: inter99 randomized trial. BMJ 2014:348. https://doi.org/10.1136/bmj.g3617(Published09June2014)Citethisas:BMJ2014;348:g3617

Nakamuro M, Tsugawa Y (2017) Gen'in to kekka no keizai-gaku - deta kara shinjitsu o minuku shikō-hō' daiamondo-sha, p 215

Nakaizumi T (2019) Igirisu no EBPM (ebidensu Based Policy meikingu) no dōkō to wagakuni e no EBPM dōnyū no kadai. Keizai keiei kennkyusho nenpo, vol 41. Research Institute of Economics and Management, Kanto-Gakuin University, pp 3–9

Ono T (2018) Ebidensu bēsutona gyōseki sokutei ni mukete. Keizaikei, vol 275. Research Institute of Economics and Management, Kanto-Gakuin University, pp 6–25

Suzuki W, Iwamoto Y, Yuda M (2015) Ta 'tokuteikenshin tokutei hoken shidō no kōka sokutei: Puroguramu hyōka no keiryōkeisaigaku kara no apurōchi. 'iryō keizai kenkyū', vol 27, no 1, pp 2–39

Sutcliffe S, Julius Court (2006) A toolkit for progressive policymakers in developing countries. https://odi.org/en/publications/a-toolkit-for-progressive-policymakers-in-developing-countries/

Part IV
Competition Assessment

Chapter 9
Competition Assessment in The UK, The US, Japan, and Pakistan

Abstract We explain competition assessment. Regulations or other government-imposed barriers unduly restrain market activities. Assessing these restraints, via a process we call competition assessment, is the first step to eliminate the burden. First, we introduce a checklist as a simple way to understand the burden the given regulation places on competition. Next, we explain competition assessment involving several countries. We emphasize the adoption of more pro-competitive regulatory proposals. This entails identifying problems at the early stage of regulation making and encourages regulatory authorities to take steps toward improvement.

9.1 Introduction

As described in Sect. 9.6—economic regulation—of Chap. 7, in a market-oriented economy, a competitive market provides the best resource allocation and allocation. Thus, without any market failure, supporting the efficient operation of the market is most effective for the development of countries and economies. Moreover, it is the primal principle to keep regulation from interfering any market activity for preserving perfect competition. Thus, all regulations interfering with price and quantity should be abolished if there is no market failure.

If market failure happens even in the competitive market, however, market does not provide optimal allocation in economy. Government intervention might be justified. Even when market intervention is a necessity, the outcome of government intervention might be worse. Thus, Impact Assessment (IA) should be done and the sufficiency to introduce a regulation checked.

Perfect competition is mainly based on four premises: (1) a large number of sellers and buyers of a product, (2) both are fully informed of the product's implications. (3) free entry and exit, and (4) there is no product differentiation. If some of these premises do not apply, some regulations might be justified. Further, some regulations violate the premises and diminish the competitive pressure. In such cases, IA or competitive assessment should be recommended. In Part 4, we describe competition assessment.

T. Nakaizumi, *Impact Assessment for Developing Countries*, Contributions to Economics,
https://doi.org/10.1007/978-981-19-5494-8_9

According to the OECD Recommendation on Competition Assessment, "increased competition contributes to higher economic productivity and growth. In many jurisdictions, however, laws, regulations, or other government-imposed barriers unduly restrain market activities. One important step to eliminate these restraints is competition assessment"—wherein you assess the regulations and find those that unnecessarily restrict competition and, if necessary, develop alternative policies that achieve the same objectives with lesser harm to competition.

Competition authorities in many OECD countries have recently created guidance for reviewing the competitive effects of regulations and developing an institutional mechanism. The OECD recommendation encourages further governmental efforts to reduce unduly restrictive regulations to competition and promote beneficial market activity.

Even in the UK government, not many IAs contain competition assessment for scrutiny, though government departments have started to consider competition assessment more seriously. Competition assessment is difficult for several reasons. One of the reasons is that the government may not have enough data about the market needed for the analysis. It is also true that it is hard to manualize.

Thus, the first step of competition assessment in the UK consists of very simple four question:

(Q1) Does it change the number of competitors?
(Q2) Does it change their ability to compete?
(Q3) Does it change their incentives to compete?
(Q4) Does it change the customers' ability to play their effective role in the market?

This is also true for other OECD countries. Most OECD countries use the checklist and conduct competition assessment. The first step of developing countries to introduce competition assessment has all the regulatory stuff make use of the checklist thoroughly. Subsequently, the checklist should be used to find issues of competition at the initial stage of the proposed regulation. After the checklist has been filled out, it is ready to go to next stage.

In contrast, formal competition procedure is not mandatory in the US. This is also the case with the UK, though IA is mandatory there. Rather than mandating the procedures for competition analysis or filling up the checklist, both the US and UK governments analyze several appropriate alternatives and choose adequate approaches that minimize the impact on competition at the early stage of regulation making. This approach minimizes the impact on competition without the need for additional assessment.

Circular A-4 (hereafter referred to as A-4), The US Regulatory Impact Analysis Guideline issued by OMB also emphasizes the adoption of more pro-competitive regulatory proposals and other measures in Section C (Consideration of Alternative Approaches), and explains them in detail with specific examples. This adoption should be considered at an early stage.

The Competition and Markets Authority (CMA) that is in charge of competition assessment in the UK, focuses on finding out problems at the early stage of regulation making and encourages regulatory authorities to fix that. To do this, the CMA has been trying to persuade other ministries to reduce the impact of regulations on competition and increase the number of their colleagues. If any further issues are found at the early stage of regulation making, they can be proactively addressed by consulting the competition authority and fixed more easily.

The importance to consider the alternatives at the early stage of regulation making can be easily understood by looking at the trend toward performance standards regulations seen in safety regulations as mentioned earlier. In the past, regulations were generally based on design-standard regulations that adopted only specific parts or parts produced by specific companies. In this case, the smaller the number of companies that can supply the product, the more competition is hampered. Even if a competition assessment were to be conducted here, the only improvement that could be expected would be an increase in the number of companies producing the specifications.

In other words, if design-standard regulations are left unchanged, the negative effects of oligopoly will inevitably remain unresolved, and the entry of new companies in the future will be closed. However, if performance-based regulations are introduced from the beginning, such problems that inhibit competition will not occur at all. Thus, it is far more effective to design a regulatory proposal that does not impede competition from the outset, to achieve sufficient competition, than to conduct a competition assessment when the regulation has been almost designed.

After briefly discussing the checklist in Sect. 9.2, we explain the consideration of impact on competition in the UK in Sect. 9.3. Subsequently, we sum up the case in the US in Sect. 9.4. Japan in Sect. 9.5, and the importance of competition assessment in developing other countries is emphasized in Sect. 9.6. Section 9.7 discusses the case of Pakistan and Sect. 9.8 provides the concluding remarks.

9.2 Checklist in Different Countries

We now introduce the competition checklist recommended by the OECD. The Competition Assessment Toolkit[1] provided by the OECD should be used as a base of finding competition issues at the early stage. The Toolkit shows how to conduct competition assessment. It provides a practical method for regulators and legislators to use it for identifying important competitive restrictions and, if possible, avoiding them.

As a first step, the method employs, a set of threshold questions—a "Competition Checklist"—that show when proposed laws or regulations may have significant potential to harm competition. This checklist helps policymakers focus on potential competition issues at an early stage in the policy development process.

While the majority of regulations do not present a risk of significant harm to competition, the competition assessment process—of which the checklist should be

[1] There are three volumes. Volume1 sets down the toolkit principles. Volume 2 provides detailed technical guidance, and Volume 3 is an operational manual.

used at the initial stage—provides the analytical framework that regulators and legislators need to mitigate or avoid potential competition problems. It does so by aiding them in identifying possible alternatives that might reduce or eliminate the potential harm to competition while continuing to achieve the desired policy objectives. The Competition Checklist probes three kinds of government restrictions on competition:

(A) Limits the number or range of suppliers
If existing businesses do not face the prospect of new competition, the possibility of collusion between them increases. Without new competition, individual businesses may also have a greater ability to raise prices.
This is likely to be the case if the proposal

1. Grants exclusive rights for a supplier to provide goods or services
2. Establishes a license, permit, or authorization process as a requirement of operation
3. Limits the ability of some types of suppliers to provide a good or service
4. Significantly raises cost of entry or exit by a supplier, which creates a geographical barrier to the ability of companies to supply goods, services, or labor; or invest capital.

(B) Limits the ability of suppliers to compete
Regulations that restrict advertising and marketing can reduce the intensity and dimensions of rivalry, yielding higher prices for consumers and less product variety.
This is likely to be the case if the proposal

1. Limits sellers' ability to set the prices for goods or services
2. Limits the freedom of suppliers to advertise or marketing their goods or services
3. Sets standards for product quality that provide an advantage to some suppliers over others or are above the level that some well-informed customers would choose
4. Significantly raises costs of production for some suppliers relative to others (especially by treating incumbents differently from new entrants).

(C) Reduces the incentive of suppliers to compete
Regulation to reduce the incentive of suppliers to compete may facilitate collusion between suppliers. They may also reduce the willingness, ability, or incentive of customers to switch between different suppliers.
Collusion between suppliers over terms of competition can restrict output and raise prices, leaving consumers worse off.
This may be the case if the proposal

1. Creates a self-regulatory or co-regulatory regime
2. Requires or encourages information on supplier outputs, prices, sales, or costs to be published

3. Exempts the activity of a particular industry or group of suppliers from the operation of general competition law.

(D) Limits the choices and information available to customers
Regulations sometimes limit the choices available to consumers could limit quality of care and mobility the consumers would be interested in reflaining from doing so. Limits on consumer choice can be harmful, because the suppliers who remain can have less incentive to satisfy consumers by delivering products of desired quality and price.
This may be the case if the proposal

1. Limits the ability of consumers to decide from whom they purchase
2. Reduces mobility of customers between suppliers of goods or services by increasing the explicit or implicit costs of changing suppliers
3. Fundamentally changes information required by buyers to shop effectively.

If a problem is found in the first step, we go to Step 2. The second step is for governments and decision-makers to revise regulations that unduly restrict competition. This phase of competition assessment involves identifying the objectives of regulations, laws, and policies that restrict competition; examining the rationales for these limits; and developing alternative, less restrictive means to achieve legitimate goals that promote more competition.

For most regulations, laws, and policies, competition assessments are not necessary or yield only minor benefits. In certain cases, some type of restriction on competition is necessary to achieve government objectives. However, for some others, a detailed competition assessment will indicate that a revision will have significant benefits. Multiple options are often available for achieving a policy goal with less harm to competiton.

Determining a preferred option can be a difficult task that requires careful analysis, creativity, and sector-specific knowledge. The toolkit's competition assessment review involves the following:

(1) Development of feasible alternative policies that achieve the government objective with less harm to competition
(2) Comparison of alternatives against each other
(3) Identification of the best option.

It is important that competition assessment should be conducted at the early stage of regulation making. This makes it easier to revise and improve the regulation. Early discussion with the competitive authority is also recommended. We introduce examples of early consideration in the CMA in the UK in Sect. 9.3, the US in Sect. 9.4, and Japan in Sect. 9.5.

9.3 Competition Assessment in the UK government

IA is mandatory in the UK, but competition assessment is not. In the UK, policy makers' obligation is to follow the "Green Book" (Treasury's guidance on IA and policymaking). The previous "Green Book" had hardly anything about competition assessment. This is because it was designed to look very closely at the intervention and its costs and benefits in its own merit. There has never been a formal requirement to conduct a competition assessment, either as part of the Green Book or as part of better regulation process.

The UK's CMA has an important role in investigating the impact of regulation on competition. Since the UK government has enough economists in each department and they understand the importance of competition, the CMA focuses on finding out problems at the early stage of regulation making and encourages regulatory authorities to be fixed. To do this, the CMA has been trying to persuade other ministries to reduce the impact of regulations on competition and increase the number of their colleagues. If any further issues are found at the early stage of regulation-making, they can be proactively addressed by consulting the competition authority and easily fixed.

Two examples from the 2010s are shown:

Example 9.1 Department for Education in relation to vocational qualifications

For qualification, a single standard is desirable but it need to be considered because single standard might restrict the competition. In response to the CMA intervention, the Department for Education paused and conducted something like a Competition Assessment on the legislation.

Example 9.2 Certification schemes for distributed electric generation (Microgeneration Certification Scheme)

Currently a single certification scheme is not competitive. And CMA encouraged them to consider competitions. They carried out some work, showed it to the CMA, and the CMA commented.

In 2015, the government gave the CMA a new power. It now has the exclusive power to make public recommendations to the ministers on proposals for legislation. Therefore, when ministers bring forward legislation, the CMA is open to write to the concerned minister (have to be done publicly) to let the minister know of it's comment. The CMA was given the power to encourage government officials to seek its advice, generally in private, at an early stage and take it seriously before receiving a letter from the CMA.

The following are two examples where the CMA's comment played an important role.

Example 9.3 Privatization of the Land Registry (CMA (2016))

It is not a legislative example but a matter of competition. The UK government proposed to privatize the Land Registry (i.e., the body that keeps the commercial register of land ownership).

The proposal was to sell a vertically-integrated business entity to supply both exclusively owned data (monopoly data) and commercial products (which use the exclusively owned data as an input). The CMA is not against privatization but privatizing the vertically-integrated body, because there is a significant risk that the business entity engaged in the supply of both monopoly data and commercial products (which use the monopoly data as an input) would not maintain or improve access to the monopoly data to other firms. Further, despite price-regulation on its monopoly activities, the company may degrade the terms of access to its monopoly data to weaken competition to its own commercial products. Therefore CMA expressed its concern to the ministers and got the right outcome as they dropped the privatization.

Example 9.4 Regulation of taxis and private hire vehicles (CMA (2017))

The CMA commented to several local authorities—because the regulation is a local responsibility in the UK—about restrictions on licenses they were seeking to impose which would place restrictions on the ability to enter. A most obvious example relates to a widespread concern about child protection in the taxi. One of the solutions proposed in this regard was to enforce authorities to ensure that drivers work only for one operator. However, the CMA knows from previous works that the principal way for new entrant operators to the market is by attracting drivers to work for them and the operators they are currently working for; that is, drivers work for more than one operator. The problem with banning them from working for more than one operator is that it makes entry difficult, if not impossible. In addition, if a driver is allowed to work for only one operator, the driver would want to work for the biggest operator, which would likely encourage an even greater concentration in that market, which profoundly restricts the competition. Most of the regulatory local authorities simply did not have a grasp of this competition aspect. As a result of the CMA's comments, most of them dropped the proposal.

Thus, even where a formal competition assessment was not carried out by the government department, it is possible for the CMA to step in and comment as a matter of advocacy. It has had some success, even in the context of local regulations.

To conduct a competition assessment at the early stage, proportionality is also important. It is clearly excessive to do a detailed, quantified competition impact assessment on every small proposal. We turn to the US Competition Analysis in the next section.

9.4 The US Competition Analysis (Competition Assessment)

When regulation suppresses competition, it itself distorts market efficiency and leads to increased social costs. In this sense, the suppression of competition by regulation is an important factor in the rise of social costs and constitutes a significant part of the assessment of costs and benefits. Therefore, competition assessment is not entirely independent of the other parts of impact assessment of regulation, but is positioned as part of the analysis of efficiency.

As derived in Chap. 7, if the demand curve is assumed to be linear and the supply curve is assumed to be horizontal and coincides with the long-term average cost curve, which is the long-term equilibrium state, the total surplus coincides with the consumer surplus, which can be estimated by calculating the area of the triangle consisting of the demand curve, supply curve, and vertical axis. The total surplus is equal to the consumer surplus. If competition is impeded for some reason, the analysis will reflect the competitive situation in the form of an upward shift in the supply curve or an increase in prices compared to competitive markets.

However, it is true that the surplus analysis itself is large and burdensome for conducting IA. It should also be pointed out that surplus analysis has its limitations as it is based on very strong assumptions. It is also true that even in the US, many competition analyses have not been explicitly conducted. For instance, E.O. 12,866 explicitly requires cost/benefit assessment, but not competition assessment. This is mainly because there are a wide range of issues and analysis methods in assessing the impact on competition, and it is difficult to create a standardized manual like the one for cost-benefit analysis, Thus, the guidelines may not function.

For this reason, presidential departments are focusing on reducing the impact on competition by designing appropriate regulations at the early regulation-making stage. The impact of regulations on the competitive situation varies greatly depending on the design of the regulation. Therefore, in the US presidential departments, whose jurisdiction is mainly social regulation, the impact of regulations on competition is considered in selecting alternatives that minimize this impact on competition.

A-4 also emphasizes the adoption of more pro-competitive regulatory proposals and other measures in Section C. Consideration of Alternative Approaches, and explains them in detail with specific examples.

Rather than presenting the procedures for competition analysis in this way, it enumerates several appropriate alternative approaches that minimize the impact on competition and encourages the selection of appropriate alternatives at the early stage of regulation making. This approach minimizes the impact on competition without the need for additional assessment.

The idea of promoting competition is deeply ingrained in the US, and the history of deregulation is comparable to the history of IAs. Therefore, even if explicit competition analysis does not always accompany IAs, the efforts described above are usually undertaken, and the ideas of competition analysis are expected to be reflected in the actual preparation of regulations.

It goes without saying that one of the main reasons few competition analyses are conducted in the presidential departments, which actively conduct RIAs even for non-critical regulations, is that they have a small impact on competition—so small that they can be ignored. In addition, the regulatory flexibility analysis, which analyzes whether there is an undue burden on small and medium-sized enterprises (SMEs), supplements the competition analysis in that it analyzes the burden on SMEs, which always face entry and exit.

Therefore, as described in Sect. 9.1 in the US presidential departments and agencies, competition analysis is basically considered at the early stage as an alternative selection to choose less impact on competition, and then supplemented by public comments if there are any additions. In some cases, the analysis of the impact on SMEs based on the regulatory flexibility analysis complements the competition analysis. The next chapter describes the US competition assessment in more detail.

9.5 Procedures for Competition Assessment in Japan

The Japan Fair Trade Commission (JFTC), in the process of IA, supported by the Administrative Evaluation Bureau of the Ministry of Internal Affairs and Communications (MIC) is currently reviewing competition assessment by each ministry through the following checklist method.

(1) In conducting IA of regulations, each ministry within the government will fill in a checklist on the impact of regulations on the competitive situation, which was prepared with reference to the checklists in Europe and OECD. For this purpose, the Administrative Evaluation Bureau of MIC will distribute a flowchart of the process and examples of how to fill in the checklist in the process of IA, and the JFTC will review the checklist and provide necessary support, including consultation on filling in the checklist.
(2) The completed checklists will be submitted to the Administrative Evaluation Bureau of Ministry of Internal Affairs and Communications (MIC) and the JFTC at the same time as the submission of the Impact Assessment to MIC.
(3) As a voluntary initiative of each government ministry, when it is judged that there is an impact on the competition situation through the completion of the checklist, the results of understanding the impact will be reflected in the IA report.

A major problem associated with IA in Japan is that IA and competition assessment begins at an almost final stage and rarely improve the regulation. The other is poor quantification of the analysis. However, it is a higher priority to conduct competition assessment from the earliest possible stage to avoid pro-competitive regulation. At the early stages of drafting a regulation, it is difficult to quantify the impact because the regulation has not been specified, and because there is not enough data. It would be difficult to finalize a competition assessment, an IA, checklist at the beginning.

Therefore, it would be possible to improve the regulations through a preliminary analysis written down in the preliminary competition assessment and IA. A clear description of the procedure is beneficial for objectification and transparency in regulation making.

The JFTC adapts the following three cases as good practices, especially as those that adequately assess the impact on competition. In that respect, although not strictly quantified, following three good practices seem to begin with a earlier stage of regulatory proposal that has been thoroughly examined to improve the regulations. All examples below are designed to strengthen the market infrastructure and promote healthy competition.

The criteria for selecting practices are as follows: (1) those that have quantitatively evaluated the impact on competition or have conducted an ex-post evaluation using quantitative indicators; (2) those for which the impact of the regulation has been properly recognized; and (3) those for which a comparison with alternatives has been made.

Example 9.5 (Japan good practice 1) Checklist for the Ministry of Agriculture, Forestry and Fisheries' (MAFF) "Proposed Law to Partially Amend the Seeds and Seedlings Law", JFTC (2022)

Name of regulation: Mandatory breeds-registration labeling

Summary of regulation: Measures shall be taken to create a trading environment in which users of propagating material of a registered breeds can easily and reliably identify whether or not the propagating material they are using is registered. Specifically, it shall be compulsory for a person who transfers, or exhibits or advertises for the purpose of transferring, in the course of business, propagating material of a registered breeds to affix the breeds-registration mark on the propagating material of the registered breeds or on the package of the propagating material of the registered breeds or on its advertisement.

Reasons for selection as a good practice: Since this proposal would require a person who transfers seeds of a registered breeds in the course of business, etc., to display the mark of the registered breeds, it is considered to impose restrictions on the activities of business operators who handle registered breeds. Although the MAFF has not quantitatively evaluated the impact of such restrictions on competition, it has analyzed that the regulation does not substantially affect the competitive situation of business operators because it uniformly requires all business operators to display the registered breeds, and is not likely to have a significant impact on the competitive situation of business operators because it does not require business operators to properly identify whether a breeds is registered or not. The case does not have a negative impact on competition, based on the analysis that the regulation will broaden the range of consumers' choice of breeds by allowing them to select breeds. Thus, the case falls under criterion (2).

As an alternative, it is suggested to require the communication of the fact that the breeds is registered and the preparation and storage of transaction records, so that accurate information is disseminated to the users. In its preliminary evaluation of the proposed regulation, the MAFF assessed that the cost burden on businesses and the government would be greater than that of the proposed regulation, and concluded that the proposed regulation would not have a negative impact on competition based on the same reasons as the proposed regulation. Thus, the case falls under criterion (3).

Example 9.6 (Good Practice 2) Checklist for the MAFF's "Proposed Law Concerning Protection of the Names of Specified Agricultural, Forestry and Fishery Products, etc." JFTC (2022)

Name of regulation: Regulations on labeling that may mislead people to believe that the product is a Geographical Indication (GI)* product (*GI refers to the labeling of the name of an agricultural, forestry, marine, or fishery product or food product, by which the origin of the product can be identified and the quality or other established characteristics of the product can be identified as being associated with the origin of the product).

Outline of regulation: In accordance with Article 14.25 of the European Union (EU) and Japan's Economic Partnership Agreement (EPA), which stipulates that the regulation shall apply to means of misleading consumers as to the true place of origin and prohibiting manipulation as if they were GI products, it is prohibited to label products in Japan in a manner that may mislead consumers into believing that they are GI products, and it is prohibited to use such labeling in advertisements and other media. Cases in which GI is used in the service sector shall also be subject to regulation.

Reasons for selection: Since this regulates product labeling, it is considered to impose restrictions on the method of advertisement or promotion by businesses that handle the product in question.

Although the MAFF has not quantitatively evaluated the impact of such restrictions on competition, it is considered that preventing misleading labeling or the improper use of GI products will protect the interests of consumers and producers of genuine GI products, and ultimately motivate the producers of GI products to increase production. Therefore, it can be said that the impact of the regulation has been properly recognized and described, and the case falls under criterion (2). In addition, since this regulation falls under the category of "a regulation associated with the ratification of an international treaty that leaves no room for discretion," an ex-ante evaluation of the simplified regulation has been conducted. Therefore, it is possible to omit the consideration of alternatives, and comparisons with alternatives are omitted in the competition assessment.

Example 9.7 (Good Practice 3) Ministry of Health, Labor and Welfare, Ministry of

Economy, Trade and Industry, and Ministry of the Environment "Draft Cabinet Order for Partial Revision of the Enforcement Order for the Law Concerning the Evaluation of Chemical Substances and Regulation of Their Manufacture, etc." JFTC (2022).

Name of regulation: Designation of chemical substances whose manufacture, import, or use is restricted; products whose import is prohibited; and products for which obligations of conformity to standards and labeling are imposed.

Regulation summary: 2,2,2 trichloro-1-(2-chlorophenyl)1-(4-chlorophenyl) ethanol and perfluorooctanoic acid or its salt are designated as Class I Specified Chemical Substances. In addition, 13 products containing perfluorooctanoic acid or its salt have been added to the list of import-prohibited products; and fire extinguishers, fire extinguishing agents for fire extinguishers, and fire foam extinguishing agents that contain perfluorooctanoic acid or its salt already exist as products in stock in other forms. The obligation to conform to the standard and labeling is imposed on the agents.

Reason for selection: Since this case newly designates certain substances as Class I Specified Chemical Substances that require a license from the Minister of Economy, Trade and Industry when manufactured or imported, it is considered to impose restrictions on the activities of business operators who handle the substances. Although the Ministry of Health, Labour and Welfare, the Ministry of Economy, Trade and Industry, and the Ministry of the Environment have not quantitatively evaluated the impact of such restrictions on competition, the 2,2,2-trichloro-1-(2-chlorophenyl)1-(4-chlorophenyl) ethanol has been used in Japan in the past. In addition, there are no operators who plan to manufacture or import perfluorooctanoic acid or its salt after FY2020, and therefore, the activities of operators will not be substantially restricted. Therefore, it can be said that the impact of the regulation is correctly recognized and described in this case, and thus, the case falls under criterion (3). In addition, since this regulation falls under the category of "a regulation associated with the ratification of an international treaty that leaves no room for discretion," an ex-ante evaluation of the simplified regulation has been conducted. Therefore, it is possible to omit the consideration of alternatives, and comparison with alternatives is also omitted in the competition assessment.

9.6 Importance of Competition Assessment in Developing Countries

In developed countries, especially in Japan, there are several markets with a sufficient number of firms, and the impact of regulations on competition is generally insignificant. However, in oligopolistic markets where there is not enough competition to begin with, the impact of regulations is quite important and special consideration is required.

In the case of a duopoly, for example, if a single firm were to leave the market due to a regulation, the situation would be so serious that competition itself would not exist. Such a case may occur in developing countries where the only companies supplying the market are public companies and foreign companies due to foreign direct investment restrictions. In such a case, foreign-investment restrictions are extremely important for competition.

In developing countries, which have smaller markets with fewer firms than the developed economies, economic regulations for rent-seeking are more likely to exist. Furthermore, the possibility of collusion among firms is more serious in oligopolistic markets. Thus, when the market size and the number of firms within the market is small, competition analysis becomes more important.

Competition policy and competition analysis in oligopolistic markets, such as the telecommunications market, is also important in developed countries. In the case of advanced technologies with a small number of suppliers, it is also effective to postpone the introduction and implementation of regulations and wait for multiple companies to enter the market before introducing regulations. For example, in the case of the regulation of albuterol MDI in the US, the implementation of the regulation was delayed until the patent expired, thereby reducing the inefficiency caused by the price increase due to the monopoly power of the regulation.

The oligopoly situation described above is also common in Pakistan. In particular, markets with only state-owned companies and foreign companies or, as in the case of the automobile industry, competition between Japanese companies and small and medium-sized second-hand importers are common. In such cases, not only the peculiarities of the market but also various measures to promote competition in an oligopolistic market have to be considered. In particular, the complementarity of the competition policy with organizational reform of state-owned enterprises, deregulation of foreign investment restrictions, and policies for the protection of childish industries must be considered.

9.7 Key Points Regarding Regulatory Reform and the Introduction of IA in Pakistan

Competition assessment is considered more important in Pakistan than Japan and, hence, would play a more significant role in Pakistan (Nakaizumi (2015)).

Regulatory analysis and reform in developing countries such as Pakistan requires not only the implantation of a system of IA or competition assessment, but also a comprehensive approach to improve market infrastructure and organizational reform of regulators and public enterprises. In addition, in Pakistan, both each ministry and independent regulatory authority has regulatory jurisdiction. In general, even if each ministry is in charge of drafting laws, the reality is that each regulatory body is responsible for specific regulations. Therefore, the question of how to improve the capacity of these regulatory bodies and the regulations themselves is not a challenge unique to Pakistan. In particular, the following points are essential:

a. Organizational reforms such as independence and transparency of regulators, in particular, the availability of budget and staff to conduct analysis.

b. Reform of public utilities to improve market health, strengthen the functioning of competition authorities, and promote competitive analysis.
c. Research and personnel exchanges with universities to ensure the quality of analysis.
d. Review of RIA to ensure its quality.

Organizational reform and the introduction of analytical methods are two sides of the same coin, and both are essential. It is also pointed out that the parallel introduction of policy evaluation with various regulatory reforms may be more complementary than the introduction of policy evaluation alone. Furthermore, the penetration of regulatory reform and evaluation is not enough to realize a single project; spreading it throughout the government agencies is also necessary.

9.8 Concluding Remarks

Assessing the impact on competition by regulation consists in the assessment of benefits and costs. If competition is restricted by regulation, price might increase and quality or quantity decreases, which cause the reduction of benefit or consumer surplus. Thus, analysis of economic surplus—also known as total welfare or Marshallian surplus within partial equilibrium analysis—can include competition effects. The US Environmental Protection Agency (EPA) conducts RIA in which they estimate total surplus considering the impact of competition see Nakaizumi (2010, 2014) and Institute of Administrative Management Japan (2008).

In the US government, however, competition analysis is not mandatory within RIA and most other agencies in the US do not conduct quantitative competition assessment. One reason is the difficulty of conducting a cost-benefit analysis of the impact on competition. It is even difficult to generalize and write guidance of competition analysis because tools and models of competition is case-based. Thus, the US government tries to consider the impact on competition in the early stage by considering the best alternatives among regulation that minimize the impact on competition (see Nakaizumi (2010, 2011, 2012, 2013)).

The case of competition assessment in the UK is also similar as described in Nakaizumi (2018). The CMA in charge of competition assessment try to find out problems at the early stage of regulation-making and encourage regulatory authorities to be fixed. In developing countries of smaller markets with fewer firms than the developed economies, competition assessment becomes more important.

References

CMA (UK Competition Market Authority) (2016) CMA response to BIS consultation on the future of the land registry, https://www.gov.uk/government/publications/cma-response-to-bis-consultation-on-the-future-of-the-land-registry

CMA (UK Competition Market Authority) (2017) Private hire and hackney carriage licensing: open letter to local authorities. https://www.gov.uk/government/publications/private-hire-and-hackney-carriage-licensing-open-letter-to-local-authorities
Institute of Administrative Management Japan (2008) Kisei no jizen hyōka handobukku yoriyoi kisei ni mukete chosha-mei. Institute of Administrative Management, 333 page
Japan Fair Trade Commission, Competition Assessment Page. https://www.jftc.go.jp/dk/kyousouhyouka/170731.html
Japan Fair Trade Commission (2022) Good practice of competition assessment. Kyōsō hyōka chekku risuto no guddopurakutisu. https://www.jftc.go.jp/dk/kyousouhyouka/220331_goodpractice/220331_goodpractice.pdf
Nakaizumi T (2010) 'Beikoku de no kyōsō bunseki jitchi chōsa hōkoku-sho' kōsei torihiki iinkai itaku chōsa, JFTC
Nakaizumi T (2011) Beikoku ni okeru kisei ga kyōsō ni ataeru eikyō no haaku bunseki shuhō ni tsuite' kōsei torihiki, No. 733, 2011–11, Kosei Torihiki.
Nakaizumi T (2012) 'Kisei sakusei ni okeru kisei eikyō bunseki (ria) no jūyō-sei: Beikoku no jirei o sankō to shite' hyōka ni tsuite no kōen gaiyō. Hyoka Q Inst Admin Manag (23):2012–2010
Nakaizumi T (2013) Progress of competition analysis in the US government, mainly focusing on environmental regulation, (in Japanese). Res Inst Econ Manag (Kanto-Gakuin University) 35:163–173
Nakaizumi T (2014) Kisei no jizen hyōka no kōjō no tame no kyōsō hyōka no hōkō-sei. Hyoka Q Inst Admin Manag (29):23–31
Nakaizumi T (2015), "Pakisutan kaikyō kyōwakoku keizai kaikaku shien adobaizā senmonka gyōmu kanryō hōkoku-sho", Japan International Cooperation Agency
Nakaizumi T (2018) Toward a better competition assessment: practice of UK government. Keizaikei, vol 275. Research Institute of Economics and Management, Kanto-Gakuin University, pp 99–109
OECD Competition assessment documents and links. http://www.oecd.org/daf/competition/reducingregulatoryrestrictionsoncompetition/competitionassessmentdocumentsandlinks.htm
OECD Recommendation on Competition Assessment. https://www.oecd.org/daf/competition/oecdrecommendationoncompetitionassessment.htm
UK Competition and Markets Authority (2015) Guidance Competition impact assessment: guidelines for policymakers Guidelines to help government policymakers assess the impact their proposals will have on competition. https://www.gov.uk/government/publications/competition-impact-assessment-guidelines-for-policymakers

Chapter 10
Competition Assessment in the US

Abstract We introduce US competition analysis. Although the EPA conducts substantial economic competition analysis, government departments focus on reducing the impact on competition through appropriate regulatory design at the earlier regulation-making stage because the impact of various regulations on the competitive landscape varies greatly depending on institutional design. We show the importance of this using several examples of competition analysis.

10.1 Introduction

As referred in Chap. 9, in the US presidential administration, analysis of impact on competition called competition analysis instead of competition assessment in the US is conducted within RIA. US Guideline A-4 by OMB (2003) clearly shows that economic regulation is undesirable:

"Government actions can be unintentionally harmful, and even useful regulations can impede market efficiency." For this reason, there is a presumption against certain types of regulatory action. Under Market Power of B. The Need for Federal Regulatory Action in A-4, it is stated that "generally, regulations that increase market power for selected entities should be avoided."

It can be said that A-4 indicates that economic regulations and regulations that inhibit competition should not be implemented. At the same time, the list of alternative regulatory measures to be considered, which is proposed in the discussion of alternatives, has as one of its main objectives the promotion of competition as described in Chap. 9.

In addition, especially when the fixed costs of compliance are large, it is worthwhile to consider the possibility that the costs of complying with regulations may be heavier for small firms, for example, by imposing different levy requirements for different firm sizes, which not only facilitates potential entry but also increases the room for future competition. In this sense, regulations that have a significant impact on a large number of SMEs should be assessed under a regulatory flexibility analysis. This analysis shares a similar aspect to competition assessment because both consider to decrease the burden to entry or future entry.

T. Nakaizumi, *Impact Assessment for Developing Countries*, Contributions to Economics,
https://doi.org/10.1007/978-981-19-5494-8_10

To complete the perfect cost-benefit analysis, it is necessary to derive consumer surplus and producer surplus of the affected market, taking into account the competitive situation. Therefore, competition analysis is not totally independent from the rest of the IA, but is positioned as a part of efficiency analysis (cost and benefit analysis). A cost-benefit analysis should include the impact on competition, in which the surplus gained in the market based on the circumstance of competition would be calculated and added to the net benefits.

Thus, the ultimate goal of competition analysis is to evaluate the competitive conditions of a market, estimate supply and demand curves sufficient for estimating surplus, and estimate the price level in the relevant market based on the number of firms or market competitiveness. This will allow for a more rigorous analysis of the surplus and improve the quality of IA. As a result, cost-benefit analysis, including the assessment of impact on competition, would be ultimate. A case where an analysis similar to this has actually been conducted is the RIA of EPA, such as new environmental regulations imposed on the cement industry.

In the interviews at the Federal Motor Carrier Safety Administration (FMCSA) in the Department of Transportation (DOT) on November 2009, even when competition analysis is not explicitly conducted, the respondents answered that variables that affect competition, such as the number of firms and market structure, are also considered in cost-benefit analysis. In other words, many competition-related factors, such as the number of drivers and transaction costs, are basically captured and reflected in the cost-benefit analysis of the FMCSA.

For example, the number of carriers must be considered, and the possibility of companies entering or exiting due to regulations is also analyzed. Competition analysis is not done specifically but is naturally taken into account and incorporated in the cost-benefit analysis. Some regulations may be modified according to the size of firms in an industry. For example, registration fees are changed according to company size. All regulations consider the size of the company, as described in the A-4 guidelines.

However, A-4 does not formalize competition analysis and does not require it with the same weighting as cost-benefit analysis. The main reason for this is that most of the regulations of the presidential administration are related to health, safety, and the environment; and few regulate market structure, which often has an indirect or rare impact on competition. Another factor is that many health and safety regulations do not meet the $100 million threshold and, therefore, have little impact on industry structure and the competitive situation of interested parties.

There is no standardized process for competition analysis in the US government, although it involves looking at changes in the market structure due to regulation and the resultant attribution of costs and benefits. The US government agencies, especially presidential departments, analyze several appropriate alternatives and choose adequate approaches that minimize the impact on competition at the early stage of regulation-making, as A-4 emphasizes the adoption of more pro-competitive regulatory proposals and other measures in Section C. Consideration of Alternative Approaches.

Another reason that the US has not adopted a standardized method for competition analysis is that the impact on competition is too diverse to be analyzed with a standardized method. Analysis of the impact on competition is likely to be on a case-by-case basis and may not work even if guidelines are developed. For this reason, there is no formal guideline that considers all the effects on competition except the basic principle to analyze the impact on competition on a case-by-case basis.

This is because the US agencies share the basic premise of promoting competition. I had a interview with several US government Officers who engage in regulation maing and conducting IA and summed up to Nakaizumi (2010, 2011, 2012, 2013, 2014). Following compilations is mostly the comments that I got in a interview with Dr. Neil Eisner and Bob Klothe at the Secretary Office of DOT in November 2009. Although they are lawyer, their understanding itself express the basic premise of promoting competition very well. Regulators mostly look at the effects of regulations on consumers and suppliers. In DOT, they look at cargo and shippers, but their analysis is limited. Competition also brings about technological progress and novelty. The basics are left to the market. The government only intervenes in case of a market failure. Economic regulations have been relaxed since the 1970s, and it is very difficult to enforce a new one. Even if a particular technology was needed for a truck, it was clear that the government would not regulate it in such a way as to fix the price, which was a prerequisite for leaving it to the market.

The regulators would rather focus on information disclosure and market transparency and ensuring that produced goods and services are better supplied than on making such regulations. To bring benefits to consumers, suppliers must ensure that information about the transaction, such as prices, is transparent and widely available.

Regarding safety regulations, safety standards should be set, but the market should be allowed to decide who participates in the market. A market economy lends itself to matching safety standards in such a way. There is no requirement for a specific technology. If a new technology is developed, ownership issues can arise. In that case, authorities could potentially restrict the use of a particular technology. Even then, they should avoid regulations that promote the spread of a particular brand's or company's product, and focus only on the technology and its performance. This will promote market progress and eliminate impediments to competition. The direct goal is to improve safety.

Even if social regulation is a central issue for most of the US presidential departments, economic efficiency should be considered at a minimum necessary amount. For example, the minimum insurance level set by Congress and to be complied with by the authorities, or the minimum level of pollution set by the EPA and the technology to guarantee it, should ideally be set by the government and met by the market.

In the DOT, competition analysis is part of the framework for enacting regulations. It gives top priority to designing regulations that avoid unnecessary burdens on competition. For example, when the Civil Aeronautics Administration installs a new safety device on an airplane, it decides at the time of enactment whether to limit the device to a specific company, require a specific specification, or make it a performance rule. In the past, the Federal Aviation Adminstration (FAA) required a specific brand of altimeter. In reality, a simple altimeter would have been fine, and it was a very problematic decision because design standard restrict suppliers. Today, the FAA uses performance standard rather than design standard. This is also dictated by A-4, which sets minimum standards with the expectation that there will be room for future improvements and the effect of more competition.

In addition, many highway-traffic rules and safety regulations are based on test results. They use crash tests with appropriate dummies, but in any case, it is simply stated that they must pass the crash test. All that is required is to pass a certain level. Note that any impact on competition can be a problem as pointed out by stakeholders during public comments. Stakeholders are the biggest watchdogs, and the departments will respond to their comments. The departments will then try to exclude any impact on competition before the regulations come into effect.

In sum, analysis of the impact on competition in each department is mainly based on considering a proposed regulation and reducing the impact on competition as much as possible at the early stage. Subsequently, additional analysis of the impact on competition is conducted as a supplement if pointed out in public comments or the Regulatory Flexibility Analysis. Therefore, in the US, many competition analyses do not get published in the Official Gazette. However, it must be kept in mind that this does not indicate a lack of competition analysis, but a phenomenon that occurs when the design is rooted in selecting best alternatives at the early stage as pointed out in A-4. There are many useful cases of competition analysis in each department, because they do not employ a stylized analysis. This chapter then provides various examples of competition analysis conducted in the US. Altough these examples are based on the interviews in 2000s, they still worth reference. But current system might be followed completely. if you need more up-dated one, please refer Viscusi et al. (2018).

The next section discusses the OMB's review on competition analysis and the cooperation between the Office of Information and Regulatory Affairs (OIRA) and the competition authorities. Then we describe the competition analysis by the US Department and Agencies of Presidential Office in Sect. 10.3. Section 10.4 disucsses how to use several analytical methods in the US government agencies. Subsequently, we introduce several analyses of an Independent Regulatory Commission in Sect. 10.5. In section 10.6 we explain the involvement of Competition Authorities and 10.7 provides the concluding remarks.

10.2 The OMB's Review of Competition Analysis

The OMB in the US Presidential Office, while reviewing RIA within the presidential departments, only requires competition analysis as a duty when there is a truly significant competition problem. Restricting competition would be an important issue, if the analysis shows that the regulation will result in a dead weight loss of welfare with less than two firms remaining in the market. However, in the case of safety and health regulations, the impact on competition is small compared to the effects of externality. Therefore, as long as the regulation do not impede competition, dead weight loss due to impeded competition will not be a serious problem, and such a significant concern will not arise.

In addition, the OMB will focus on examining regulations if they are designed to directly regulate the market, for example, mortgage disclosures for loans. In this case, they require a basic competition analysis to determine whether or not there is an impact on market structure and whether there is an increase in market power.

Social regulations can also create barriers to entry, especially through increased fixed costs. In such cases, a separate category of analysis is required under the Regulatory Flexibility Act, namely, a regulatory flexibility analysis, to analyze the impact on small businesses. This is not a competition analysis, but it is expected to take into account the issue of such barriers to entry. From the interview with Dr. Mancini, Dominic at OMB in November 2009, A parliamentary report on cost-benefit analysis in 2008 analyzes the impact of regulations on trade in a similar way to competition analysis.

Further, they turn to the cooperation between the OMB/OIRA and the competition authorities. The OMB collaborates with the Department of Justice (DOJ) in cases where market power is concerned, such as antitrust and monopoly. The DOJ's Antitrust Division is larger than the OIRA, especially in terms of the number of economists. Cooperation is done on a case-by-case basis, and if a regulation affects competition, the proposed regulation is also sent to the DOJ.

In the US, knowledge, background, and thinking in economics are widespread and work on a common framework. Resultantly, there is a lot of informal cooperation and coordination, which is reflected in the analysis even if it is not appeared explicitly.

Though there is no formal collaboration regarding the review of RIA (economic analysis) between OMB and competition authorities, competition authorities are also interested in economic analysis and discuss it a lot. The Antitrust Division of the DOJ evaluates regulations and cooperates only informally with the OMB. The Antitrust Division has a number of economists who monitor the regulations. They also like to be informally involved in the regulation-making and are willing to exchange views with the OMB. They do not like to act overtly as the DOJ. However, the DOJ's economics experts are excellent, and the OMB appreciates the fact that such opinions are often very useful.

10.3 Competition Analysis Within RIA in Some Departments of the US Presidential Office

As mentioned earlier, the US presidential administration is in charge of "so-called" social regulations, which mainly deal with externalities such as health, safety, and the environment. As for how those agencies take competition into account in setting regulations, the principle is to design regulations in such a way that they are compatible with the desirability of promoting competition. This is indicated in C. Consideration of Alternative Approaches in A-4, which emphasizes the adoption of more pro-competitive regulatory proposals and other measures, and gives examples of such measures. This is also evident in the aforementioned example of whether to adopt performance-standard regulations or design-standard regulations. The latter would be more restrictive to competition. Therefore, at the early stage of regulation-making, one must consider which one will promote competition. Economists are also involved in the regulation making from the beginning, analyzing which alternative is desirable and where the problems lie at the drafting stage, and providing feedback to the regulation-making.

While there is no stylized description of competition analysis in A-4, as noted above, there are many examples to analyze the impact of regulation on competition by each department. The most complicated one is made by the EPA, and there are some interesting cases. In the following subsections, Sect. 10.3.1 presents an example of the EPA modeling an oligopolistic market in a market analysis embedded in a cost-benefit analysis. Sect. 10.3.2 describes the basic concept to conduct competition analysis in the DOT and presents an example of competition assessment in the FMCSA's regulation of Brokers of Household Goods Transportation of 2010 and the FAA's regulation of Limiting Chicago International Airline Access to 88 Aircraft per Hour (2005a, b). In Sect. 10.3.3, we will present an economic analysis of the regulation of emissions of ozone-depleting substances related to the Montreal Protocol and, as an example, the regulation of CFCs in metered dose inhalers (MDIs) using albuterol.

10.3.1 Analysis of Distributional Effects in the EPA

The ultimate goal of competition assessment is to evaluate the competitive conditions in a market and to estimate the supply and demand curves sufficient for estimating the surplus and the price level in the relevant market based on the number of firms. This will allow for a more rigorous analysis of the surplus and improve the quality of the RIA. As a result, cost-benefit analysis, including the impact on competition, would be ideal. Some of the RIAs by the EPA belong to such a complicated analysis. We introduce below an environmental regulation imposed by the EPA on the cement industry, from Environmental Protection Agency (2009a, 2009b).

In the first half of 2009, the EPA submitted its final proposed regulations (National Emission Standards for Hazardous Air Pollutants From the Portland Cement). In its impact analysis, the EPA is looking at how the regulation will change the structure of the industry, how market share will change, and whether there will be entry or exit due to the additional costs of the regulation. The OMB seems to call this "distributional effects analysis." It refers to partial equilibrium analysis, which is the analysis of the distribution of tax and regulatory cost burdens between consumers and producers based on market prices.

The US cement industry is regionally fragmented and limited in the number of producing companies due to transportation costs and large fixed costs. As a result, the market is not perfectly competitive, but rather an oligopoly for each region. This RIA analyzes the impact of such regulations, the fact that regulations on pollution control lead to increased costs and higher prices using an oligopoly model, and how the increased costs due to regulations affect prices and whether they can also affect competition.

It is theoretically shown that in a competitive market, the supply curve is determined in the long run, including entry and exit, and the price matches the average cost. In this case, the change in price is consistent with the average cost, and the market can be easily analyzed by making certain assumptions about the demand function.

To analyze how the increase in costs due to regulations in the short term will be passed on to prices, it is necessary to derive a right downslope supply curve. Further, we must assume diminishing returns in terms of the firm's production function in the short run and estimate a cost function with increasing costs. Therefore, it is at least necessary to estimate a Cobb-Douglas type production function and a cost function and supply curve is derived from it. Such estimation is not easy in a real market where multiple factors of production are actually required. Therefore, it is a difficult task to directly analyze the impact of cost increase on prices and market structure in a competitive market.

In the case of an oligopoly model, since marginal revenue is diminishing, equilibrium prices can be derived even using a linear cost function with constant marginal cost. Therefore, the oligopoly model has the advantage that it is easier to perform comparative statics, and the change in price due to the change in cost can be analyzed using a linear cost function or demand function. A simple explanation of the above using the model is as follows.

Let the price be P, the quantity of output be x, the quantity of derivative production inputs required to produce x be Li(x), and the price of each production element be wi; then, the total cost $C(x)$ = wi Li(x). From this, the firm maximizes the following problem. In this case, due to the competitive market assumption, the output of individual firms is assumed to have no effect on the price.

$$\Pi(x) = Px - C(x)$$

Maximizing this, from $\Pi'(x) = P - C'(x) = 0$

$$P = C'(x) \Leftrightarrow S = S(p)$$

is obtained. Therefore, if $C(x) = \mathrm{cx}$, $C'(x) = c$ and only a horizontal supply curve can be obtained with $P = c$. On the contrary, to obtain a right ascending supply curve, $C''(x) > 0$ is required, and the corresponding derived factor demand function and production function become complicated.

In contrast, in the case of the oligopoly model, the production function of the firm concerned affects the price, and by making certain assumptions on the demand function, we can obtain.

$$\Pi(x) = P(x + y)x - C(x)$$

$\Pi(x)$ is maximized with x. Here, y is the total production of other companies. Strictly speaking, production is determined based on the estimated production volume of other companies. It also has the effect of depending on the company's own production volume, and $y = y(x)$. In general economics, we would assume a Nash equilibrium here, but the EPA assumes that the response is inelastic ($y'(x) = 0$), which simplifies the analysis. Thus, we obtain the following conditions.

$$\Pi'(x) = P'(x + y)x + P(x + y) - C'(x) = 0$$

This is because the marginal revenue itself is a linear function of x. Therefore, even if the marginal cost is constant, the price is endogenously determined. Now, assuming a linear cost curve cx with a cost per unit of c and a linear demand curve D(x+y) = −d(x+y)+A, the above equation becomes.

$$c = -2\mathrm{d}x - \mathrm{d}y + D$$

From this, when the cost per unit increases due to the Δc ($c \to c + \Delta c$) regulation, the decrease in the output of individual firms due to the increase in cost, Δx ($x \to x - \Delta x$), can be obtained quantitatively as $\Delta x = \Delta c/2\mathrm{d}$. By summing up these decreases in supply in the market, it is possible to calculate the range of price increases.

Under the simplification described above, we use a linear cost function to analyze the price shift due to rising costs. In addition, we estimate the likelihood of the exit of SMEs with higher costs and a higher proportion of fixed costs, and the expected volume of imports. Based on this, an examination of the impact on SMEs is also conducted. The regulatory flexibility analysis under the Regulatory Flexibility Act also analyzes the impact on such marginal plants and estimates the plants that may exit due to rising costs. In addition, the IA also estimates the impact of regulation on domestic prices, and the amount of export growth that would result from higher domestic prices due to regulation.

In this analysis, we identify the market as a regional market, consider price shifting using an oligopoly model, and analyze the possibility of entry and exit. Moreover, the steps of identifying which areas have strong competition impediments and examining the extent to which regulation will increase deadweight loss are used even in the Federal Communications Commission's (FCC) review of satellite broadcasting mergers. This will be discussed in Sect. 10.5 as a reference example of competition analysis.

10.3.2 Some Practices in the DOT

As shown above, a large-scale market analysis requires a certain amount of cost. Furthermore, it is more desirable and efficient to design a system with appropriate alternatives to fully consider the impact on competition. For this reason, presidential administrations that deal with social regulations, such as the DOT, focus on adopting appropriate alternatives in regulatory design. As one example of this, the DOT introduced the deregulation of aircraft repair and the elimination of monopolies on web-based ticket purchasing sites.

Aircraft repair has been limited and monopolized by Airbus and Boeing. Airbus and Boeing have had a monopoly on aircraft repair because both companies have refused to make their repair manuals available to the public (this belongs to their intellectual property). The FAA enacted regulations to make the repair manuals public, allowing other companies to enter the repair business.

Further, there was market power on airline ticket purchasing websites, where the three companies' main web pages were unfairly manipulated to always rank high in search engines for airline ticket fares, thus maintaining market power. Thus, the DOT passed regulations to promote competition and prevent this from happening.

Although most of the regulations under the DOT's jurisdiction are related to safety, some regulations were taken over from the Interstate Commerce Commission (ICC) about 20 years ago that are more like economic regulations regarding the entry and exit of carriers. In what follows, Example 10.1 provides a competition analysis of the FMCSA's regulations on the transportation of household goods, such as sundries, and Examples 10.2 presents a competition analysis of Chicago International Airlines' regulations on limiting departure and arrival slots to reduce congestion.

Example 10.1 Competition Analysis of Regulations Related to the Transportation of Miscellaneous Goods and Other Household Goods (Brokers of Household Goods Transportation Regulatory Evaluation, FMCSA)

The FMCSA's regulation imposing obligations on brokers was prompted to be reconsidered from the perspective of promoting competition, and this regulation and its history are described below.

Since shippers do not often transport goods, they do not have enough information to choose a carrier. When brokers use the Internet to quote prices, they sometimes cheat shippers and carriers out of their money and get away with it. Alternatively, brokers may raise the price once they have secured the shipment and threaten to return the shipment if it is not paid. Therefore, a motion was filed to require more disclosure and to try to resolve the issue. This was in response to market failures related to the issue of information asymmetry.

Consumers are not informed and may suffer losses along with the carriers. This is because neither of them knows what the brokers are doing. Therefore, the authorities have decided to promote disclosure and protect the consumers. They enacted regulations that require brokers, like shipping companies, to be notified to conduct business, impose deposits, require them to actually see the goods when giving estimates, and require them to use registered and authorized carriers.

The proposed regulations would require brokers to disclose material information to individual shippers, use only properly licensed and insured carriers, impose penalties for providing quotes without a contract with the carrier or for not using the proper carrier, and raise the registration fee for brokers to $10,000 to conform to the status quo.

The economic analysis considers three options—(1) maintain the status quo, (2) require audits by the FMCSA, and (3) impose further obligations, including an increase in the minimum registration deposit—and quantitatively estimates their costs and qualitatively examines their effects on benefits and competition.

The second option is to require an audit of household goods (HHG) brokers on the above issues and require them to perform their duties properly. Since HHG brokers are already required to register and keep transaction records for three years, no new paperwork is needed except for the obligation to comply with audits. The FMCSA conducts audits of such records and charges fees for these audits as expenses. In addition, state authorities will work with the FMCSA to ensure that brokers are in compliance with regulations, and training costs have been included. As a result, an annual cost of $65,771 will be incurred throughout the US, according to the competition analysis.

The third option is to increase the minimum guarantee from $10,000 to $25,000 in line with rising prices, and to use only registered and authorized carriers, precisely identified as HHG brokers. It requires the signature of the parties and a notary public to maintain records of the contract and to negotiate agreements with the carrier, and requires the user to specify the conditions for cancellation. Regarding the above costs, we estimate all the costs incurred by this option in the entire US by, for example, estimating the cost for HHG brokers to find a registered and authorized carrier. The result is an average cost of $750,000 per year.

In terms of benefits, shippers would be better informed and would have more legitimate bargaining power in negotiating prices and other issues prior to transportation. The benefits of each option are as follows.

(Option 1) This is a baseline; there are no additional benefits as it maintains the status quo.
(Option 2) This will have the effect of curbing the illegal behavior of HHG brokers, and the benefit is that it is stronger than the previous regulation.
(Option 3) This will increase the likelihood that shippers will be able to avoid the illegal behavior of HHG brokers, which will strengthen the protection of the shippers' rights and allow them to negotiate on a fairer footing in pricing decisions.

The economic analysis estimates that the benefits will include a reduction in the amount of damage estimated from existing complaints, and this will lead to benefits (reduction in damage) of $6.25 million per year.

Next, the analysis also mentions the impact on competition. The proposed regulation consists of five elements.

(1) Requires HHG brokers to provide adequate information to shippers.
(2) Requires the use of properly registered HHG carriers.
(3) Imposes the same obligations as HHG carriers with respect to transportation quotes.
(4) Imposes additional penalties on those who quote without contracting with an HHG carrier or who perform services without registering with the FMCSA.
(5) Increases the minimum registration guarantee amount in response to inflation.

The disclosure requirements are designed to ensure that individual shippers are fully informed to facilitate transportation, facilitate minimum deposit and refund procedures in the event of cancellation, and ensure that appropriate HHG brokers and carriers are able to handle the business.

Therefore, the disclosure of information in the proposed regulation tends to be pro-competitive in the sense that consumers can choose HHG brokers who can offer higher quality services at lower prices. Ensuring that HHG brokers use licensed and appropriate carriers is also intended to ensure that carriers compete in an appropriate environment and customers enjoy better service. Interstate carriers are required to register with the FMCSA, make minimum contributions and insurance, and charge less than the legal limit. Unregistered carriers are likely to be uninsured and may be able to offer lower prices. Speculative nature encourages carriers to register, reduces the number of unregistered carriers who can operate at unreasonably low prices, and provides a more level playing field for registered carriers.

It also imposes the same legal obligation on carriers by requiring that all quotes be in writing and based on an actual valuation of the household goods to be transported. However, since HHG brokers commonly quote over the phone, this would promote competition by standardizing the rules of quotation to provide a more reliable quote and ensure that consumers are not ultimately surprised by the high price. However, the reality is that brokers generally do not have agents to make such actual quotations; therefore, FMCSA invited comments on the impact of these regulations. The increase in the minimum deposit is based on the inflation rate and does not have a suppressive effect on competition.

In assessing the impact on competition, the use of illegal carriers may result in lower prices, but this will not ensure safety and will not lead to fair competition. Only the problem of adverse selection arises. In addition to curbing illegitimate activities, we believe that requiring information disclosure through regulations will reduce the problem of such asymmetric information and promote competition.

It is also pointed out that these regulations should reduce the burden on good brokers as much as possible, and this point may be taken into account in the comments. Since it is very difficult to analyze these points quantitatively, the impact on competition will be examined by reflecting and considering public comments.

Example 10.2 Competition Analysis of the Regulation Limiting Chicago International Airline Access to 88 Aircraft per Hour

FAA (Federal Aviation Administration) analyzed the allocation of slots with respect to the regulation limiting flights to Chicago International Airlines to 88 aircraft per hour to reduce congestion in 2004 (Docket FAA-2004-16944).

There are many airport-related issues that need analysis. There are two philosophies in the allocation of slots: one is to promote maximum competition so that consumers can use the airport at the lowest possible price. The other is to recognize that existing companies are also investing heavily in airport facilities. It is on the basis of the tension between the two that regulations are designed. The general tendency is to balance rents from monopolies with spending on airport slots by comparing price changes with those in similar markets where no such slots are allocated. For example, a fare from Chicago to Pittsburgh might be compared to a fare from St. Louis to Atlanta. The former does not charge as much for a slot. If the two are the same, that is good; however, if they are different, it is likely that monopoly rents are being generated. Therefore, there is a possibility that more competitive measures will be taken.

Specifically, an evaluation of competition in the economic analysis of Chicago airport regulation (Impact on Competition and Air Fares at O'Hare) is outlined below.

The proposed regulations would restrict landings, but the FAA is trying to reduce congestion by restricting them. In the six months since the regulations were issued, this has resulted in a rather large increase in the number of passengers using the Chicago airport. In addition, the two airlines that use Chicago as their hub have enough slots to coordinate and decentralize their landings to the Midway airport (Midway). Therefore, it is concluded that although there will be an undeniable increase in prices for passengers with Chicago as their final destination, the allocation of slots will be efficient based on the philosophy described above, and the fact that the regulation is time-limited will limit the impediment to competition.

10.3.3 Economic Analysis Related to the Regulation of Ozone Depleting Substances Related to the Montreal Protocol[1] in the Food and Drug Administration (FDA) of the Department of Health

Example 10.3 Economic analysis of the US Food And Drug Administration (FDA) regulation of albuterol MDIs

Albuterol MDIs, an ozone-depleting substance, are subject to the Montreal Protocol. Although the production of ozone-depleting substances was banned in principle before the 1990s, the use of ozone-depleting substances in MDIs has been allowed because of the risk to human life. However, in April 2005, the FDA banned all inhalants containing chlorofluorocarbons (CFCs, specified CFCs) (including albuterol). However, in April 2005, the FDA announced that the production of all inhalants (including albuterol) containing chlorofluorocarbons (CFCs, specified CFCs) would be banned in the US by December 31, 2008. At the time, it was expected that pharmaceutical companies would produce adequate supplies of hydrochlorofluoroalkane (HFA, CFC substitutes) inhalants by the end of 2008. However, because hydrochlorofluoroalkane (HFA, CFC substitute) inhalers were still under patent, they were more expensive than the existing CFC albuterol inhalers, resulting in lower demand, especially for low-income individuals who could not afford them. Further,

[1] https://www.federalregister.gov/documents/2008/11/19/E8-27436/use-of-ozone-depleting-substances-removal-of-essential-use-designation-epinephrine.

due to existing patents, generic HFA albuterol inhalers are not expected to hit the market any earlier than 2017.

In addition, at the time of the 2008 ban, there were only two companies producing hydrochlorofluoroalkane inhalants (HFA-albuterol MDI), an alternative CFC, if the ban were to be lifted in 2008, and there was concern about an oligopoly problem. To examine these issues, the price elasticity of the substitute good (HFA-albuterol MDI) was estimated in the economic analysis. Subsequently, we attempted to quantify the extent to which price increases due to patents and lower competition would lead to lower users. In other words, RIA of the regulation states that the cost of the regulation is that the use of the substance within the term of the patent right and the price increase resulting from the fact that the producing company is a duopoly will reduce the consumption of the drug in question, resulting in a dead weight loss. To estimate this decrease in consumption, the price elasticity of demand for the substitute good (HFA-albuterol MDI) was calculated using the price elasticity estimated from the change in demand based on the change in the patient's basic window payment (co-payment) obtained in Goldman et al. (2004). As a result, the price elasticity of these demands was calculated. It is estimated to be between −0.15 and −0.33, which is used to estimate the decrease in demand. From this, FDA estimate that this will result in a decrease in health care spending of between $40 million and $60 million. However, these rising costs will be lowered by the expiration of patents in 2017 and increased entry. Therefore, postponing the implementation date is more likely to lead to lower costs. However, this would lead to a decrease in benefits and also be problematic from the perspective of compliance with the Montreal Protocol.

As a result of these considerations, the date of the ban, which was originally set for the end of 2008, was shifted by one year to the end of 2009. In consideration of the competitive situation and the price increase caused by patents, the "adoption of a longer transitional measure," which is introduced in the discussion of alternative measures in A-4, was chosen. However, from the perspective of compliance with the Montreal Protocol, the abovementioned regulation is considered to be essential, and the conclusion has been reached that no further deferral is possible.

Example 10.4 Attempts to address competition considerations regarding regulations related to the Montreal Protocol

According to the hearings at the OMB, regulations related to the Montreal Protocol on ozone-depleting substances are designed to preserve the industrial structure. However, when the draft regulations were first developed, an attempt was made to give emission rights to the entrants, but it failed due to the problems of the system design and criticism from the viewpoint of fairness. The result is the current regulatory system, which allows existing companies to operate. Moreover, while many regulations related to the Montreal Protocol require the phasing out of destructive substances, the number of existing companies seems to be kept constant.

10.4 Viewpoints of Analysis Refering the US Government

This book does not explain the econometric methods of analysis in detail as various other works on the subject have already covered it. However, we explain the extent to which such analytical methods are being used. In particular, it is instructive to explain the methods used in the US, where most advanced analysis is being conducted in the world, is instructive. Therefore, in this section, we will introduce examples to use such analytical methods in the US, especially FCC and FERC.

10.4.1 Market Identification

Market identification is an important analytical step in competition policy, including merger review for those who are responsible for both ex ante regulation and ex post competition policy such as the FCC regulation. A minimum level of market identification is also necessary when conducting partial equilibrium analysis, as in the case of the EPA's regulation of the cement industry.

However, in most regulations of the presidential departments, where social regulations are mainly enacted, market identification is not necessary, one of exceptions is the allocation of departure and arrival slots. There is a debate on how market identification and price elasticity should be estimated in the aviation market, which uses a hub-and-spoke system. In particular, it is even more difficult to take into account the possibility that airlines may change their hubs. There are also airlines that do not use the hub-and-spoke system, such as Southwest Airlines, which must also be considered. Some airports are still running out of slots, and these issues must also be taken into consideration. Though the Federal Trade Commission (FTC) will be more involved in such market specific issues, market identification and definition is often not an issue for the DOT.

In addition, the Federal Energy Regulatory Commission (FERC) identifies markets, that is, the definition of a particular electricity market, on a regional basis based on transmission capacity. For example, in the PJM region, sales can be made almost anywhere at any time, but when supply capacity is impaired during peak periods, the impaired region is then considered a segmented market. Specific product markets are identified based on two factors: short-term and capacity. The market for power-generation capacity is determined based on where the power plant is located. Energy markets encourage entry through a function of price, but as a market for derived services, electricity must always balance supply and demand at any moment. Determining the market will depend on these unique properties of electricity, namely supply capacity constraints and the nature of the power plant and the nature of electricity that is unable to store.

10.4.2 Cross-Elasticity Between Each Market

In market identification, it is usual to consider substitutability with similar markets. But the FCC and FERC can assume that there are few substitutes and that cross-elasticity is small due to the specific nature of the telecommunication and electricity.

For example, the FERC may consider cross-elasticity if there is a problem in the two preliminary screenings explained in 10.5.2. However, in electricity, the market is very clearly defined and there are very few substitute goods. Peak and off-peak periods are considered different for different goods, and it is difficult to substitute between them. In the case of smart grids, the cross-elasticity will be greater because consumption patterns can be changed. If substitution between the two is possible, it should be considered as a valid indicator, but it is usually assumed to be perfectly inelastic.

The FCC also considered the substitutability of cable TV and satellite TV. These were difficult because they did not have enough data. In the case of canned soups and breads, all supermarkets use POS and other systems to collect data. Therefore, they have accumulated data on which products are purchased at what price and what happens if the price is a promotional price, and it is easy to understand changes in demand due to such price changes. Therefore, it will be easy to measure cross-elasticity through appropriate quantitative analysis. Although it is more difficult to identify markets for food products in terms of the degree of product differentiation. Obtaining data is difficult, and if the data are not appropriate, proper competitive analysis cannot be done. This requires adjustments, judgments, and compromises. Mistakes can also be made.

10.4.3 Use of the Hirschman-Herfindahl Index (HHI)

The FERC uses the HHI as a key indicator with respect to the market review described in next section. It follows the DOJ and FTC guidelines for mergers. It is used for preliminary screening to see if there is any harm to competition. If there are problems, a detailed economic analysis estimating the price elasticity at the margins is conducted to see if any firms have the ability to influence prices. If there are firms with low elasticity and high potential to exercise market power, the FERC will take action such as restricting mergers or imposing other additional regulations.

At the FCC, competition analysis differs in each category of regulation, but for deregulation analysis and review of transactions such as wireless transactions, traditional analysis begins with (a) an analysis of market structure, (b) market identification with respect to output and geographic spread, (c) calculation of market share and the HHI, (d) analysis of barriers to entry and potential entry, (e) looking at the dynamics of market share, (f) looking at price trends and costs, and (g) looking at the impact of the regulation on the market. It will (f) look at price trends, costs, and profits; and (g) investigate the possibility of collusion.

From the interviews in November 2009 with Mr. Stockdale, Donald at FCC, the he suggested the importance of market identification, using the example of the European Commission's (EC) competition policy, which allows the imposition of ex ante regulation only when there is strong market power. As it was, 18 markets were suspected of having such dominance, and each country was asked to conduct an analysis with appropriate market identification; subsequently, regulation was adopted.

Initially, the EU divided regional markets by national borders. Eight years later, however, EU member states had come to realize that increased competition in urban commercial areas requires broader market identification. Thus, market identification within each nation, which is easy for governments to handle, can be problematic in terms of economics. Regulators must choose markets that reflect the actual market. It cannot be a single country or household. Regulators must analyize properly.

10.4.4 Effectiveness of Creating Criteria

Creating criteria is important for conducting competition analysis. At the interviews with Dr. Ennis, Sean at OECD headquater he introduced us an interesting case study on radio station mergers in the US. In reviewing radio station mergers, the DOJ and FCC use either revenue or audience share. The revenue share is the most commonly used. The basic principle is that it is desirable to have at least three radio stations operating in a given area, and the criteria were then set to ensure that the share would not exceed 40% at the time of the merger. Although some have argued that 33% is preferable, unifying such a standard across the country would be an easy way to achieve consensus.

10.4.5 Relationship Between Regulatory Flexibility Analysis and Competition Analysis

If the increase in costs due to regulations leads to an increase in fixed costs, including set-up costs and sunk costs, this will have a restraining effect on competition through barriers to entry and exits, especially by SMEs. Based on the Regulatory Flexibility Act in the US, regulatory flexibility analysis is conducted to analyze the impact on SMEs.

The flow of the regulatory flexibility analysis will be outlined based on A Guide to the Regulatory Flexibility Act.[2] The regulatory flexibility analysis indicates whether the company has considered alternatives that would minimize the serious impact of the regulation on SMEs. The analysis should explain the purpose of the

[2] This statement was based on the 1996 version. Current version is as follows: https://cdn.advocacy.sba.gov/wp-content/uploads/2019/06/21110349/How-to-Comply-with-the-RFA.pdf.

regulation and its direct and indirect impacts on SMEs, and state the reasons for proposing that particular regulation among the various alternatives.

According to the regulatory flexibility analysis guide, the draft regulatory flexibility analysis should first include five items: (1) the need for the regulation, (2) the purpose and legality of the regulation, (3) the nature and number of SMEs to be regulated, (4) the paperwork and other tasks required for the regulation, and (5) consistency with other regulations. As will be understood, it is the first priority that the individual analysis shows which of the various alternatives to achieve the regulatory objectives would have the least impact on SMEs, and that the causes and consequences of the various alternatives are communicated to policy makers and reflected in their policy decisions.

In addition, as soon as the proposed final regulation is submitted, the final regulatory flexibility analysis or the reason for not conducting the regulatory flexibility analysis must show the small impact of the regulation on SMEs. The final regulatory flexibility analysis must provide a response to public comments and a rationale for why the proposed regulation is preferable to other alternatives. The final regulatory flexibility analysis must then include the following five items.

It may seem difficult to prove that the impact is small before conducting a detailed analysis. However, as for the regulatory flexibility analysis, the criteria for whether or not it should be conducted are vague, which are listed below; therefore, discretionary judgment is allowed.

(1) The purpose and simple necessity of the regulation.
(2) The important issues raised in the public comments, their analysis, and the parts of the regulation that have been changed in response to them, if any.
(3) An estimate of the number of firms the regulation will affect, and if this cannot be estimated, explain why not.
(4) The duties and tasks imposed by the regulation. If it requires specialization, provide details.
(5) Of those that would achieve the objectives of the regulation, the review process that minimized the burden on SMEs, and the reasons for excluding other than the current regulatory proposals.

The validity of the final proposal in question and the analysis of its merits and demerits are the most important. Regulators do not simply use regulatory flexibility analysis to justify the final proposal. Regulatory flexibility analysis requires an argument to reduce the burden on SMEs and to increase the effectiveness of the regulation-making process. The above is a summary of the regulatory flexibility analysis based on the above guide. Again, it is apparent that they emphasize how important it is to consider and adopt more desirable options from the outset of regulatory design.

In addition to reduce the cost burden on marginal firms and facilitate their entry and exit, consideration for SMEs can lead to increase competition and technological progress in the future.

However, as noted in the guide, there is no set of criteria for requiring an analysis, and it is completely up to the regulator to decide what impacts require a regulatory flexibility analysis. At the US Government Auditing Office (GAO) hearing in 2004, the GAO has repeatedly asked Congress to develop such standards, but Congress has not. Therefore, it is left to the discretion of the regulators to decide whether or not an analysis will actually be conducted.

In the end of the subsection, we present an example of a proposed regulatory flexibility analysis of the FMCSA regulations on brokers (2004) that was prepared in accordance with these ideas. This analysis is in the draft stage, and the description follows the above items, and it is helpful to see what description is provided for each item.

(1) Need for regulation
The American Moving and Storage Association (AMSA) has requested the DOT to require HHG brokers, who take charge of the transportation of household goods, to provide consumers with the same information that carriers provide, plus information indicating that they are brokers. The DOT has enacted regulations requiring them to do so. The necessity of the regulation is that there is a limit to how much such information can be provided by the private sector, and it addresses the problem of asymmetric information.
(2) Purpose and legality of the regulation
This regulation is based on the ICC's economic regulation of HHG brokers under the Motor Carrier Act of 1935, which regulated brokers until it was abolished in 1995. The ICC regulated brokers until it was abolished in 1995, when jurisdiction was transferred to the DOT.
This regulation ensures that shippers requesting interstate transportation receive proper information about the client and about their rights and responsibilities when they go through a broker instead of going directly to the carrier. The regulation also aims to prevent consumer harm by ensuring that HHG brokers use only properly registered carriers.
(3) Nature and number of SMEs subject to the regulation
In 2004, there are 615 brokers operating in the US and 394 dormant ones. The number of unregistered brokers cannot be ascertained, but it is estimated to be around 75 based on interviews and other research. As a result, the number of brokers in operation is estimated at 690. Almost all of them belong to SMEs as defined by the Small Business Administration (SBA), with an average turnover of $23.5 million. Carriers will also be indirectly affected.
(4) Documentation services and other services required for regulation
Option 1 is the baseline and imposes the same obligations as the current situation. In contrast, Option 2 strengthens regulatory compliance and audits of brokers (HHG brokers), and does not require additional paperwork, but requires that records be kept in a form that can be provided. As such, no special technology is required.
Option 3 would impose additional regulations on HHG brokers, requiring them to keep records and submit them during audits and regulatory compliance reviews. In this case, the additional document storage costs would be $1,378,000 per year and the opportunity cost increase due to the increase in the minimum

capital for registration would be $300,000 per year. No special technology would be required.

(5) Consistency with other regulations
The FMCSA is not aware of any regulations that overlap with this regulation, and states that consistency with other regulations has been ensured. However, similar regulations must be imposed separately on brokers (HHG brokers), although they are similar to those imposed on HHG carriers.

10.4.6 More Advanced Analysis

We conclude this section with a discussion of the more sophisticated economic analysis with which the OMB is concerned in the interviews in November 2009. First, one thing that the OMB does not do well enough is to evaluate vertical and horizontal industry structure and long-term contracts. However, these are fixed costs and difficult to incorporate into an RIA. Next, the issue of asymmetric information, such as adverse selection, was generally a more important concern for the OMB 20 years ago.

One example to consider in behavioral economics 10 years ago was the exclusion of retirement savings plans that allow firms to automatically enroll people in retirement savings plans with respect to conditions on default and financial investment, giving them the opportunity to exit the plan freely. The classic behavioral economic consequence is that if the decision set is the same, the ability to exit freely is known to increase retirement savings by far.

Another example is the standard setting in resource economies. In setting socially optimal standards that take into account resource depletion, one must consider the trade-off between rising current costs and uncertain future resource constraints. However, it is difficult for consumers to fully assess future uncertainty, which leads to irrational biases analyzed in behavioral economics. It is explained in Chapter 11 in detail.

10.5 Economic and Competition Analysis at an Independent Regulatory Commission

Most economic regulations are under the jurisdiction of independent regulatory agencies and Section 3(b) of Executive Order 12,866 excludes "Independent Regulatory Agencies" from the list of agencies that are required to conduct RIAs. Thus IA or economic analysis of economic regulations in the US seems less strict than and fall behind the RIA by presidential agencies that are required to conduct RIAs under Presidential Executive Order 12,866.

However, even regulations by an independent regulatory commission are subject to obligations of assessment similar to Presidential Decree 12,866, based on laws and regulations relevant to independent regulatory commissions (establishment laws, internal documents, etc.) from the perspective of accountability, etc. The GAO be consults when the independent regulatory commission enacts regulations, though the summary of the GAO's analysis that is not quantitatively analyze the costs and benefits.

In addition, an independent regulatory commission is not given complete discretion in its analysis. Under the Congressional Review Act, significant regulations with an impact of $100 million or more must be reported to Congress, and Congress also has the authority to overturn the regulation. This delays the regulations from taking effect for 60 days. In practice, the OMB has the authority to decide whether a regulation is "significant regulation with an impact of $100 million or more." Therefore, even an independent regulatory commission may have to provide sufficient information to the OMB to show whether it does or does not exceed $100 million, and may require additional analysis to show the basis for doing so.

Under the Administrative Procedure Act, each agency must have a reasonable basis for enacting regulations. These may or may not require a cost-benefit analysis, but in any case, it is suggested that an analysis should be conducted if the enactment of the regulation and the imposition of costs on the parties are critical to the policy decision. In enacting regulations, if the analysis of whether there is a reasonable basis for the regulation is judicially determined, the independent regulatory commission's regulation may be overturned in a judicial forum.

For example, although the FCC is not subject to the RIA mandate under Executive Order 12,866, it is required by the Communications Act to conduct an RIA-like analysis of the regulations under its jurisdiction. This is because the US Communications Act requires that telecommunications rates be reasonable, and the FCC must demonstrate that they are. When Congress passed the US Communications Act of 1996, it introduced competition into the local telecommunications market and promoted competition in other markets. The aim of the amendment was to reduce barriers to entry into local markets and promote competition in local markets. As a result, the FCC has revised its regulations and at the same time has shifted its analysis from traditional monopolies to competition analysis, such as that done with respect to mergers.

Similar procedures are followed for deregulation: under the US Communications Act of 1996, the FCC has the authority to decide not to implement obligations imposed by a regulation if it deems that prices are reasonable and that no specific regulation is needed to protect consumers. Therefore, to make a decision not to require the performance of obligations for regulatory compliance, it is necessary to evaluate the impact on competition.

For example, the FCC has decided that the long distance market has become sufficiently competitive that it is no longer necessary to enforce the obligations imposed by the regulations and has eliminated the reporting requirements on long distance carriers. Since there is more competition in the local telephone market these days, the 1996 US Communications Act imposes substantial obligations on certain companies, especially those with existing switching operations, but there are calls to eliminate such obligations. Such requests for deregulation must be addressed after conducting a competitive analysis.

The FERC is also conducting competition analysis to keep the market competitive from the standpoint of complying with the Energy Act. When Congress deregulated the wholesale electricity market, the FERC, as a government entity, was legally obligated to ensure that the prices were reasonable. For prices to be set reasonably, the wholesale market must be competitive. If it is not, consumers and businesses harmed by high power prices can take the FERC to court. Therefore, the FERC must ensure that the wholesale market is competitive to the extent that the court finds it to be. If competition functions well in the local market, the court is likely to find that pricing is reasonable.

In the following subsections, the FCC (in Sect. 10.5.1) and FERC (in Sect. 10.5.2) will be discussed separately and the methods of analysis will be discussed. As described in Chap. 6, cost-benefit analysis of the regulation was not systematic and common practice in the FCC before 2019. Thus, we pick up several economic analyses based on the established law or other requirement both in the FCC and FERC. We emphasize that they are not competition assessments, but the economic analysis applied to other competition assessment.

10.5.1 Economic Analysis and Competition Analysis at the FCC

(1) The FCC's competition policy

It would not be an exaggeration to say that most of its regulations affect competition. For example, when Congress passed the US Communications Act of 1996, it introduced competition into the local telecommunications markets and promoted competition in other markets; the aim of the revised US Communications Act of 1996 was to reduce barriers to entry into local markets and promote competition in local markets. Therefore, the FCC's economic analysis has shifted from the traditional analysis of monopolies to an economic analysis closer to competition policy, such as that on mergers, see Kwerel et al. (2004). Spectrum allocation is related to competition policies, where the FCC is obligated to ensure that spectrum is allocated in a manner that preserves a competitive market. For example, when the FCC allocated spectrum for cell phones to the first two companies in 1980, the two companies were considered competitive enough for cell phones. However, by 1993, the FCC's economist director asked Congress to change the law and allow the FCC to allocate more spectrum through auctions, which resulted in the FCC allocating spectrum for five additional personal communications services (PCS, the cell phone service offered in North America). As a result, the FCC auctioned off five additional PCS spectrums and their licenses. This led to increased competition in the market, a significant decrease in prices, and a significant increase in penetration. The

FCC also has jurisdiction over the transfer of such spectrum, and companies must obtain its approval for the transfer of any spectrum. The FCC analyzes the effects of the spectrum transfer and assesses the impact on consumers due to market concentration in markets such as mobile phones that use the spectrum. If there is a concern that spectrum will be used exclusively, concentration will increase, or competition will be unduly suppressed, it will not be permitted.

In addition, the FCC has a great deal of authority over media ownership in the laws governing media regulations under its jurisdiction. Congress has given the FCC the power to (1) limit ownership, that is, regulate the number of households served by a single cable TV, (2) limit joint ownership of newspapers and television, and (3) limit the number of radio and television stations owned by local companies. In the international sector, the FCC's approval is required when a satellite communications company wants to resell its license.

The FCC also makes rules to introduce and promote competition; the US Communications Act of 1996 requires that local competition be maintained. For example, the issue of computers was raised: in the 1970s, companies began to realize that a variety of computer application software could be used for telecommunications. The FCC was trying to determine whether the market for these new computer services would be more competitive than the market for information processing services, which was then dominated by the telephone, and to establish rules to promote competition.

(2) Basic Premise for competition in the FCC

When deregulation occurs, the FCC analyzes whether it will lead to an increase in a particular company's market power or not. Several other competition analyses of deregulation are also presented in annual reports. Competition analysis is also conducted and written in regional market competition reports, broadband reports, and wireless-related and media-related annual reports. There are also regulatory enactments that are not included in these categories, but may be subject to competition analysis in some circumstances. For example, with respect to the Internet, there are regulations to ensure neutrality on the Internet, and additional regulations imposed on broadband Internet access services to ensure an open Internet.

In the FCC's case, due to the proximity to economic regulation and the deregulated market, the focus has shifted to measures closer to so-called ex-post competition policy, such as merger review, rather than ex-ante regulation, and to economic analysis of the associated rule changes. However, they have also enforced regulations that impose a cap on spectrum ownership on individual companies.

The general procedure in such cases is that Congress may request the enactment of regulations, in which specific issues are detected and a determination is made as to whether the enactment of such regulations is appropriate. Before proposing a regulation, it is normal to analyze it internally. Similar to the procedure for other regulations, once the internal analysis is done, public hearings and public comments are held, following which a regulatory proposal is made. Subsequently, a final proposal is made and the regulation is approved.

Though the regulation to impose a cap on spectrum ownership has been thoroughly examined internally, it is difficult to explain because it is not a standardized process. It would be better to enforce such regulations on media ownership and caps on spectrum ownership, as the information would be disseminated in advance, making it easier to understand and more certain to market participants. However, such ex ante regulations can also bring down costs. For example, if the FCC wants to issue additional licenses to five companies under the initial presence of two cell phone companies, new entrants will want to start at the same level as the existing companies. With that in mind, the FCC thought it would be best to add at least two more companies and have four competitors, and granted licenses to two new companies. However, a few years later, it decided to allocate licenses to a total of seven companies. In some areas, one company overwhelmed the others, and if the number of customers increased by another 15%, there would not be enough spectrum. Therefore, the FCC allocated the new spectrum to be distributed for cell phones; the FCC decided to increase licenses due to the increase in available spectrum and the decrease in spectrum due to increased competition. This is also done on a case-by-case basis. Whether ex ante regulation or ex post competition policy is preferable is a matter of debate. Ex-post coordination on a case-by-case basis is more flexible, but requires more work from the FCC.

When creating regulations, the Paperwork Reduction Act must be followed first. This means that excessive paperwork must not be imposed on those who are subject to the regulation. The OMB's approval is needed to require a certain number of entities to provide data. Similarly, a regulatory flexibility analysis of the impact on small businesses may have to be done. Other than that, the FCC has a lot of discretion regarding its analysis. Internally, however, there is an accumulating belief in the importance of competition. This makes the internal analysis very efficient. There is also a lot of personnel exchange among economists; in addition, the FCC, FTC, and DOJ each hosts university economists on sabbatical. Such positions play an important role in improving the quality of economic analysis. Accepting young economists can improve the creation of regulations.

(3) Analysis of Market Identification and the FCC's Merger Review

Market identification is a key element in the FCC's merger review process. The scope of the appropriate regional market must be determined. In the case of the US, the price elasticity of demand can be taken into account to determine the market identification and regional market. For example, in the case of a merger of gasoline retailers to identify a local market, if the firm is a monopoly and increases the price marginally, it can find out how many customers will avoid the price increase and go to other gas stations. Customers who do not go to other markets will be identified as participants in that market.

As for mergers in the telecommunications industry, for example, if Verizon (a US cell phone company) raises prices by 10% in a monopoly area, it is unlikely that consumers will move to avoid it. Thus, the market is identified as the area covered by the company's signal. This would be a very broad market identification, but in practice, a smaller market may be appropriate.

An example of this type of market identification is the case of the merger review of the proposed merger of two satellite broadcasters, EchoStar and DirecTV. In this case, how should the relevant market be identified? Should it be satellite broadcasting only, multi-channel cable TV, cable TV with less than 30 channels, or the entire television industry? In general, it is safe to assume that the two merging companies offer the same satellite TV service. Multichannel cable TV can be considered a close substitute depending on how competition is handled; it would be delicate to consider cable TV with less than 30 channels as a close substitute. Moreover, there are areas in the US where cable TV does not exist at all. Therefore, the regions are classified into three categories: satellite broadcasting only; satellite broadcasting and small channel cable TV only; and satellite broadcasting, small channel cable TV, and multi-channel cable TV.

Based on this idea, FCC studied the market share of cable TV companies covering the regions. Since the coverage area of cable TV companies is small, the survey covered about 7,000 markets in the US. The HHI was then calculated for each. The results of these analyses are summarized in the FCC (2002).

The FCC (2000) concluded the following about the effect of mergers on competition. The structural analysis shows that the merger of the two companies will have a serious impact on competition, which requires a more detailed investigation. Therefore, it was concluded that the merger would impede competition and that an administrative hearing was appropriate. As a result, both parties decided to withdraw the merger.

10.5.2 Economic Analysis of the FERC

We had several interviews with the officer in the FERC in 2000s and this subsection was written based on that information. Although it has not be updated, it is still useful while considering competition assessment. The FERC is responsible for the regulation of energy-related sectors at the federal level in the US, with a focus on electricity and gas. In this subsection, we will focus on the electricity market and discuss the economic analysis of its regulation and market research activities. In the past, electric power was an established industry where transmission and generation were carried out by the same company and the cost base of regulation was mainly based on the total cost. After deregulation in 1990s, the generation and transmission sectors have been separated, and the transmission sector, which is a strong natural monopoly, remains regulated on a cost basis in an increasing number of regions, while the generation sector is a competitive market.

Power plants are under the jurisdiction of state governments, and the same is true for the retailing of electricity. However, it comes under the FERC jurisdiction if either of the two things are true: (1) it owns and operates a transmission network for wholesale sales; or (2) it resells in the wholesale market or price control exists over sales in the wholesale market (which is different from price control over consumers).

Mostly, large scale companies that supply electricity spin off and own companies for electricity distribution in each state, which is under the jurisdiction of the state government. The FERC regulates the affiliates involved in the distribution of large companies that supply electricity, often imposing (cost-based) pricing.

Even in a well-functioning market, where power is bought and sold at market prices and prices change in real time, costs are broken down into two: transmission costs and costs as a commodity. For example, in the Pennsylvania-Maryland-New Jersey Power Market (PJM), under market pricing, cost-based pricing is used for transmission costs. It is the commodity portion of the price that fluctuates, which reflects the value of transmission, but transmission costs are priced on a cost basis.

If an independent power producer sells power in the wholesale market, it is allowed to set a market price, which would be a reasonable market price in a highly organized wholesale electricity market such as the PJM even if market power existed in the day-ahead market for trading power for delivery the next day. In other words, among the series of prices offered by each seller or buyer in the bidding, those accepted in the previous day's market are allocated in the market, and the equilibrium price is calculated by the computer using the cheapest price offered and moving up. Bids for the same time period presented to the market are set at the same price. The price is not based on cost, but on market demand and supply at the moment.

However, lessons learned from the California power crisis of the late 1990s have shown that even in the power generation sector, where multiple companies exist, it is possible for certain companies to exert market power during peak hours, due to the inability to store electric power. Therefore, when market power exists in a power generation company, if the company is judged to be highly concentrated in the market in a preliminary assessment, it cannot sell at market prices and cost-based pricing is applied. How to appropriately detect companies with such market power and impose cost-based regulation has become the biggest challenge in the 2000s. As for the examination of price control in the power generation sector, there are the market share screen and Pivotal Supplier Screen, which are modifications of the recent Supply Margin Assessment (SMA), and the Delivered Price Test (DPT), which is imposed on companies that are found to have monopoly power in these examinations.

Regarding the examination of mergers, a preliminary examination (screening) is conducted first to check whether there is any harm to competition. If there are no problems, fine. If there are problems, a detailed economic analysis should be conducted. Estimating the elasticity at the margins to see if any firms have the ability to supply that would affect prices. If there are companies with low elasticity and high potential to exercise market power, the FERC will take action such as restricting mergers or imposing other additional regulations.

Finally, transparency is of utmost importance when it comes to the process of making regulations and economic analysis. All information is available on the web and is fully responsive to public comments. The public is welcome to comment on the regulations as they are prepared. Conference information will also be posted on the web.

(1) Analysis of the wholesale market for electricity conducted by the FERC
In important regions in the US such as California and the Eastern District, electric power companies have separated their transmission and distribution divisions from their generation divisions and have become separate companies. In this case, the power transmission and distribution sector, where the so-called essential facility exists, is a natural monopoly (a state in which a monopoly is justfied because increasing the number of companies would be rather inefficient) and, therefore, is subject to total cost regulation. In contrast, the power generation sector is competitive in nature and has traditionally been thought to require no economic regulation.
The FERC used the Supply Margin Assessment (SMA) until 2004 as an indicator to determine whether a company has market power in the wholesale electricity market. However, because the SMA required strict application, there was a strong demand for a more flexible response to individual cases. As a result, a new method was considered, and a two-step check and a more flexible response method was introduced in 2004.
Factors that is unique to the electricity market include the following: (1) very low price elasticity of demand in the short term; (2) almost no storage of electricity; (3) when demand exceeds supply capacity even slightely, the entire supply stops; and (4) the capacity of the entire market matters. Therefore, even when the supply of a particular company is small compared to the supply capacity of the entire market, if the latter falls below the expected demand due to that company available stopping supply, it is necessary to consider that market power exists.
There is a possibility that market power exists even in companies with low market shares, which is not a problem in other goods markets, and how to detect it is one of the biggest problems in the FERC's electricity-related regulations. If it is determined that monopoly power exists, cost-based regulation will be imposed.
The following is an introduction to the methodology and the process of preparing the Market Share Screen and Pivotal Supplier Screen, which are modifications of the SMA and DPT for companies that are found to have market power.

(2) Overview and application of the new tests
In the 2004 decision, a more flexible measure using indicators was adopted instead of SMA that had been used previously. First, the market in the region supplied by the company in question is identified, the number of companies is determined, and two indicators—the pivotal supplier screen (analysis) and the market share screen (analysis) —are examined. If the target company is able to prove that it does not have market power, there is no problem. However, if the company is found to have market power, it will be subject to cost-based regulation.
The reason for using both the pivotal supplier screen (analysis) and the market share screen (analysis) is that using both makes it possible to measure market power during both off-peak and peak periods, and clarify whether the company has market power or not.

The reason for adopting such a multi-step test format is that—after considering the public comments as described below—it was determined that a single criterion would not be flexible enough to make an appropriate assessment.

If the existence of market power is indicated by either of the two tests above, a more detailed analysis centered on the DPT is conducted. In general, if the HHI is less than 2,500 at the peak of all seasons and the market share is less than 20%, market power is considered absent.

(3) Pivotal Supplier Analysis

The Pivotal Supplier Analysis evaluates the potential market power of the target company in the supply area during the peak period. It checks whether the supply in the target company's supply area will be able to meet the demand at the peak if the target company does not supply at all. In this sense, Pivotal Supplier Analysis looks at the market power of the target company during peak periods, especially in the spot market. If the target company does not exist and the demand cannot be met by the supply of all other companies, the target company is considered pivotal. When the price elasticity is very small, as in the case of electricity during peak hours, the pivotal firm can exercise serious price control and obtain monopoly profits.

Thus, Pivotal Supplier Analysis follows the SMA's idea, which identifies pivotal sellers in advance based on their transmission capacity, and checks whether they have sufficient supply capacity during peak hours. A power flow study must be done by adding up the power for each transmission capacity.

A power flow study is a more accurate estimate of transmission capacity by taking all the power plants in and out of the market and increasing the supply of power to the limit, up to the point where the transmission capacity reaches its limit, or the point where outside power purchases begin. It will be more clear who will actually supply the power.

(4) Market Share Screen

The market share screen evaluates the share of unused production capacity on a seasonal basis. It checks whether the supplier has a dominant position and does not exercise market power in conjunction with other companies. The test also measures the market share of the target company. The quantity supplied during the minimum peak hour of each season is specified, taking into account the amount of planned outages.

(5) Delibered Price Test (DPT)

The DPT is imposed when one of the two aforementioned tests is violated. In addition, the company may submit historical data as evidence of non-exclusive power. DPT defines potential suppliers based on price, cost and transmission capacity, and calculates the production capacity of individual firms in each season, taking into account the transmission capacity.

In other words, DPT is a structural model that first identifies and defines a regional market based on the limits of transmission capacity. Next, it identifies all the expected suppliers; estimates the operating costs of all the plants; and derives a market supply curve using historical data on fuel costs, efficiency, and fuel types. The market price is then estimated for each season, peak, off-peak, and maximum peak periods. Further, it identifies companies whose prices increase during the summer months and who can be profitable at that price plus 5%. In addition, the supply capacity of each seller is added based on generation capacity, location of the plant, and running costs. From the supply capacity, the market share, HHI, and structural parameters are calculated (e.g., 200 per megawatt for high peak in summer). Note that the winter peak is 35 per megawatt and, therefore, is very different. Only competitive plants (hydro, nuclear, coal-fired) are incorporated as base quantities. A different market picture can be drawn for different situations. The calculation is based on supply capacity, not actual supply.

(6) Design process for tests (importance of public comments)

It is difficult to formalize the analysis of such tests, and feedback from the public, especially public comments, is important. At the FERC hearings, the Commission developed an analysis methodology, made it available to the public, and left it to public discussion, including the opinions of sellers and buyers. We are currently making significant improvements to the SMA described above and made available on the web. The FERC has its own ideas on how to evaluate the accuracy of the analysis and study the market, and to codify them into regulatory policy, listening to industry, to buyers who demand rigorous testing, and to sellers who demand easy testing. The process is open, and feedback is taken. The FERC believes that this is the best way.

Technical conferences are also held, and details are posted on the web, and past conferences can be viewed. Actual research and models are also posted on the web. They puts a lot of effort into publicizing their works, and if they do not agree with the FERC, they can make their own proposals. For example, UC Davis in California and the Energy Institute at Haas in UC Berkeley have accumulated a lot of research directly related to California, which they send to the FERC.

In addition, any region must seek approval from the FERC for any rule changes. For example, Regional Transmission Organizations (RTOs) have designed auctions for supply capacity. There have been a great deal of controversy over what type of auction design is desirable. The result is different designs for different regions. The advantages and problems of different auctions has been discussed. These are also stored in the FERC's e-library system.

10.6 The Involvement of Competition Authorities: The DOJ and FTC

In the section, we summarize the involvement of competition authorities based on the interview at the DOJ (November 2009) and the speech by the FTC Chair Deborah Platt Majoras at the AEI-Brookings Joint Center (2007).

10.6.1 The DOJ's Involvement in Regulatory Enforcement

The DOJ deals with competition issues, based on both legal and economic perspectives. It can contribute both formally and informally to regulation making when there are competition issues. In such cases, the DOJ informs the regulator of its view on the impact of the regulation on competition, and will not act as a decision-maker on issues that need to be revised or reconsidered, but will remain in a position to persuade the regulator to reconsider and revise such issues. All issues found by the DOJ will be made public. Each department will have to respond to the DOJ's comments as well as all other comments.

There is a lot of informal cooperation and coordination with the OMB, as mentioned above, although there is less about RIA (economic analysis) and no formal collaboration at the RIA review stage, which will be reflected in the analysis. Furthermore, although the FTC/DOJ's guidelines on merger standards are concerned with ex-post competition policy, they are naturally taken into account and have an impact on regulation-making.

10.6.2 The Role of the DOJ in the Preparation of Regulations

First, we pick up the example of railroad industry. The DOJ also has a role regarding competition policy with respect to the railroad industry. While the Surface Transportation Board (STB) has jurisdiction over the industry in question, including the preparation of regulations, approval of mergers, and receipt of consumer complaints, the DOJ may conduct reviews and competition analyses, and exchange information on these points with the STB on a formal and informal basis. However, the decision making is done by the STB.

If the STB does not make any comments, it is endorsing that the regulation does not pose a problem for competition. If the DOJ is commenting on the regulation during the enactment process, it is also essential for the regulator to respond, as this will draw more public attention. However, in most cases, there is informal discussion and cooperation prior to the public comment process.

10.6.3 Collaboration with Independent Regulatory Commission

The FERC and DOJ are very interconnected and meet regularly on a quarterly basis. The DOJ works with the FERC on the deregulated power industry, particularly in the power generation sector, and the FTC works with the FERC on gas. Whenever there is a proposal for regulation of power transactions, the DOJ, along with the FERC, evaluates it internally. As for mergers in the power generation sector, the DOJ has the authority to approve them because of its jurisdiction. Mergers in telecommunication sector are also under the DOJ's jurisdiction; therefore, even if the FCC grants a license, the DOJ must approve it.

In the late 2000s, the FERC has addressed its authority over market manipulation in the 2005 amendments to the Energy Act. It allows the DOJ to assess prices for market operations in supervised markets. The DOJ observes the prices offered by market participants in the wholesale market for generation, transmission, and retail. If there is a suspicious price quote, it can be observed by both the DOJ and FERC. The DOJ will look for antitrust activity, while the FERC will look for market manipulation and fraud, each monitoring the same issue from a different perspective. The FERC is more open to concessions and compromises than the DOJ. However, the DOJ has the authority to review mergers, and the FERC approves them.

Thus, there is a rough line as to the extent to which regulators will incorporate antitrust considerations into their regulatory enactments, and it varies depending on the case and industry. Violation of this rule is a violation of the obligation. Whether or not the DOJ will actually intervene and fine them is another matter. In any case, when you set up regulations, you are more or less involved in antitrust issues. In economic matters, if the lawmakers say they will look into it, they will look into it and engage with the regulators both formally and informally.

In general, there are two channels in the creation of regulations: the formal one, like Star Alliance, where the alliance makes the material public and the DOJ comments on it. The other trend is to consult informally with regulators and regulatory agencies for comments and informal discussions during the process of establishing regulations.

10.6.4 The Role of the FTC

The role of the FTC in regulatory development is discussed below, which is based on a presentation of the FTC and DTC at the 2007 workshop, The Role of Competition Analysis in Regulatory Decisions, sponsored by the AEA-Brooking Joint Center. The role of the FTC in regulatory decisions is discussed in the following excerpts from the keynote speech of Mr. DEBORAH PLATT MAJORAS, FTC.

While the FTC is often called upon to comment on legislative actions and regulatory decisions of other agencies, it is important to show that it is not commenting casually. Rather, the FTC takes a careful, empirical, fact-based analytical approach that considers the cost-benefit to the consumer. On top of that, it is aware of three problems.

The FTC looks for empirical evidence of such harm to consumers. Second, it checks whether the regulation explicitly addresses such harm to consumers and, to answer that question, whether there are restrictions that inadvertently discourage pro-competitive behavior. The third is to consider whether such restrictions are causing more harm to consumers than they are restraining, and whether they are reducing the benefits of competition. Here, the FTC helps agencies conduct cost-benefit analyses and emphasizes that it is generally preferable to promote competition rather than protect consumers through regulation.

The FTC also tries to select areas where there is sufficient internal consensus on the benefits of competition, or similar areas, rather than accumulating past know-how. Specifically, there are cases where deregulation can (1) promote entry, (2) eliminate deception and misrepresentation in the market, and (3) make it easier for consumers to obtain useful information about goods and services.

First, the FTC has been advising the FERC on deregulation of the electricity market, emphasizing the importance of accurate and timely information to ensure benefits to consumers. The FTC has also paid close attention to regulatory decisions on entry. For example, in 2004, when Eurex, a futures exchange founded by German and Swiss companies, was licensed to operate a commodity futures market and entered the US to compete with the Chicago Board of Trade, the incumbents opposed it, citing concerns about predatory pricing by incumbents. The FTC commented that such entry would be beneficial to consumers and desirable from the perspective of promoting competition.

Finally, regarding the importance of adequate disclosure, in the area of diet and nutrition, the FTC has encouraged companies to provide more accessible and useful information to consumers. In 2006, the FTC commented on the FDA's guidelines for labeling grains to allow producers to include additional quantitative information on the label to provide consumers with more effective and understandable information.

In addition, efforts are being made to publicly disclose information through various means. In particular, it is to put the guidelines into effect. The FTC/DOJ guidelines on horizontal mergers are probably the most well-known and influential. These merger guidelines provide companies with a useful roadmap for how the FTC and other governments will evaluate mergers and help companies make decisions that do not violate antitrust laws.

Further, the guidelines will be influential in guiding courts and other agencies on how to analyze deals. Although the guidelines are not legally binding, judges also rely heavily on the way the guidelines are analyzed. The FERC has agreed to this method and uses it in its merger reviews of power markets. Naturally, the FTC's and DOJ's guidelines on merger standards should be taken into account in the development of ex ante regulations, and should have an impact.

Finally, all departments that make economic decisions face issues related to competition. Therefore, when designing regulations related to such issues, all departments should be able to improve their regulations in a way that promotes competition and avoids companies from taking advantage of such regulatory designs. The FTC is always ready to help with that.

10.6.5 Cooperation and Division of Roles Between the DOJ and the FTC

There is no clear reason for the two agencies to exist for the same purpose. The main difference is that the DOJ deals with cartels and the FTC does not. Convicted cartel price-fixing practices are subject to prosecution by the DOJ. This can lead to imprisonment, but only the DOJ has the authority to imprison.

The FTC also provides consumer protection. Each has a different procedure, but the idea is essentially the same. The FTC can bring charges in court, but also has a judge who makes judicial decisions within the organization. The case may then be appealed to the courts. Both the DOJ and FTC have the same authority over mergers, downstream/upstream corporate alliances, and unilateral actions of a single company. However, the two sides never look at the same cases. For example, in monopolies, both sides will never accuse Intel.

It is customary for either side to follow what is called the "clearance procedure," and if either side wants to investigate a matter, it is communicated to the other side and the more experienced side is assigned. For example, the DOJ has a comparative advantage in transportation and telecommunications, the FTC has a comparative advantage in pharmaceuticals, and both are skilled in real estate; therefore, it is done on a case-by-case basis. Sometimes a joint statement is issued. This is especially the case at the state level.

Conflicts between the two sides are also very rare. Ninety-five to ninety-eight percent of the time, an agreement is reached. In some cases, differences may arise due to the organizational differences between the FTC and the DOJ, where the FTC is an independent regulatory commission and the DOJ is a department of the presidential office. This is especially true in the final stages of the proceedings. For example, during the Bush administration in the 2000s, the Justice Department put into effect the DOJ Antitrust Enforcement Guidelines for unilateral conduct, which were based on the Sherman Act's Sect. 10.2. In other countries, it is called abuse of a dominant position. It is an attempt by one company to gain a dominant market share position and use it to gain an advantage in trade and competition with other companies.

Three of the FTC's directors have announced in the press that they do not agree with the guidelines because they believe they do not properly comply with the law. There was a slight difference in focus and emphasis. A change of administration occurred and the Assistant Attorney General of the DOJ withdrew the guidelines. As a result, the guidelines are no longer the compliance policy of the Antitrust Division. In this case, it appears that the focus of the two organizations was different.

According to newspaper reports, the opinion of three of the four dissenters (one retired) was that the DOJ was too lax in dealing with the actions of the same companies. Further, they said that if the DOJ does not, the FTC will continue to use its authority to protect consumers. However, while there have been such cases, these situations are rare and the agreement between the two parties is generally very strong.

10.7 Conclusion

Competitive analysis has a wide variety, making it difficult to create a standardized guideline or manual. Further, while checklists are useful in that they identify problems, it is not clear how to solve or analyze them. Therefore, analysis of the impact on competition in each agencies of the US government is mainly based on considering a proposed regulation and reducing the impact on competition as much as possible at the early stage. Thus, even if many competition analyses do not get published in the Official Gazette in the US, this does not indicate a lack of competition analysis. Instead, it has almost done the analysis at the early stage of regulation making by selecting best alternatives as pointed out in A-4. And additional analyses of the impact on competition is conducted as a supplement if pointed out in public comments or regulatory fexibility analysis.

Most regulations of the presidential office are mainly related to health, safety, and environment. Most of these regulations do not affect competition, for example, environmental regulations on road construction or not to fly three miles closer to an Empire State Building. In such cases, costs are imposed but there is no impact on competition.

It should be noted that the philosophy behind so-called social regulations is mainly to counter externalities at the expense of market efficiency. Therefore, there is a strong belief that regulations are enacted to improve externalities, even if they impose a burden on the economy, and that it is unavoidable to interfere the market, including competition.

If competition can be an important issue, it will be incorporated at the early stage of regulation making. This approach has the advantage in that it does not require extensive analysis, but reflects the need to minimize the impact on competition in actual regulations. After the regulations are prepared, the draft regulations are submitted for public comment. The comments from the actual interested parties obtained are helpful and often supportive. In addition, the comments often point out problems that were not anticipated at first. While reflecting such comments, the regulations are revised to a form that is economically sound. This process may be repeated twice or third. When a regulation is submitted for public comment, some departments may consult the competition authority.

In contrast, the Independent Regulatory Commission, which is mainly in charge of economic regulation, has been imposing cost-based regulations on firms that are natural monopolists to deal with the problem of natural monopolies. However, deregulation in recent years has led to the adoption of measures to introduce market competition rather than traditional regulation, and the emphasis has shifted to ex-post competition policies, such as analysis for deregulation, merger review, and checking whether the market is competitive, rather than ex-ante traditional regulation. As a result, competition analysis is often conducted in such a context, which is similar to the competition policy conducted by the Antitrust Division of the DOJ. An example of a merger review is the FCC's analysis of satellite broadcasting company mergers, in previous section.

Next, in the electricity market, since the California electricity crisis, the unique nature of electricity has given rise to market power that would not occur in ordinary goods. The FERC conducts primary tests such as the Pivotal Market Screen and Market Share Screen to check whether such markets are competitive, and a secondary check using DPT.

Since these checks on whether the market is competitive or not and the merger review are at the heart of competition analysis, if an RIA were to be conducted, it would have to be imposed on the analysis of the analysis method itself, and the formal procedures may become rather restrictive. Therefore, it can be considered that the agency is making efforts to make the analysis as open as possible to the public and is ensuring transparency in the analysis and methodology by reflecting the findings from public comments, including those from the DOJ or other departments.

Regulatory flexibility analysis under the Regulatory Flexibility Act, which analyzes the impact of regulations on SMEs, has been used to analyze the effects of regulations on marginal enterprises; and to derive the effects of entry and exit. It also paves the way for future technological progress. The same effect can be seen in the consideration of SMEs in regulations on procurement. By easing the conditions under which SMEs can bid and increasing the likelihood that they will bid, the regulations will help promote future competition. Even if this increases government spending in the current situation, it is expected that more suppliers will emerge in the future, thereby promoting competition.

References

Environmental Protection Agency (2009a) Industrial sector integrated solutions model—Documentation for peer review. Document ID: EPA-HQ-OAR-2002-0051-2007, Docket ID: EPA-HQ-OAR-2002-0051

Environmental Protection Agency (2009b) Industrial sector integrated solutions (ISIS) technical support document. EPA-HQ-OAR-2002-0051-2009b. Docket ID: EPA-HQ-OAR-2002-0051

Environmental Protection Agency, U.S., Office of Air Quality Planning and Standards (OAQPS) Air Benefit and Cost Group (MD-C439-02) (2009) Regulatory impact analysis: national emission standards for hazardous air pollutants from the Portland Cement Manufacturing Industry Final Report. https://www.epa.gov/sites/default/files/2020-07/documents/nonmetallic-minerals_ria_proposal-cement-neshap_2009-04.pdf

Federal Aviation Administration, DOT (2006) Final regulatory evaluation—Congestion and delay reduction at Chicago's O'Hare international airport. Document ID: FAA-2005-20704-0034-0002. Docket ID: FAA-2005-20704

Federal Aviation Administration, DOT (2005a) Congestion and delay reduction at Chicago O'Hare international airport. A Proposed Rule by the Federal Aviation Administration on 03/25/2005a. https://www.federalregister.gov/documents/2005a/03/25/05-5882/congestion-and-delay-reduction-at-chicago-ohare-international-airport

Federal Aviation Administration, DOT (2005b) Congestion, delay reduction and operating limitations at Chicago O'Hare international airport. Proposed Rule and Notice Friday, March 25, 2005b Part IV. https://www.govinfo.gov/content/pkg/FR-2005b-03-25/pdf/05-5882.pdf

Federal Aviation Administration, "competition analysis". http://ostpxweb.ost.dot.gov/aviation/aviatanalysisprog.htm#competition

Federal Communication Commission (2002) EchoStar-DirecTV merger page. https://www.fcc.gov/general/echostar-directv-merger-page
Federal Energy Regulation Commission (2004) Order on rehearing and modifying interim generation market power analysis and mitigation policy. 107 FERC 61018. http://www.pulp.tc/FERCOrderModifyingSMA5-1404.pdf
Federal Energy Regulation Commission (2007) Market-based rates for wholesale sales of electric energy, capacity and ancillary services by public utilities. (Docket No. RM04-7-000; Order No. 697)
Federal Motor Carrier Safety Administration US department of Transportation, Analysis Division (2004) Proposed rule regulatory evaluation initial regulatory flexibility analysis unfunded mandates reform act analysis brokers of household goods transportation. Document ID, FMCSA-2004-17008-0018. Docket ID:FMCSA-2004-17008
Federal Motor Carrier Safety Administration, US department of Transportation (2007) Brokers of household goods transportation by motor vehicle. (Docket No. FMCSA-2004-17008-0022), Notice of proposed rulemaking, request for comments
Federal Motor Carrier Safety Administration, DOT, Analysis Division (2004) Proposed rule regulatory evaluation initial regulatory flexibility analysis unfunded mandates reform act analysis brokers of household goods transportation
Federal Motor Carrier Safety Administration, DOT (2010) Final rule regulatory evaluation final regulatory flexibility analysis unfunded mandates reform act analysis brokers of household goods transportation. RIN 2126-AA84 By Analysis Division Federal Motor Carrier Safety Administration August 2010. https://omb.report/icr/202204-2126-002/doc/120396500
Federal Trade Commission (2004) Comment before the commodity futures trading commission regarding the application of U.S. futures exchange, LLC for contract market designation. http://www.ftc.gov/os/2004/01/040113c/FTCcommenttext.pdf
Federal Trade Commission (2007a) The role of competition analysis in regulatory decisions. Opening Remarks of Chairman Deborah Platt Majoras at the workshop on AEI/Brookings Joint Center, Washington, D.C. http://www.aei-brookings.org/events/page.php?id=163
Federal Trade Commission (2007b) The role of competition analysis in regulatory decisions. Opening Remarks of Chairman Deborah Platt Majoras at the workshop on AEI/Brookings Joint Center, Washington, D.C. http://www.ftc.gov/speeches/majoras/070515aei.pdf
Federal Trade Commission and Department of Justice (1997) FTC/DOJ horizontal merger guidelines. http://www.justice.gov/atr/public/guidelines/hmg.htm
Food and Drug Administration, DEPARTMENT OF HEALTH AND HUMAN SERVICES (2007a) Use of ozone-depleting substances; removal of essential-use designations-proposed rule
Food and Drug Administration, DEPARTMENT OF HEALTH AND HUMAN SERVICES (2007b) Use of ozone-depleting substances; removal of essential-use designations-proposed rule. http://www.epa.gov/Ozone/title6/downloads/FDA_rule_3.pdf
Goldman DP, Joyce GF, Escarce JJ, Pace JE, Solomon MD, Laouri M, Teutsch M. Pharmacy benefits and the use of drugs by the chronically ill. Journal of the American Medical Association. 2004;291(19):2344–2350
Kwerel E, Levy J, NEEDY C, Perry M, Uretsky M, Waldon T, Williams J (2004) Economic analysis at the federal communications commission. Rev Ind Organ 25:395–430
Nakaizumi T (2014) Kisei no jizen hyōka no kōjō no tame no kyōsō hyōka no hōkō-sei. Hyoka Q Inst Adm Manag (29):23–31, 2014-04
Nakaizumi T (2010) 'Beikoku de no kyōsō bunseki jitchi chōsa hōkoku-sho' kōsei torihiki iinkai itaku chōsa, JFTC
Nakaizumi T (2011) Beikoku ni okeru kisei ga kyōsō ni ataeru eikyō no haaku bunseki shuhō ni tsuite' kōsei torihiki, No. 733, 2011-11, Kosei Torihiki
Nakaizumi T (2012) 'Kisei sakusei ni okeru kisei eikyō bunseki (ria) no jūyō-sei: Beikoku no jirei o sankō to shite' hyōka ni tsuite no kōen gaiyō. Hyoka Q Inst Adm Manag 23:2012–2110

Nakaizumi T (2013) Progress of competition analysis in the US government, mainly focusing on environmental regulation, (in Japanese). Res Inst Econ Manag (Kanto-Gakuin University) 35:163–173

OECD Competition assessment documents and links. http://www.oecd.org/daf/competition/reducingregulatoryrestrictionsoncompetition/competitionassessmentdocumentsandlinks.htm

OMB (2003) Circular A-4. http://www.whitehouse.gov/omb/circulars/a004/a-4.pdf

Office of Information and Regulatory Affairs/OMB,The U.S. (2009) Report to congress on the benefits and costs of federal regulations and unfunded mandates on state, local, and tribal entities. http://www.whitehouse.gov/omb/rewrite/inforeg/costs_benefits/2008_draft_cb_report.pdf

UK Competition and Markets Authority (2015) Guidance competition impact assessment: guidelines for policymakers guidelines to help government policymakers assess the impact their proposals will have on competition. https://www.gov.uk/government/publications/competition-impact-assessment-guidelines-for-policymakers

Viscusi WK, Harrington JE Jr, Sappington DEM (2018) Economics of regulation and antitrust, Fifth edn. MIT Press, 1000 page

Part V
Current Issue and Concluding Remark

Chapter 11
How to Incorporate Behavioral Science and Using Nudges in Regulation and IA

Abstract Behavioral science is useful to improve regulation. We explain how to incorporate Nudge into Impact Assessment. There are several ways to check Nudge, BASIC (Behavior, Analysis, Strategies, Intervention, and Change) by the OECD, FEAST (Fun, Easy, Attractive, and Timely by the U.K., and (Sunstein 2014a, b)). Though nudge is based on behavioral economics extending rationality assumption, assessment of the cost and benefit of nudge should be based on traditional neoclassical criteria as other mandatory measures and economic incentive, because it is compared with the maximum social welfare which is the ultimate goal of IA.

11.1 Introduction

Building regulation, assuming that people behave rationally as defined in economics, is a prerequisite. However, there are cases where people have habits that prevent them from acting more rationally.

Thus, the findings of behavioral science and psychology have been incorporated into economics and verified through economic experiments and empirical studies based on causal inference. Based on these findings, effective measurement making use of the habit could be considered as one of the options in the proposed regulation.

It is possible to improve the effectiveness of regulations by making use of such habits. Nudge belongs to these measures. Thaler and Sunstein (2008) defined a nudge as any aspect of the choice architecture that alters people's behavior predictably without forbidding any options or significantly changing their economic incentives. Nudge is easy and cheap. Nudges are not mandates. Putting fruit at eye level counts as a Nudge, while banning junk food does not.[1]

In this Chapter, we explain nudge in regulation making and IA. There is a vast literature regarding Behavioral Economics and nudge regarding Regulation making. Thus, we sum up briefly the characteristics of nudge and how to analyze it in Impact Assessment.

[1] https://en.wikipedia.org/wiki/Nudge_theory.

T. Nakaizumi, *Impact Assessment for Developing Countries*, Contributions to Economics,
https://doi.org/10.1007/978-981-19-5494-8_11

The most important point is that the conventional cost/benefit analysis should be applied straightforwardly. In the case of effective nudges, cost-effectiveness is higher than traditional measurement because of low cost. Therefore, it is particularly important to ensure the effectiveness and consider the degree to which the effectiveness is greater than compulsory measures or economic incentive schemes.

Next section, we briefly sum up the aspects of nudge and introduce Sunstein's insight regarding nudge, based on Parilli and Scartascini (2020). And in Sect. 11.3, we incorporate nudge or Behavioral Economics in Impact Assessment.

11.2 A Brief Summary of Nudge and How Nudges Could Be Incorporated Into the Regulatory Design

Thaler and Sunstein (2008) popularized nudge, defining it as in previous section. Any approach that guides people's behavior without forbidding any options or significantly changing their economic incentives is regarded as nudge. Nudge covers a broader category including economics. Only when it affects economics or policy, it will become the subject of economics or policy analysis. While adequate nudge is less costly than compulsory measures and economic incentives, the effectiveness of nudge tends to last less as shown in Otake (2022). Thus, compulsory measure and economic incentives should take precedence over nudge if effectiveness of nudge and other mandatory measures or economic incentives is indifferent nudge-like methods should be reccommended because of low cost. Assessment of the effectiveness of nudge is more important than general regulatory measurement. Negative effects could happen. It is opposite of nudge and called sludge.

OECD shows how to find a nudge and incorporate it to improve regulation on the "behavior insight" webpage. To design adequate nudge, OECD recommends the Behavior, Analysis, Strategies, Intervention, and Change (BASIC) framework. Though they use behavioral insight instead of Nudge, it is equivalent. On the webpage, BASIC is an overarching framework for applying behavioral insights to public policy from the beginning to the end of the policy cycle. It consists of five stages that guide the application of behavioral insights and contains a repository of best practices, proof of concepts, and methodological standards for behavioral insights practitioners and policymakers who are interested in applying behavioral insights to public policy.

The Nudge Unit in the U.K. government introduces the factor of EAST which is useful to check nudges. The Behavioral Insights Team (BIT) designed EAST framework in the U. K Nudge Unit. EAST has the following elements: (i) Easy—the messages and nudges have to be simple; (ii) Attractive—the messages should catch the attention of the recipient; (iii) Social—they must emphasize existing social norms that promote the desired behavior; and (iv) Timely—messages need to be presented on time, ideally when individuals are most susceptible to changing their behavior.

Prof. Cass Sunstein, who is the first advocate of nudge, insists on adding, "F," for Fun, making the acronym "FEAST." Messages or minor changes that can add an element of fun to the daily routine can contribute to taking measures. He showed an example of New Zealand's government during Easter in quarantine period of COVID-19 Pandemic, introducing a fun element to the government's narrative by declaring the Easter Bunny an "essential worker" and urging families to continue celebrating the holiday at home. "Fun theory" has been applied to a diverse set of behavioral interventions.

11.3 How to Assess the Impact of Nudge in IA

The most important point in assessing the benefit and cost of nudge is that the conventional cost/benefit assessment must be retained. In the case of effective nudges, cost-effectiveness is high because they are effective despite their low cost. Therefore, it is particularly important to consider the degree to which the effectiveness is greater than that of costly compulsory measures and economic incentives. Economic welfare should be based on rationality economics depends on. Assuming a hyperbolic or other utility function within a wider class that behavioral economic insight based on will lead to a deviation from the socially optimal level. If the socially optimal level is realized, more gains can be achieved and welfare can be improved shown in Chapter 2. Thus even if the nudge measurement is based on wider class of rational welfare function, it must be evaluated accoding to traditional rational economic theory.

However, some of the policies might be difficult to explain solely based on classical economics theory. One example is the pension system. In Knoll (2010), they discuss several issues in Behavioral Economics in saving behavior, although it is still controversial to extend the criteria to assess benefit and cost to wider class than neoclassical welfare theory.

11.4 Concluding Remark

It is useful to consider nudge in regulation making because it is highly cost-effective if it is effective and not sludge which brings negative effects. The most important point is that the conventional cost/benefit analysis must be applied straightforwardly. And it is particularly important to ensure the effectiveness and consider the degree to which effectiveness is greater than that of mandatory measures or economic incentives. And generally, nudge does not continue so much as mandatory measure and economic incentives. Thus, if nudge is one of the alternatives and it is compared with mandatory measures and economic incentives, a longer period should be considered to assess effectiveness.

References

Knoll MAZ (2010) The role of behavioral economics and behavioral decision making in Americans' retirement savings decisions. https://www.ssa.gov/policy/docs/ssb/v70n4/v70n4p1.html

OECD Behavioural insights webpage. https://www.oecd.org/gov/regulatory-policy/behavioural-insights.htm

OECD BASIC—The Behavioural Insights Toolkit and Ethical Guidelines for Policy Makers. https://oecd-opsi.org/toolkits/basic-the-behavioural-insights-toolkit-and-ethical-guidelines-for-policy-makers/

Otake F (2022) Anatawo kaeru koudou keizaigaku, Tokyo Shoseli, 248 page

Owain Service et al (2014) EAST: four simple ways to apply behavioural insights. UK Behavioural Insights team. https://www.bi.team/publications/east-four-simple-ways-to-apply-behavioural-insights/

Parilli C, Scartascini C (2020) A conversation with Cass Sunstein on behavioral science and using nudges: recommendations for overcoming covid-19. https://blogs.iadb.org/ideas-matter/en/a-conversation-with-cass-sunstein-on-behavioral-science-and-using-nudges-recommendations-for-overcoming-covid-19/

Sunstein CR (2014a) Nudging: a very short guide. J Consum Policy 37:583–588. https://doi.org/10.1007/s10603-014-9273-1

Sunstein CR (2014b) Sludge audits. In: Behavioural public policy. © Cambridge University Press, pages 1 of 20. https://doi.org/10.1017/bpp.2019

Thaler RH, Sunstein CR (2008) Nudge: improving decisions about health, wealth, and happiness. Yale University Press

Chapter 12
COVID-19 Pandemic and Impact Assessment

Abstract In the crisis period, it is inevitable to settle immediate and temporal measures and ex-post evaluation of those regulations and to revise and ex-post evaluate than to ex-ante rigorous analysis. But it is far more effective to conduct a initial simplified analysis than to conduct no assessment at all. Thus, we explain the superiority of conducting IA even in a simplified manner.

12.1 Introduction

In a crisis such as the novel coronavirus pandemic (COVID-19), settling immediate and temporal measures is inevitable. But a crisis lasts only a few years at most, and ex-post evaluation of those regulations is essential for the preparation of regulations after the convergence of the crisis. Thus, it is more important to revise and ex-post evaluation than ex-ante rigorous analysis.

The book explains Impact Assessment, that is ex-ante evaluation, and does not explain ex-post evaluation that is key during a crisis. It is out of scope. However, the principles described in the book can apply to regulation making during a crisis period, especially proportionality and earlier rough estimation is highly recommended. We briefly discuss the IA and regulation making during a crisis, based on the lessons learned from the COVID-19 pandemic.

Even if the crisis is short-lived, the social impact can be exceptionally large. Especially, the COVID-19 pandemic has led to lockdowns and other coercive measures that have also curbed human rights. A large several-trillion-dollar budget, including subsidies for lockdowns and budgets for vaccines and so forth, was spent in a short period. Policies might be implemented that have a longer social impact, such as exemplified by Japan's immigration restrictions. Delays and failures in implementing countermeasures also cause tremendous social losses.

It is exceedingly difficult, however, to conduct an ex-ante evaluation of regulations accurately and rigorously in a crisis, when urgent measure is required. This is because (1) there is insufficient evidence, to begin with, and (2) there is often not enough time for analysis. Therefore, the IA itself has to be a simplified one with many unsolved contingencies in a crisis.

T. Nakaizumi, *Impact Assessment for Developing Countries*, Contributions to Economics,
https://doi.org/10.1007/978-981-19-5494-8_12

However, it is far more effective to conduct a simplified analysis based on stilized fact at the moment than to conduct no assessment at all. The effectiveness of sensitivity analysis is enhanced in uncertain situations. In COVID-19 pandemic, it can be appropriate to use SUR model explored by Acemoglu et al. (2020) or stylized fact by Oshitani (2020). Therefore, this chapter is not a proposal to prepare a rigorous IA for a crisis, but rather to explain that it is more effective in critical situations to conduct an IA in a simplified manner by using the sensitivity analysis to deal with uncertainty.

In the next section, we introduce the OECD report (2022) and show the several policy lessons about the COVID-19 pandemic in various countries. In Sect. 12.3, we will explain the importance of proportionality and earlier analysis of regulation in the COVID-19 pandemic, based on specific examples, and Sect. 12.4 concludes.

12.2 Government Evaluations of COVID-19 Responses by OECD

We introduce the OECD report (2022) of the evaluation of Policy Responses to COVID-19 and share the stylized facts. OECD summed up lessons from government evaluations of COVID-19 responses: in January 2022 it provides a synthesis of the evidence from 67 such evaluations produced in OECD countries during the first 15 months of the pandemic. The study does not aim to evaluate countries' COVID-19 responses but to provide useful insights in the hopes that these can feed into ongoing policy efforts and future resilience. Particularly, the evaluations analyzed in this study underline that:

1. Pandemic preparedness was generally insufficient, chiefly considering the major human and financial costs associated with global health crises like the COVID-19 pandemic.
2. Governments took swift and massive action to mitigate the economic and financial effects of the pandemic but should carefully monitor the longer-term budgetary costs of these measures.
3. Trust requires transparency, not only through frequent and targeted crisis communication but, more importantly, by engaging stakeholders and the public in risk-related decision-making.
4. Important gaps remain in the evidence base available to date and would warrant further investigation: There is insufficient evidence on critical sectors' preparedness for pandemics, whereas early evaluations suggest that they were crucial to effective crisis response. For example, the effectiveness of lockdown and restriction measures should probably be further assessed, given their impacts on individual liberties.
5. Finally, issues relating to policies' proportionality and coherence are still largely under-explored by these first evaluations, despite their usefulness for policy

debate, especially when resources are scarce and cross-government coordination is crucial.

While the COVID-19 pandemic has hit different countries with varying intensities, responding to the crisis has presented an unprecedented challenge to most governments in the OECD—both in scale and in the depth of its impact on health, the economy, and citizens' well-being. At the same time, the pandemic has brought structural and social issues to light, including the erosion of public trust in government and in expert advice, which was compounded by a wave of misinformation and disinformation. To respond to these challenges, OECD governments have deployed, relatively quickly, significant human, financial, and technical resources to manage and mitigate the impacts of the crisis.

12.3 The Importance of Proportionality and Earlier Analysis

In a crisis, emergent measure is an important decision-making factor. The evidence may not be able to keep up with the rapid response to the crisis, and it is important to explore how to evaluate and make decisions in such cases.

Some of the measures that have been taken to date, while initially desirable, can be considered problematic thereafter. Others, however, have been much more effective than initially anticipated. For example, it is well known that in Sweden, at the beginning of the COVID-19 pandemic, priority was given to measures that ensured mass immunity. However, with the subsequent increase in infections, it is fair to say that the Swedish method has been rated as a failure.

The use of masks was, on the other hand, initially regarded as less effective. Masks were highly regarded as leading to quarantine when worn by an infected person, but not when worn by a non-infected person. However, in the summer of 2020, it became the mainstay of non-medical countermeasures worldwide as a very cost-effective measure.

As for the speed of vaccine development, it was initially thought to be based on traditional inactivated vaccines, which would require at least three years from development to become operational at the earliest. Several innovations were developed to make mRNA practical at an astonishing speed, six months after the pandemic. Moreover, it has significantly higher efficacy than past inactivated vaccines and has been supplied worldwide.

Concerning the face-to-face meetings in elementary schools, many studies initially showed that the younger age groups were less likely to be infected with SARS-COV-2. However, as research progressed, the view was confirmed that younger children are less likely to develop SARS-COV-2, and although they do not show symptoms, they can be infected and transmit the disease to others. Especially with the Delta or Omicron variant spreading worldwide in 2021, the probability of not only being infected but also transmiting has increased, making the strengthening of measures for minors the biggest challenge in the world.

Some of the most effective measures that have been proposed from the beginning and are still in place today are maintaining social distance and thorough hand washing and hand sanitizing. Furthermore, infection and transmission among university students have been a problem since the early days of the COVID-19 pandemic, and university lectures have been online worldwide since the beginning of 2020. Moreover, situations where droplets are spread indoors, specifically in live music venues, large group dinners with alcohol, and church chorus services, have been regulated from the beginning.

Although the mRNA vaccine has been more effective than expected, rejection of the vaccine is higher than expected, and the uptake rate is in the 60% range even in developed countries by mid 2021, making it difficult to achieve herd immunity with the vaccine.

Among the OECD countries, Japan was slow to get a higher vaccination rate because of the limited provision of mRNA vaccine, especially for the younger generation. Thus, the Tokyo Municipal government planned to provide mRNA vaccines to a younger generation in the Tokyo area in August 2021. They opened a venue where young people could have received vaccines without an appointment. Although it might have ideal purpose, the provision was far from sufficient. It is easy to estimate how many vaccines should be provided to young people who can take the vaccine without an appointment.

For example, we know that Tokyo has a population of about 3.5 million people under the age of 30 (2017). If we assume that 60% of them want to consume the product and 1% of them visit the store daily, the number of visitors can be about 20,000. Even this low level of estimation is much more effective than doing nothing at all. As it is, just 200 vaccines have been prepared. Of course, with this number of people, there must undoubtedly be lineups and potentially COVID-19 inflectional clusters if the system was not changed to require reservations. There was a long queue on the first day of the event. The local government finally decided to revise the plan and implement a reservation system was introduced.

As can be said for policy evaluation in general, especially in the case of ex-ante analysis, everything is just a prediction, and it is impossible for the prediction to be completely accurate. Rather, the goal is to show that the benefits of regulation exceed the costs under various assumptions, as in the epidemiological prediction model. In such cases, it is necessary to show the probability of the predicted values being applicable. However, if it is difficult to estimate such a probability distribution, a distribution such as a uniform distribution or normal distribution may be assumed which called sensitivity analysis. Furthermore, when the uncertainty is extremely high, it is also effective to give examples of changes in results because of changes in possible parameters. Furthermore, even in cases where forecasting is exceedingly difficult and even estimating a specific value is difficult, just show whether the digits are correct or not. It is more effective for policymaking than no analysis at all. What is important is that the attitude of trying to be as specific and quantitative as possible, with the proviso of uncertainty, is itself beneficial for policymaking.

12.4 Concluding Remark

A crisis lasts only a few years, and ex-post evaluation of those regulations is essential for the preparation of regulations after the convergence of the crisis. Thus, it is more important to revise, and evaluate ex-post than to analyze regously ex-ante.

The book explains ex-ante analysis, not an ex-post evaluation, which is key during a crisis, is out of scope. However, proportionality and earlier rough analysis to select adequate alternatives are still important. As described in the next chapter, it is more important to design flexible regulations promoting cost-effectiveness.

References

Acemoglu D, Chernozhukov V, Werning I, Whinston MD (2020) Optimal targeted lockdowns in a multi-group SIR model. https://economics.mit.edu/files/19698

OECD (2022) First lessons from government evaluations of COVID-19 responses: a synthesis. https://www.oecd.org/coronavirus/policy-responses/first-lessons-from-government-evaluations-of-covid-19-responses-a-synthesis-483507d6/

Oshitani H (2020) COVID—19 e no taisaku no gainen shingata koronauirusu ni kanren shita kansenshō taisaku ni kansuru kōsei Rōdōshō taisaku suishin honbu kurasutā taisaku han Tōhokudaigaku daigakuin igaku-kei kenkyū-ka. https://www.jsph.jp/covid/files/gainen.pdf

Chapter 13
Regulation for the Digital Era and IA for Smart Regulation

Abstract In times of great change, the structure of the economy itself could change drastically. It is considered necessary to show and share the apparent direction and to move toward that direction. Fairness, transparency, and flexibility are important, and the process should involve repeated trial and error. But in conducting IA, the basic principle could be applied and should be based on a proportional principle as explained in the book.

13.1 Introduction

In recent years, technological progress has been advancing at an even faster pace, and the past 20 years have seen a radical transformation of the world. To fully reap the benefits of such technological innovations, flexible organizations are needed. The marketplace can keep pace with technological progress with new companies entering and old ones exiting. The public sector, however, has no mechanism other than elections in a democracy, and without strong top-down leadership, it is difficult to change the old ways. This is especially true in a society such as Japan, where change is difficult.

Therefore, in the U.K. and the U.S. in the 2010s, there were attempts to reduce a number of regulations in the form of "one in one out," "one in two or more out," etc. Deregulation itself began in the U.S. in the 1980s and other OECD countries followed it. In Japan, it began in the 2000s, but the recent resurgence of deregulation seems to be a response to such social changes, see Department for Business, Innovation, and Skills, the UK government, (2010–2015), Smith et al. (2021).

In times of great change, the structure of the economy itself could change drastically. In regulation making and conducting IA, it is important to proactively consider how the digital economy should be evolved, including the business environment and technological trends. Although earlier commitment to analysis in regulation making is the priority for conducting IA, it is difficult for anyone to foresee the future in such a period of change at the early stage of regulation making. Therefore, it is considered necessary to show and share the apparent direction and to move toward that direction, assuming what could happen in the future. The process should involve repeated trial

T. Nakaizumi, *Impact Assessment for Developing Countries*, Contributions to Economics,
https://doi.org/10.1007/978-981-19-5494-8_13

and error, flexibility, and a multifaceted viewpoint instead of strict analysis at the earlier stage.

It is still on the way to developing a desirable Impact Assessment in the Digital Era and how to assess the flexibility providing future technological progress and change in society and the economy. But basic principles could be applied, and it is desirable to conduct IA based on a proportional principle in which analysis is proportionate to the importance of the regulation and to assess properly the flexibility of the regulations enough to withstand regulatory changes. It is important to specify which part is flexible and derive the reason at the earlier stage in the regulation making.

Because the recent development of telecommunication regulation in Japan is one of the best practices of updated regulation based on the principle, we introduce the "Act on Improving Transparency and Fairness of Specified Digital Platforms" in the Ministry of Internal Affairs and Communication and show the concept of the regulation addressing the rapid development of digital technology in the next section.

Digital technology requires all the regulatory systems to change primarily, because the legal system or regulatory system must be examined at an early stage to determine if it can be digitalized. Thus, an earlier analysis should be required. And even IA can be conducted following the assessment of digitalization. The "Team for the Study of Digitalization of Legislative Affairs" in the Japanese government introduced the "Checklist of Regulations under Consideration from the Viewpoint of Digitalization" in FY2021. It contains the Digital Principles in which all the regulations should be reviewed at an earlier stage, from the viewpoint of the availability of digitalization. It is a useful approach to commit not only assessment for Digitalization but also earlier Impact assessment itself for all the countries that try to conduct IA as early as possible. Thus, we explain the case study and linkage between the assessment of digitalization and IA in Sect. 13.3. Section 13.4 concludes.

13.2 The Act on Improving Transparency and Fairness of Specified Digital Platforms in the Ministry of Internal Affairs and Communication

As an example of flexible regulation, we introduce the "Act on Improving Transparency and Fairness of Specified Digital Platforms" in the Ministry of Internal Affairs and Communication Japan. It is based on the principle that measures for improving transparency and fairness of digital platforms should be implemented, primarily based on voluntary and proactive initiatives by digital platform providers, with government involvement or other regulations kept to a minimum. It adopts a "co-regulation" approach, in which the general framework of regulations is defined by law, but the details are left to the voluntary efforts of service providers.

Among digital platforms, businesses that provide platforms are highly required the transparency and fairness of transactions designated as "Specified Digital Platform

Providers" by a Cabinet Order and the government regulates them. They are mandatory to notify information such as terms and conditions of business transactions and voluntary procedures and systems and to submit a yearly report stating the outline of the business and the measures taken for mutual understanding, together with a self-conducted evaluation (Headquarters for Digital Market Competition, Prime Minister Japan and His Cabinet web page).

A review of the operation of the platform by the government will be conducted based on the report, and the results of the evaluation will be published along with a summary of the report. At that time, the opinions of product providers, consumers, academics, etc., will be heard, and challenges will be discussed to promote mutual understanding among the parties involved. If a case is identified that may violate the Antitrust Law, the Minister of Economy, Trade and Industry request the JFTC to act in accordance with the Antitrust Law (Secretariat of the Headquarters for Digital Market Competition, Cabinet Secretariat, Japan (2020a, 2020b, 2021)).

From the standpoint of ensuring the sound development of the digital advertising market, the following are key elements: (1) securing "fairness," (2) improving "transparency," and (3) ensuring the "availability of choice" for the parties concerned in the market, including general consumers.

These elements are important analytical viewpoints in the Impact Assessment. To assess the benefit and cost of these factors, these factors should be quantified or monetized. As described in Chapter 7, if the other benefits and costs of these new regulation are the same as that of exisiting regulation, fairer, more transparent, and more flexible regulations are preferable.

However, other benefits and costs are different, benefits and costs of transparency, flexibility must be be quantified or monetized. But it is exceedingly difficult or even impossible to assess the impact. Flexibility, for example, is beneficial for inhibiting innovation. It is a rapidly changing market that builds a framework that encourages solutions through innovation. But it is almost impossible to estimate the benefits and costs of the induced innovation.

It is also difficult to estimate the impact of transparency. The regulation improves the transparency of transactions by requiring users to be notified in advance of condition of transactions. This promotes mutual understanding with business partners and prevents antitrust activities. It is recommended that these effects might be quantified with the methods or techniques explained in Part 3, though it is an ongoing research issue still unsolved.

13.3 Promoting Earlier Analysis of IA in Accordance with Digitalization

Digital technology requires all the government organizations and the procedures to change as a primary reason. The legal system or regulatory system must be examined at an early stage to be digitalized. Thus, an earlier assessment should be required regarding how the regulation can be digitalized or what kinds of policy and regulation should be digitalized at the each stage.

One of the primary premises in the book is that IA should be conducted in accordance with regulation making from an earlier stage. But some countries have been struggling to conduct IA at the earlier stage of regulation making. There are still difficulties and opposition to conduct IA earlier. But the assessment of digitalization should be conducted earlier, and the process can be conducted in accordance with IA. And the introduction of an assessment of digitalization may provide the opportunity to conduct IA at an early stage as an assessment of digitalization.

In Japan, the Digital Agency was established in 2021 and the "Team for the Study of Digitalization of Legislative Affairs" (2022a, 2022b) within the Digital Agency introduced the "Checklist of Regulations under Consideration from the Viewpoint of Digitalization" in FY2021 to check conformity with the Digital Principles at an earlier stage, and all the regulations should be reviewed from the viewpoint of digitalization availability. In conjunction with this trend, discussions are underway to be compulsory the submission of both IA and competition assessment as well.

13.4 Concluding Remarks

Digital technologies may extend gray areas within existing regulatory regimes and cause legal uncertainties. Existing regulatory frameworks are beginning to have more negative repercussions. The government's ability is also limited, and regulations should be changed. "Fairness," "transparency," "Flexibility," and "Availability of choice" is important in regulation in the Digital era.

Regarding IA, it is still on its way to developing into a desirable Impact Assessment in the Digital Era. It is difficult to derive a method to assess costs and benefits of fairness, transparency, flexibility. However, basic principles such as proportionality and the alternativeschoice at the earlier stage of regulation making should be applied, though ex-post evaluation and up-dating of regulation seems more important.

References

Department for Business, Innovation & Skills, the UK government, 2010–2015 government policy: business regulation. https://www.gov.uk/government/publications/2010-to-2015-government-policy-business-regulation/2010-to-2015-government-policy-business-regulation

Dejitaru rinji gyōsei chōsa-kai sagyō bukai hōsei jimu no dejitaru-ka kentō chīmu (Team for the Study of Digitalization of Legislative Affairs) (2022a) Hōrei no dejitaru gensoku e no tekigō-sei kakunin purosesu taisei no kakuritsu ni mukete. https://www.digital.go.jp/assets/contents/node/basic_page/field_ref_resources/a91f8fa3-2752-47d1-a135-f5408b607228/bc319391/20220513_meeting_administrative_research_working_group_process_03.pdf

Dejitaru rinji gyōsei chōsa-kai sagyō bukai hōsei jimu no dejitaru-ka kentō chīmu (Team for the Study of Digitalization of Legislative Affairs) (2022b) Hōsei jimu no dejitaru-ka ni muketa kōtei-hyō ni tsuite, https://www.digital.go.jp/assets/contents/node/basic_page/field_ref_resources/a91f8fa3-2752-47d1-a135-f5408b607228/e40a48fc/20220513_meeting_administrative_research_working_group_schedule_02.pdf

Headquarters for Digital Market Competition, Prime Minister Japan and His Cabinet. https://www.kantei.go.jp/jp/singi/digitalmarket/index_e.html

Secretariat of the Headquarters for Digital Market Competition, Cabinet Secretariat, Japan (2020a) Report on medium-term vision on competition in the digital market: summary. https://www.kantei.go.jp/jp/singi/digitalmarket/pdf_e/documents_200616-2.pdf

Secretariat of the Headquarters for Digital Market Competition, Cabinet Secretariat, Japan (2020b) Dejitaru rinji gyōsei chōsa-kai sagyō bukai hōsei jimu no dejitaru-ka kentō chīmu. https://www.kantei.go.jp/jp/singi/digitalmarket/kyosokaigi/dai4/siryou3s.pdf

Secretariat of the Headquarters for Digital Market Competition, Cabinet Secretariat, Japan (2021) Evaluation of competition in the digital advertising market, final report: summary. https://www.kantei.go.jp/jp/singi/digitalmarket/pdf_e/documents_210427.pdf

Smith D, Villiers T, Freeman G (2021) Taskforce on innovation, growth and regulatory reform independent report. The UK Independent report from the Taskforce on Innovation, Growth and Regulatory Reform. https://www.gov.uk/government/publications/taskforce-on-innovation-growth-and-regulatory-reform-independent-report

Chapter 14
Concluding Remark

Abstract We show three examples to emphasize the importance of IA. One is the example of the Japanese Ministry of Health, Labor, and Welfare (MHLW), which only considers how influential stakeholders distort and fail to achieve the goal of regulation. Second is the Tokyo Metropolitan Government's study group on the ivory trade, in which the introduction of quantitative analysis is beneficial for future regulation making. The last one is my experience in Pakistan Regulatory reform, explaining the difficulty of changing person-specific ability to organizational ability to solve the issue in IA and regulation making.

IA can be an excellent tool to make regulatory decisions more cost-effective and reduce the number of low-quality and unnecessary regulations. It can make decisions more transparent and encourage consultation and the participation of affected groups, and it contributes to improving governmental coherence and intra-ministerial communication.

To integrate IA into the regulation-making process, however, requires a significant cultural change among regulators, politicians, interest groups, and the public. Some countries, including past Japan, tend to make regulations by bureaucrats without transparency or public disclosure in the regulation-making process. It has been the opposite of the goal of IA, that is, public involvement.

Considering just influential stakeholders and conceding their pressures will distort social welfare and prevent the economy from growing. As noted in Chap. 2, the surplus from optimal policy brings maximum welfare. It is possible to increase the surplus from sub-optimal to socially optimal changing from considering only strong stakeholders' interests to a socially optimal outcome. Thus, one significant benefit of IA is that it is not influenced by any particular stakeholder.

Ministry of Health, Labour and Welfare Japan tends to overly reflect the opinions of medical professionals and the medical industry. When it takes certain actions to expand, it asks only medical professionals and institutions without consulting patients, and raises the medical service fees. If the fee becomes higher, medical institutions may be willing to supply those services. However, consumers, in this case patients, will tend to decline such services. Despite decreasing demand and

T. Nakaizumi, *Impact Assessment for Developing Countries*, Contributions to Economics,
https://doi.org/10.1007/978-981-19-5494-8_14

failing to achieve the purpose, it considers only the interests of supply side, in this case, medical professionals and institutions.

For instance, it is desirable to promote DX and the digitization of medical data. The Digital Agency tried to attach the function of a health insurance card to a social security number card. It is rather desirable to make it cheaper to use a social security number card than to use conventional medical treatments, which is obvious without a strict IA.

However, since the introduction of attachment, Ministry of Health, Labour and Welfare Japan has made fees higher and patients who use Social Security number card have been charged an additional 21 yen for the first visit and 12 yen for a follow-up visit. It has been decided that the spread of the Social Security number card requires hospitals and other institutions to invest more in equipment (Nikkei Shinbun (2021). Obviously they must prioritize the increase of the fee who does not use Social Security number card in order to promote Social Security number card and incur the cost of investment.

One of the major objectives of the introduction of IA is to take measures that maximize the overall social welfare, not merely for the direct stakeholders. From the viewpoint of maximizing social welfare, it is expected to consider not only the providers of medical services but also the demand side, the patients who use the services.

It is a long-term process that requires consistent, sustained support for IA and must be strengthened at the political level until it becomes a systematic part of a country's political and administrative culture. Designing and applying a comprehensive IA program is not an easy task. OECD countries have had long and complicated experiences in this area. It is vital to any successful IA system to follow these steps to (1) ensure compliance and adequate scope of coverage. (2) devise high-quality IA and data collection strategies; (3) institute an effective training program, and (4) assure the required level of political support.

In the case, designing and applying effective IA requires special consideration of several issues. First, methodological and operational difficulties can easily arise in the decision-making processes of developing countries. Second, in many cases, the use of regulatory tools requires a high level of expertise and access to extensive resources and information. Many low and middle-income countries do not yet meet these pre-conditions. Finally, consultation process is more challenging than developed countries in which public can access information more easily and have more knowledege to understand the analysis.

Regulation in developing countries could contribute to poverty reduction. Since context specificity matters, it is not only a question of promoting market efficiency but also ensuring that the benefits of more efficient market processes are distributed following social welfare.

Furthermore, IA should be conducted as early in the process as possible in the regulation making. In such cases, the assessment of costs and benefits tends to be vague, but fundamental measures can be taken. Additionally, depending on whether or not quantitative consideration is included concerning the basic policy, it can be used as a guideline for future objective analysis and regulatory enactment. When there are conflicting interests, it is difficult to produce quantitative estimates without accurate evidence. Even in such cases, it is necessary to at least leave room for consideration of evidence base and quantification in the future.

I participated in the Tokyo Metropolitan Government's study group on the ivory trade from 2020 to 2022, which considered ways to prevent ivory smuggling and poaching in Japan. The custom of using seals utilized ivory in Japan is still practiced. Compared to the stock that currently exists in Japan, the total amount consumed in Japan annually is statistically about 1/20, and it is difficult to believe that it is directly the cause of smuggling and poaching, but it is also true that there are businesses that process and sell ivory using the existing stock.

From the viewpoint of preventing ivory smuggling and poaching, demand for seals made from Ivory should be controlled and diminished in the future. There is an opinion, however, that elephant exports should be allowed at a minimum for countries where elephant conservation and management are properly implemented. Without any dependable data and solid analysis, it is quite difficult to decide whether to reduce demand, increase demand, or wait for the natural decrease as it is. In this case, although no conclusion can be drawn, it would be necessary to examine current demand trends to provide a minimum direction. The worst decision is made without any consideration of demand. Based on the importance of controlling demand, we successfully added the statement to maintain the adequate demand level in the Japanese Ivory in the final report, although the first draft of the study group had no statement of demand at all (Advisory Council on Regulation of Ivory Trade (2022)).

As for organization design in developing countries, review authority of IA and competition assessment is essential to improve the quality. The ex-ante evaluation of regulations is conducted by the regulatory authority that prepares the regulations simultaneously. To improve the quality of the analysis, it is essential to review and check the IA by review organization different from the regulatory body. Especially, given the importance of competition assessment in developing economies, it is important to involve the competition authorities to review and consult competition assessment.

I worked in the Economic Reform Unit (ERU) of the Finance Division in the Ministry of Interior, Pakistan. ERU has been active in introducing IA and improving fiscal discipline as well as focusing on reforming the governance of the regulatory authority. When I worked for ERU from 2013 to 2015, it played a central role in resolving the most important issues in Pakistan, such as organizational reform of independent regulator and electricity reform (Implementation and Economic Reform Unit, Ministry of Finance, Government Pakistan (2014)). However, it is heavily dependent on person-specific ability. After important people left the government, not only ERU but all the regulatory reforms stagnated. Thus, maintaining organizational ability instead of person-specific ability is a key issue, especially in developing countries.

Even in the United States, where the highest standards are subject to twists and turns. The principle of referring to it, rather than relying on it, will increase the robustness of the decision-making of the regulation.

In the end although we have updated the information as much as possible, this is not necessarily the latest information. The book intends to show the history of trial and error and to serve as a still excellent reference for countries that will develop in the future. For this reason, some of the examples from the past are actively used to illustrate the state-of-the-art at the time, so I would like readers to get a sense of how the people in charge of production at the time were working on the project.

References

Advisory Council on Regulation of Ivory Trade (2022) Report of the Advisory Council on Regulation of Ivory Trade. Tokyo Metropolitan Government, Final Report. https://www.seisakukikaku.metro.tokyo.lg.jp/cross-efforts/2022/03/images/zouge_houkokusho.pdf

Implementation and Economic Reform Unit, Ministry of Finance, Government Pakistan (2014) Institutional design of regulatory bodies: diagnostic and reform directions

Nikkei Shinbun (2022) "Dejitaru-chō meisō 'dare ga kimete iru no ka' hossoku kara hantoshi mogaku dejitaru-chō (1)" April 17th 2022

Printed by Printforce, the Netherlands